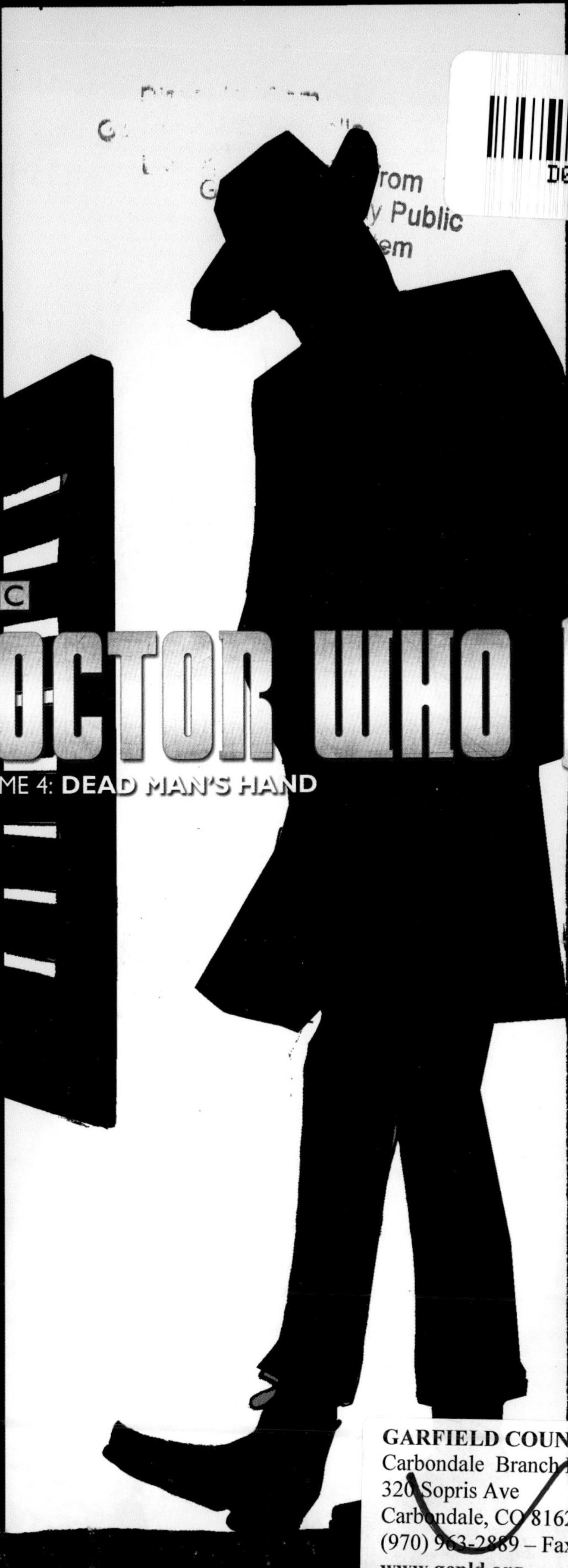

BBC

DOCTOR WHO

VOLUME 4: DEAD MAN'S HAND

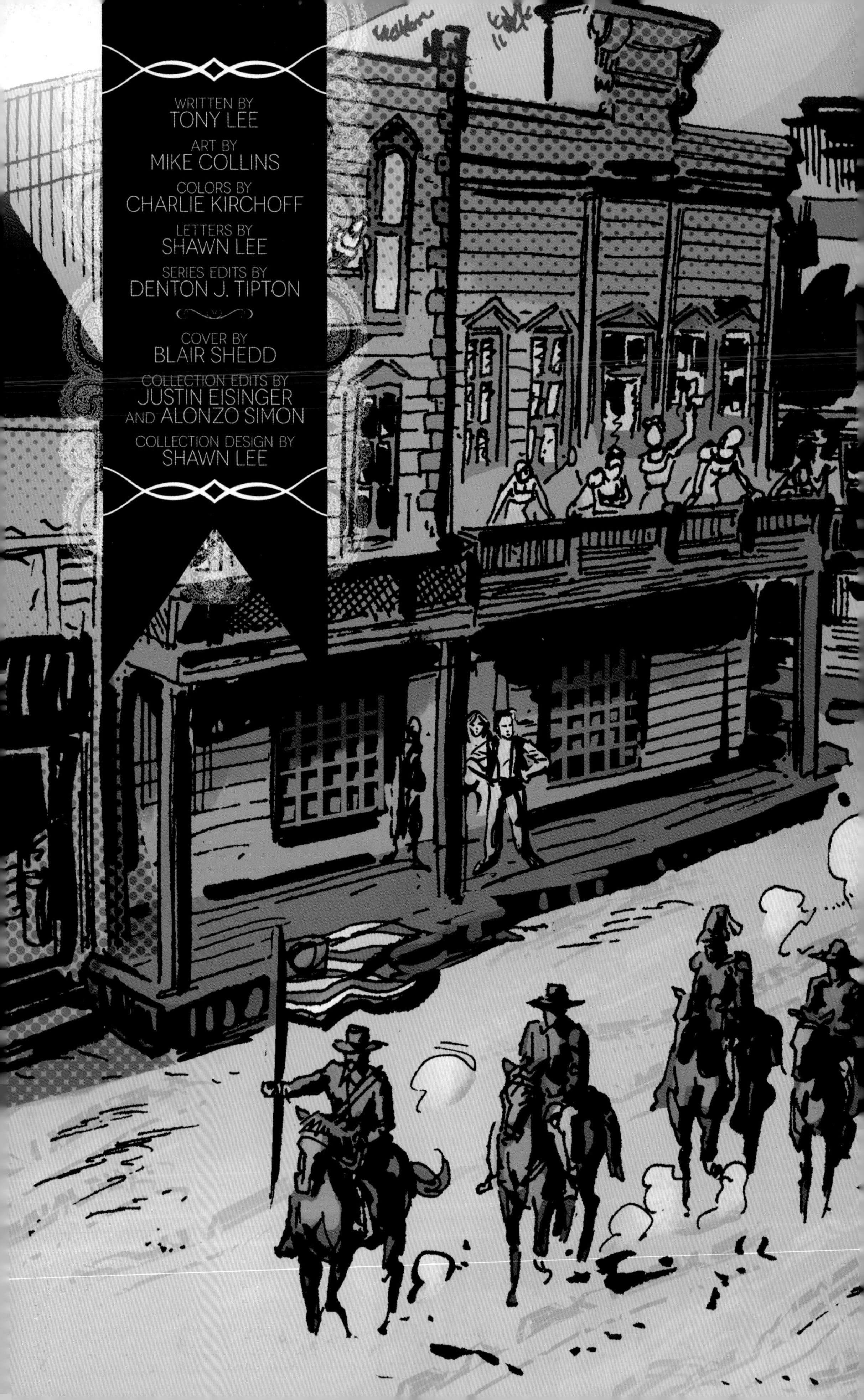

WRITTEN BY
TONY LEE

ART BY
MIKE COLLINS

COLORS BY
CHARLIE KIRCHOFF

LETTERS BY
SHAWN LEE

SERIES EDITS BY
DENTON J. TIPTON

COVER BY
BLAIR SHEDD

COLLECTION EDITS BY
JUSTIN EISINGER
AND ALONZO SIMON

COLLECTION DESIGN BY
SHAWN LEE

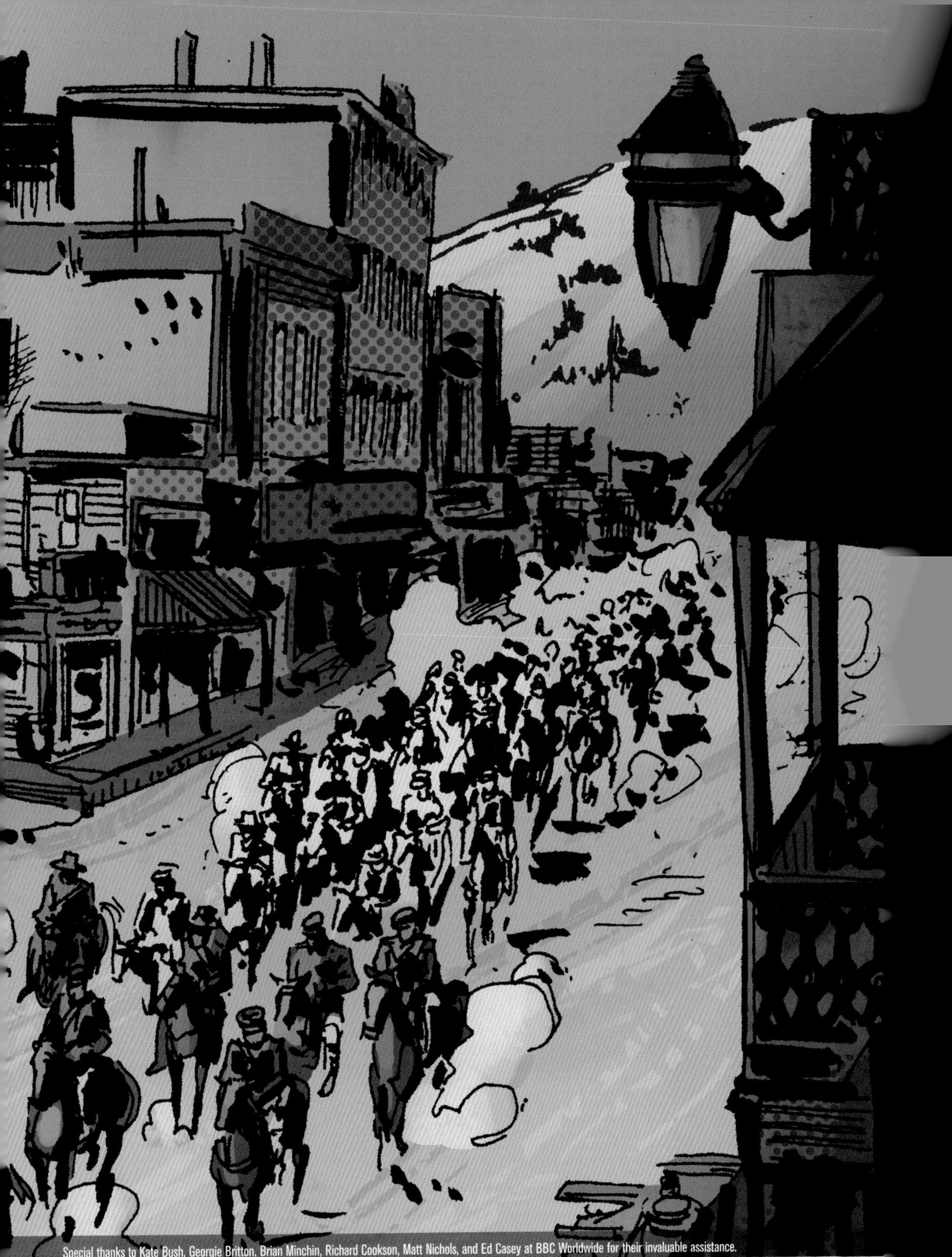

Special thanks to Kate Bush, Georgie Britton, Brian Minchin, Richard Cookson, Matt Nichols, and Ed Casey at BBC Worldwide for their invaluable assistance.

IDW founded by Ted Adams, Alex Garner, Kris Oprisko, and Robbie Robbins

ISBN: 978-1-61377-823-4

16 15 14 13 1 2 3 4

IDW®

Ted Adams, CEO & Publisher
Greg Goldstein, President & COO
Robbie Robbins, EVP/Sr. Graphic Artist
Chris Ryall, Chief Creative Officer/Editor-in-Chief
Matthew Ruzicka, CPA, Chief Financial Officer
Alan Payne, VP of Sales
Dirk Wood, VP of Marketing
Lorelei Bunjes, VP of Digital Services

Become our fan on Facebook **facebook.com/idwpublishing**
Follow us on Twitter **@idwpublishing**
Check us out on YouTube **youtube.com/idwpublishing**
www.IDWPUBLISHING.com

Originally published as DOCTOR WHO VOLUME 3 issues #13–16 and "ESCAPE INTO ALCATRAZ" from DOCTOR WHO SPECIAL 2012.

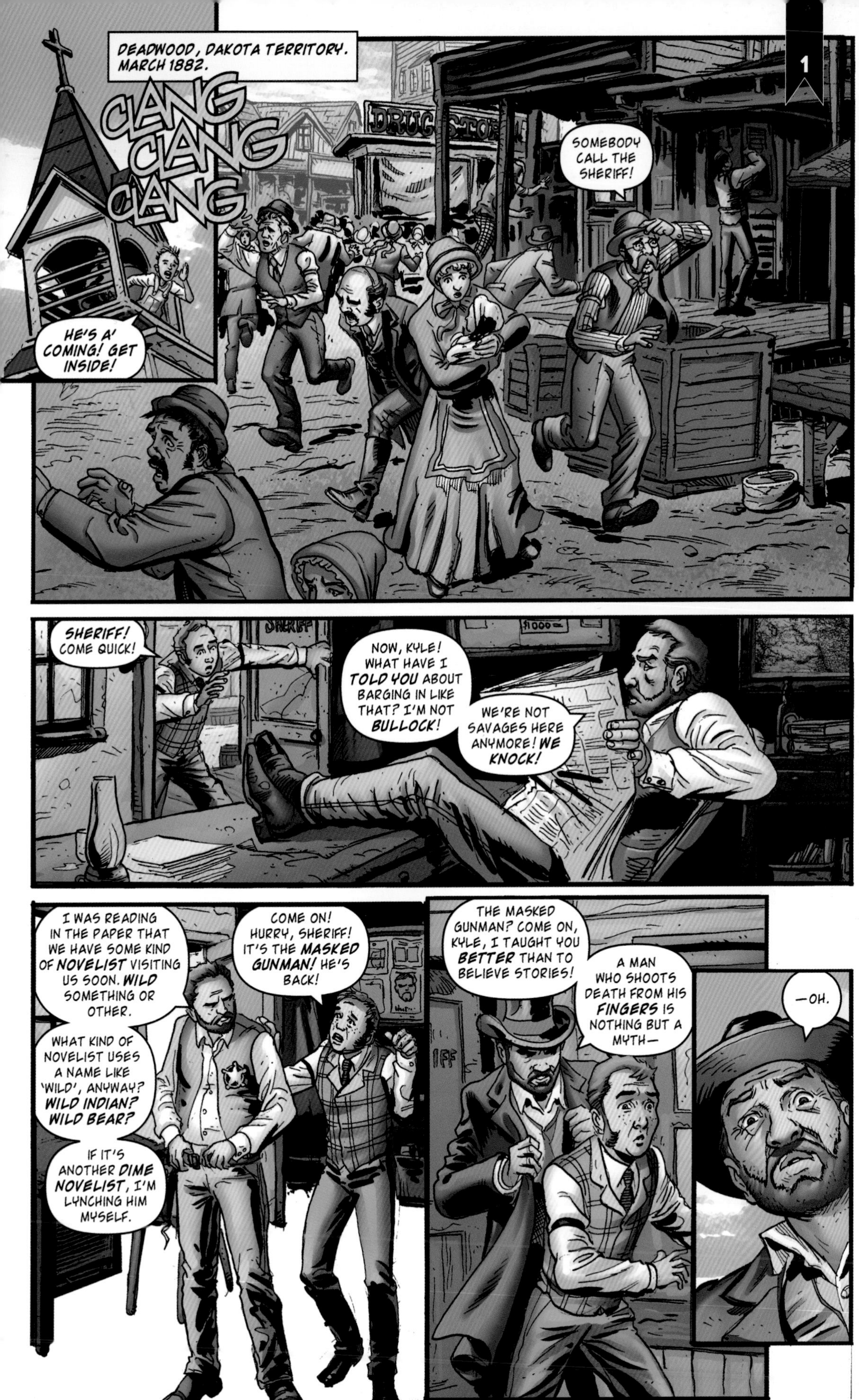
DEADWOOD, DAKOTA TERRITORY. MARCH 1882.
CLANG CLANG CLANG
SOMEBODY CALL THE SHERIFF!
HE'S A' COMING! GET INSIDE!
DRUG STORE
SHERIFF! COME QUICK!
NOW, KYLE! WHAT HAVE I TOLD YOU ABOUT BARGING IN LIKE THAT? I'M NOT BULLOCK!
WE'RE NOT SAVAGES HERE ANYMORE! WE KNOCK!
I WAS READING IN THE PAPER THAT WE HAVE SOME KIND OF NOVELIST VISITING US SOON. WILD SOMETHING OR OTHER.
WHAT KIND OF NOVELIST USES A NAME LIKE 'WILD', ANYWAY? WILD INDIAN? WILD BEAR?
IF IT'S ANOTHER DIME NOVELIST, I'M LYNCHING HIM MYSELF.
COME ON! HURRY, SHERIFF! IT'S THE MASKED GUNMAN! HE'S BACK!
THE MASKED GUNMAN? COME ON, KYLE, I TAUGHT YOU BETTER THAN TO BELIEVE STORIES!
A MAN WHO SHOOTS DEATH FROM HIS FINGERS IS NOTHING BUT A MYTH—
—OH.

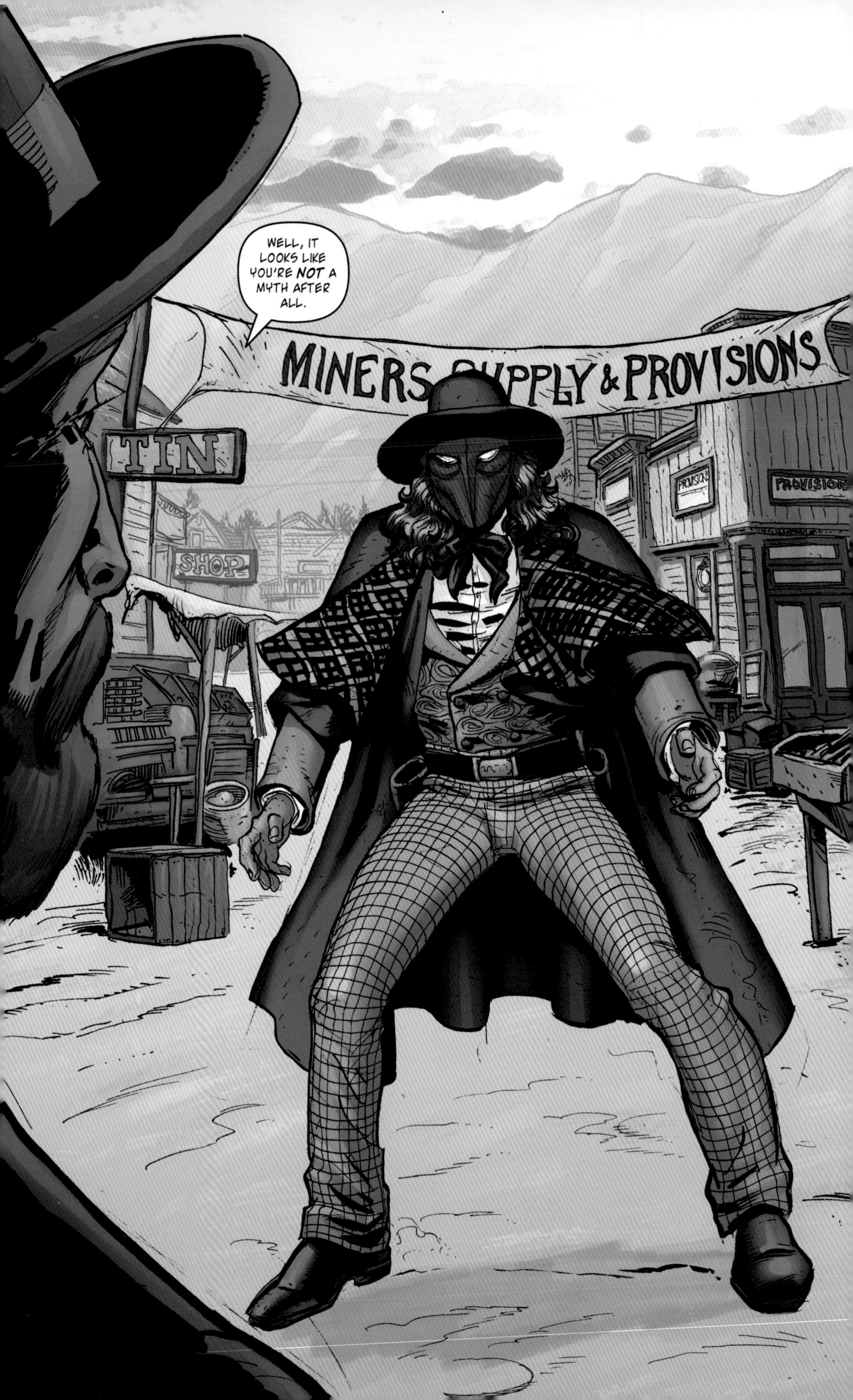
WELL, IT LOOKS LIKE YOU'RE NOT A MYTH AFTER ALL.
MINERS SUPPLY & PROVISIONS
TIN
SHOP
PROVISIONS
PROVISION

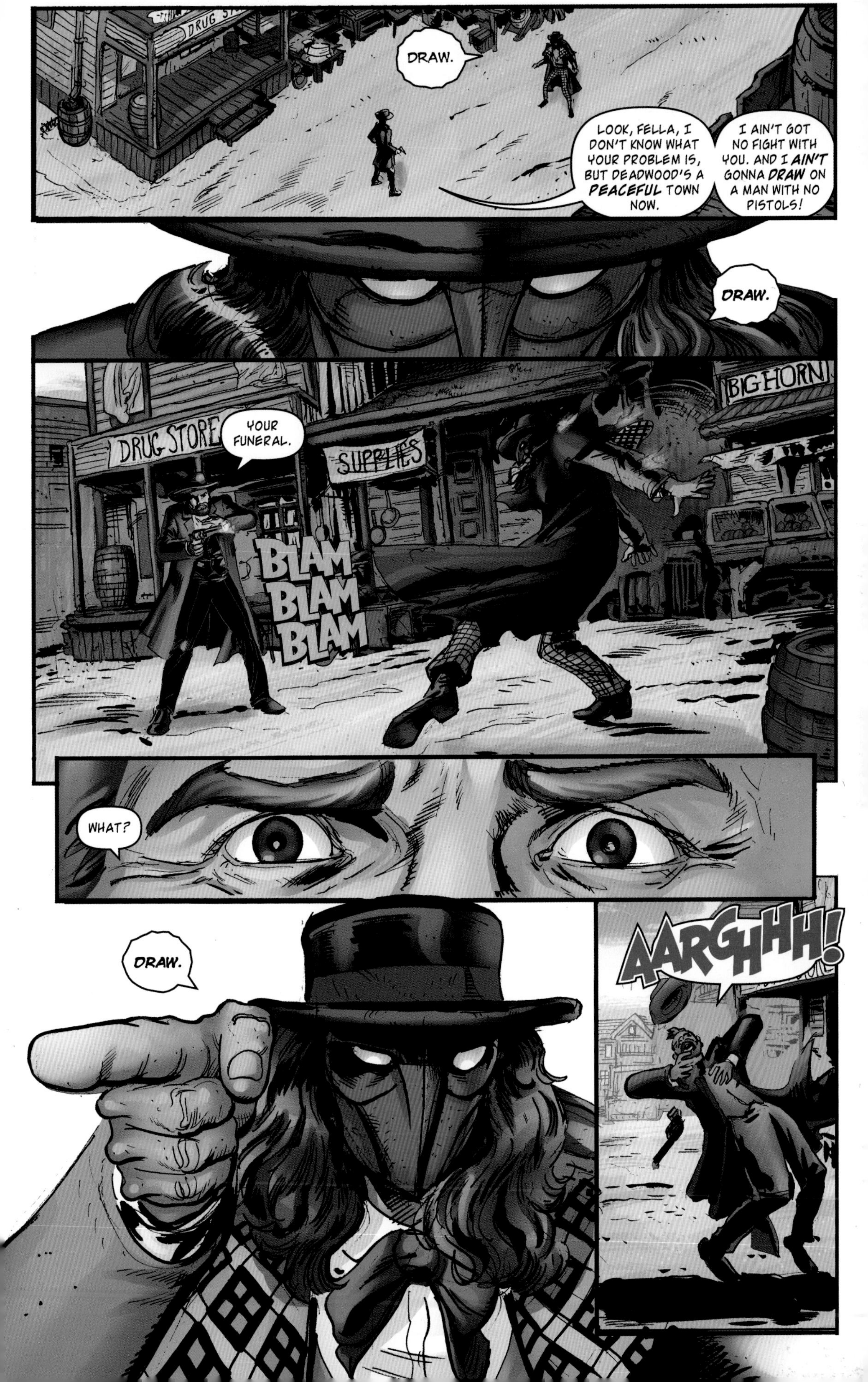
DRUG STORE
DRAW.
LOOK, FELLA, I DON'T KNOW WHAT YOUR PROBLEM IS, BUT DEADWOOD'S A **PEACEFUL** TOWN NOW.
I AIN'T GOT NO FIGHT WITH YOU. AND I **AIN'T** GONNA **DRAW** ON A MAN WITH NO PISTOLS!
DRAW.
BIG HORN
DRUG STORE
SUPPLIES
YOUR FUNERAL.
BLAM BLAM BLAM
WHAT?
DRAW.
AARGHHH!

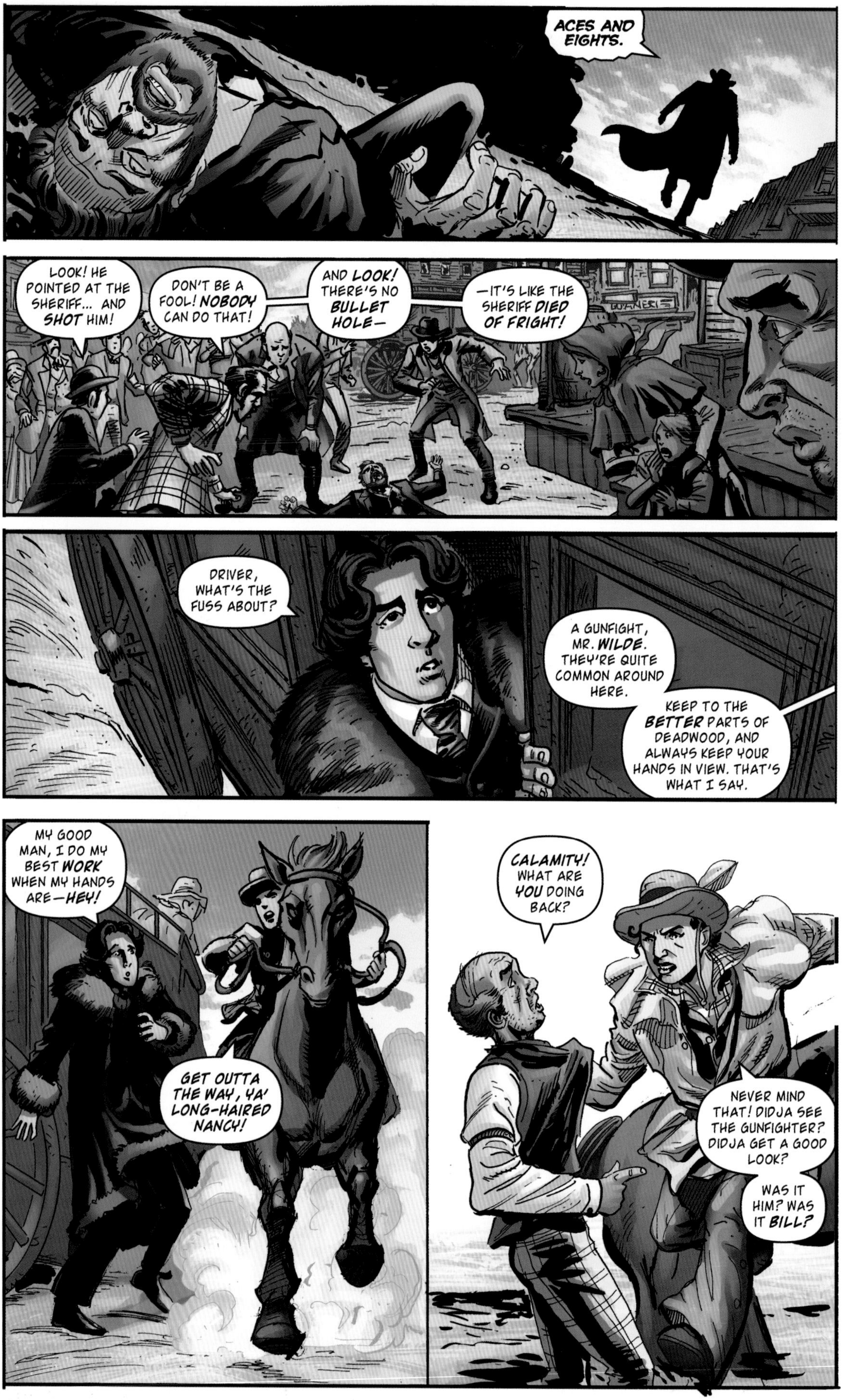
ACES AND EIGHTS.
LOOK! HE POINTED AT THE SHERIFF... AND SHOT HIM!
DON'T BE A FOOL! NOBODY CAN DO THAT!
AND LOOK! THERE'S NO BULLET HOLE—
—IT'S LIKE THE SHERIFF DIED OF FRIGHT!
DRIVER, WHAT'S THE FUSS ABOUT?
A GUNFIGHT, MR. WILDE. THEY'RE QUITE COMMON AROUND HERE.
KEEP TO THE BETTER PARTS OF DEADWOOD, AND ALWAYS KEEP YOUR HANDS IN VIEW. THAT'S WHAT I SAY.
MY GOOD MAN, I DO MY BEST WORK WHEN MY HANDS ARE—HEY!
GET OUTTA THE WAY, YA' LONG-HAIRED NANCY!
CALAMITY! WHAT ARE YOU DOING BACK?
NEVER MIND THAT! DIDJA SEE THE GUNFIGHTER? DIDJA GET A GOOD LOOK?
WAS IT HIM? WAS IT BILL?

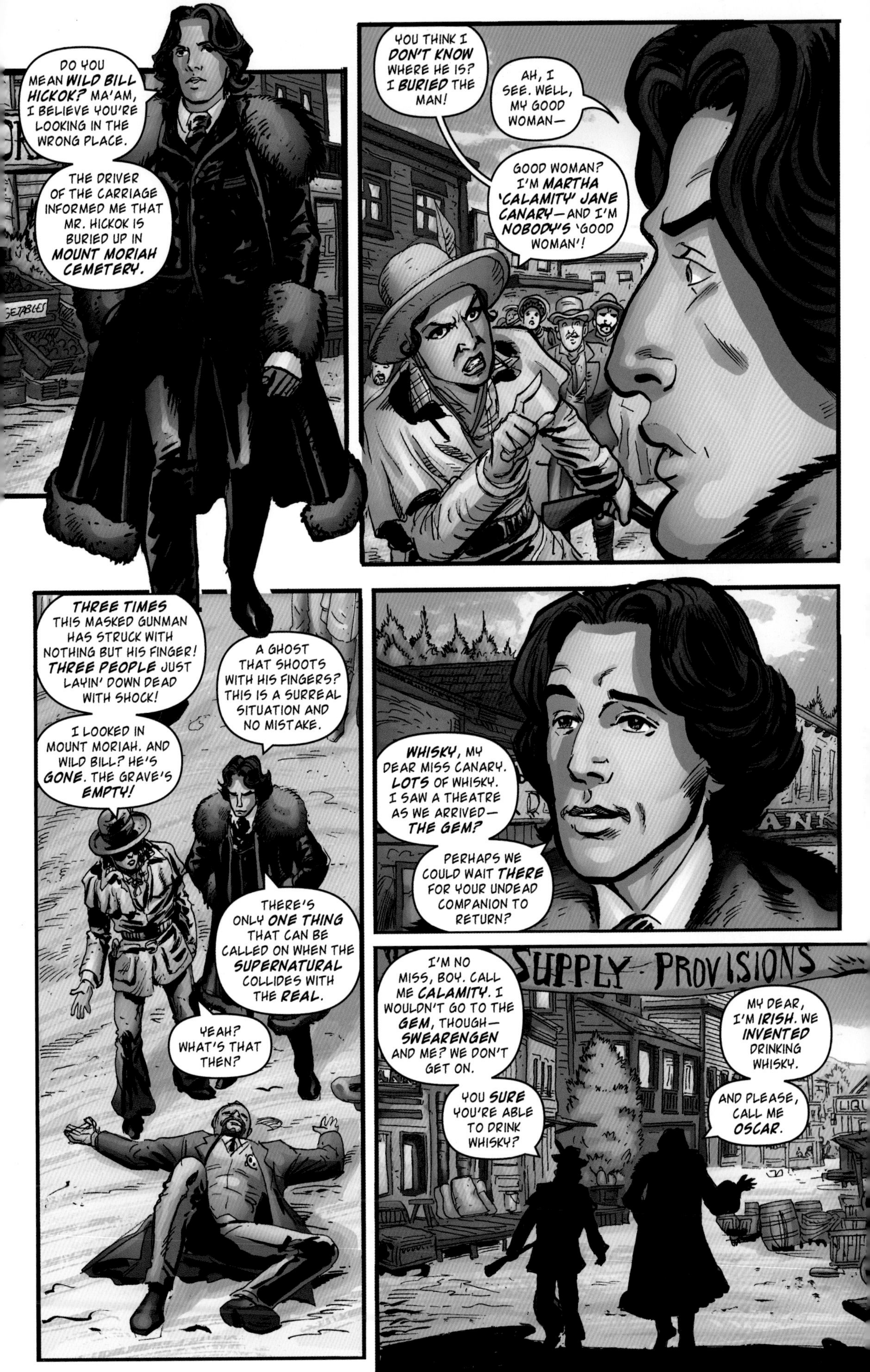
DO YOU MEAN WILD BILL HICKOK? MA'AM, I BELIEVE YOU'RE LOOKING IN THE WRONG PLACE.
THE DRIVER OF THE CARRIAGE INFORMED ME THAT MR. HICKOK IS BURIED UP IN MOUNT MORIAH CEMETERY.
YOU THINK I DON'T KNOW WHERE HE IS? I BURIED THE MAN!
AH, I SEE. WELL, MY GOOD WOMAN—
GOOD WOMAN? I'M MARTHA 'CALAMITY' JANE CANARY—AND I'M NOBODY'S 'GOOD WOMAN'!
THREE TIMES THIS MASKED GUNMAN HAS STRUCK WITH NOTHING BUT HIS FINGER! THREE PEOPLE JUST LAYIN' DOWN DEAD WITH SHOCK!
I LOOKED IN MOUNT MORIAH. AND WILD BILL? HE'S GONE. THE GRAVE'S EMPTY!
A GHOST THAT SHOOTS WITH HIS FINGERS? THIS IS A SURREAL SITUATION AND NO MISTAKE.
THERE'S ONLY ONE THING THAT CAN BE CALLED ON WHEN THE SUPERNATURAL COLLIDES WITH THE REAL.
YEAH? WHAT'S THAT THEN?
WHISKY, MY DEAR MISS CANARY. LOTS OF WHISKY. I SAW A THEATRE AS WE ARRIVED— THE GEM?
PERHAPS WE COULD WAIT THERE FOR YOUR UNDEAD COMPANION TO RETURN?
SUPPLY PROVISIONS
I'M NO MISS, BOY. CALL ME CALAMITY. I WOULDN'T GO TO THE GEM, THOUGH— SWEARENGEN AND ME? WE DON'T GET ON.
YOU SURE YOU'RE ABLE TO DRINK WHISKY?
MY DEAR, I'M IRISH. WE INVENTED DRINKING WHISKY.
AND PLEASE, CALL ME OSCAR.

LONDON. EARTH. NOW.

OH, COME ON. IT'S *WEDNESDAY*. YOU *KNOW* I TURN UP EVERY WEDNESDAY.

SO WHY ARE YOU STILL BEING *NASTY* TO ME? WHAT DID I EVER DO TO YOU?

CLARA OSWALD! YOU'RE LATE!

THE TARDIS WOULDN'T OPEN UP. I'VE SPENT *HALF AN HOUR* TRYING TO BRIBE IT.

TELL ME, WHAT *DO* YOU BRIBE A LARGE WOODEN BOX WITH?

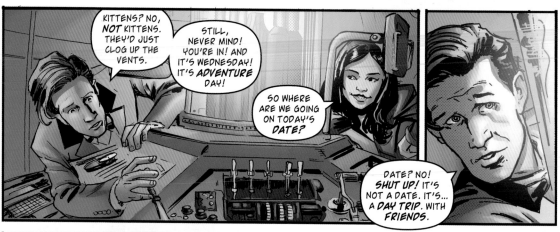

KITTENS? NO, *NOT* KITTENS. THEY'D JUST CLOG UP THE VENTS.

STILL, NEVER MIND! YOU'RE IN! AND IT'S WEDNESDAY! IT'S *ADVENTURE* DAY!

SO WHERE ARE WE GOING ON TODAY'S *DATE?*

DATE? NO! *SHUT UP!* IT'S NOT A DATE. IT'S... A *DAY TRIP*. WITH FRIENDS.

REALLY? THEN YOU SHOULD TELL *ANGIE* AND *ARTIE* THAT.

THEY STILL THINK YOU'RE MY *ECCENTRIC*, TIME-TRAVELLING *BOYFRIEND*.

AND THAT'S WHY YOU SHOULDN'T TRAVEL WITH *CHILDREN*. I MADE THAT MISTAKE WITH ANOTHER PAIR A LONG TIME AGO.

YEARS OF 'ARE WE THERE YET' AND 'WHOOPS, I ACCIDENTALLY PRESSED THE SHINY RED BUTTON'.

THOUGH I COULDN'T BLAME THEM FOR THAT. I MEAN, WHO *DOESN'T* WANT TO PRESS A *SHINY RED BUTTON?*

AS LONG AS IT'S NOT A *BIG FRIENDLY BUTTON*—I'VE HAD ENOUGH OF *THOSE* FOR A WHILE!

SO WHERE ARE WE GOING TODAY?

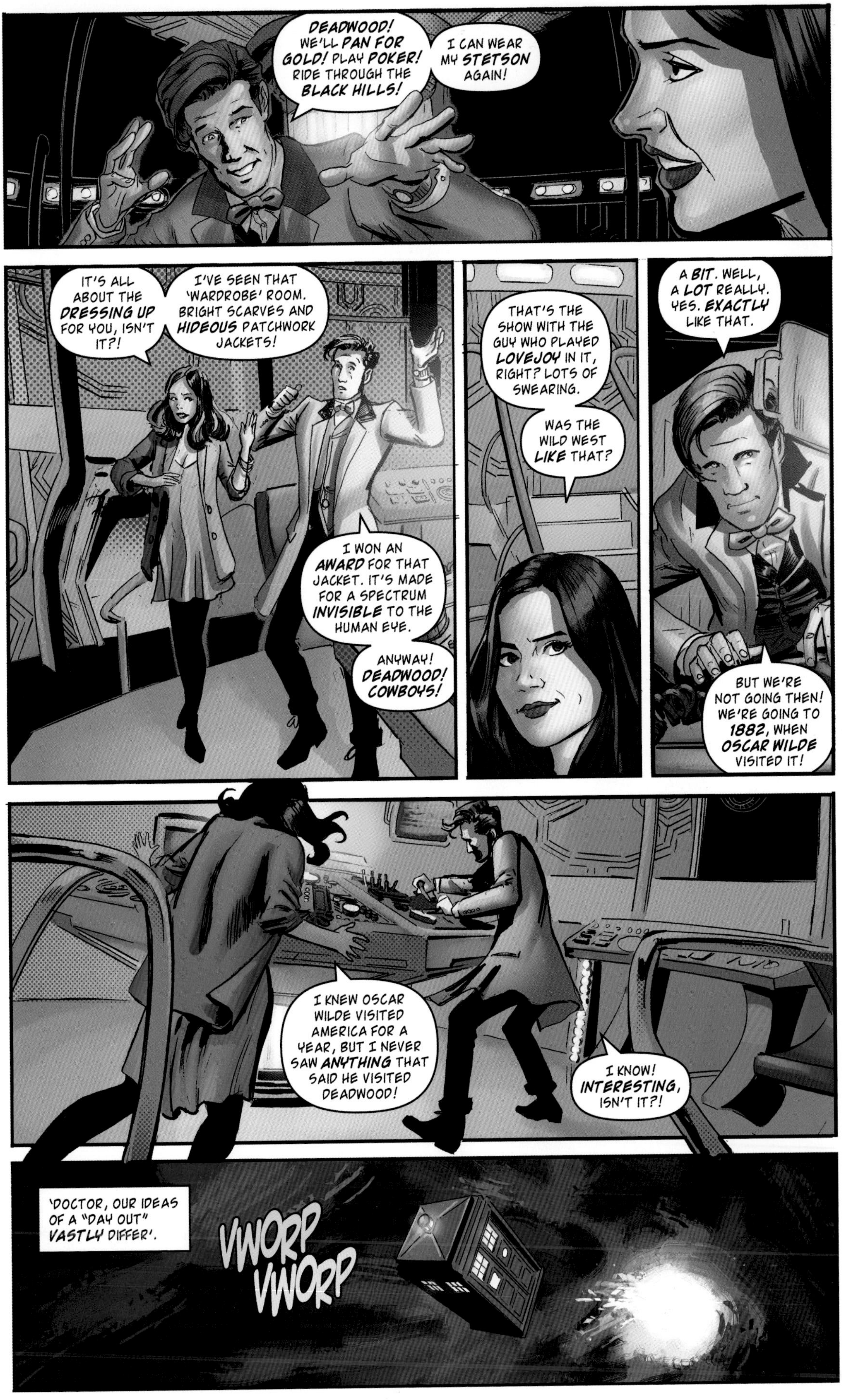
DEADWOOD! WE'LL PAN FOR GOLD! PLAY POKER! RIDE THROUGH THE BLACK HILLS!
I CAN WEAR MY STETSON AGAIN!
IT'S ALL ABOUT THE DRESSING UP FOR YOU, ISN'T IT?!
I'VE SEEN THAT 'WARDROBE' ROOM. BRIGHT SCARVES AND HIDEOUS PATCHWORK JACKETS!
I WON AN AWARD FOR THAT JACKET. IT'S MADE FOR A SPECTRUM INVISIBLE TO THE HUMAN EYE.
ANYWAY! DEADWOOD! COWBOYS!
THAT'S THE SHOW WITH THE GUY WHO PLAYED LOVEJOY IN IT, RIGHT? LOTS OF SWEARING.
WAS THE WILD WEST LIKE THAT?
A BIT. WELL, A LOT REALLY. YES. EXACTLY LIKE THAT.
BUT WE'RE NOT GOING THEN! WE'RE GOING TO 1882, WHEN OSCAR WILDE VISITED IT!
I KNEW OSCAR WILDE VISITED AMERICA FOR A YEAR, BUT I NEVER SAW ANYTHING THAT SAID HE VISITED DEADWOOD!
I KNOW! INTERESTING, ISN'T IT?!
'DOCTOR, OUR IDEAS OF A "DAY OUT" VASTLY DIFFER'.
VWORP VWORP

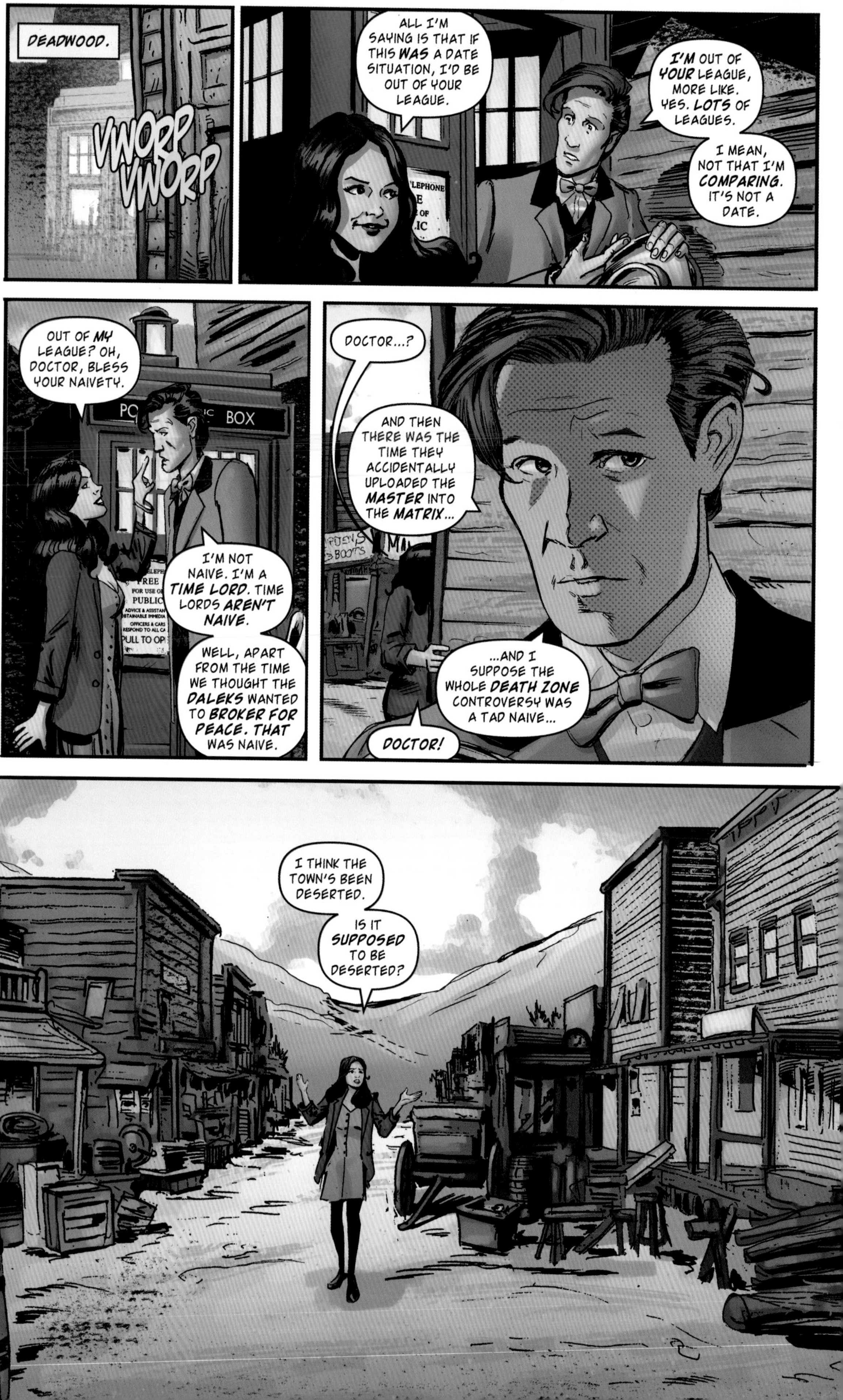
DEADWOOD.
VWORP VWORP
ALL I'M SAYING IS THAT IF THIS WAS A DATE SITUATION, I'D BE OUT OF YOUR LEAGUE.
I'M OUT OF YOUR LEAGUE, MORE LIKE. YES. LOTS OF LEAGUES.
I MEAN, NOT THAT I'M COMPARING. IT'S NOT A DATE.
OUT OF MY LEAGUE? OH, DOCTOR, BLESS YOUR NAIVETY.
I'M NOT NAIVE. I'M A TIME LORD. TIME LORDS AREN'T NAIVE.
WELL, APART FROM THE TIME WE THOUGHT THE DALEKS WANTED TO BROKER FOR PEACE. THAT WAS NAIVE.
DOCTOR...?
AND THEN THERE WAS THE TIME THEY ACCIDENTALLY UPLOADED THE MASTER INTO THE MATRIX...
...AND I SUPPOSE THE WHOLE DEATH ZONE CONTROVERSY WAS A TAD NAIVE...
DOCTOR!
I THINK THE TOWN'S BEEN DESERTED.
IS IT SUPPOSED TO BE DESERTED?

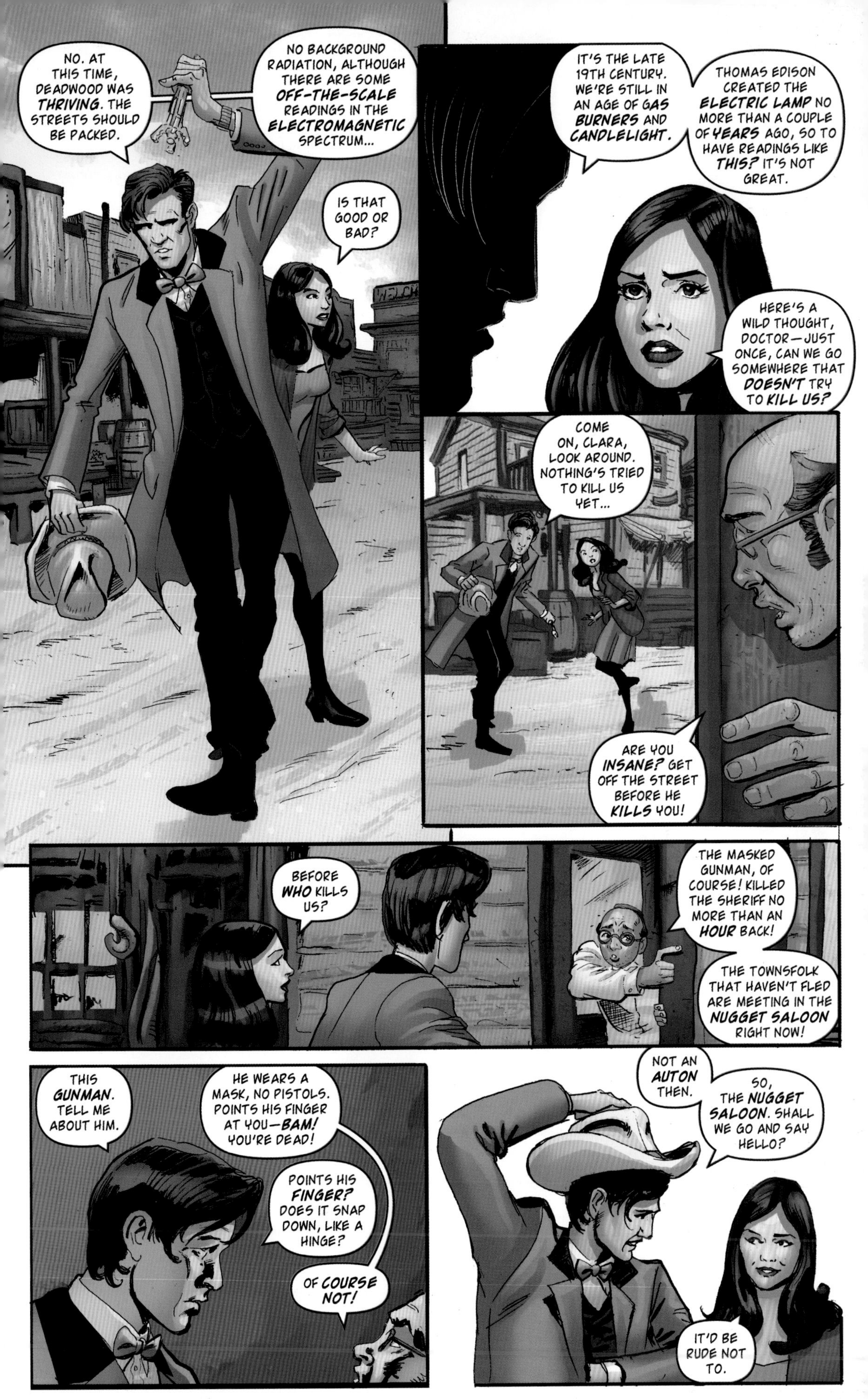
NO. AT THIS TIME, DEADWOOD WAS THRIVING. THE STREETS SHOULD BE PACKED.
NO BACKGROUND RADIATION, ALTHOUGH THERE ARE SOME OFF-THE-SCALE READINGS IN THE ELECTROMAGNETIC SPECTRUM...
IS THAT GOOD OR BAD?
IT'S THE LATE 19TH CENTURY. WE'RE STILL IN AN AGE OF GAS BURNERS AND CANDLELIGHT.
THOMAS EDISON CREATED THE ELECTRIC LAMP NO MORE THAN A COUPLE OF YEARS AGO, SO TO HAVE READINGS LIKE THIS? IT'S NOT GREAT.
HERE'S A WILD THOUGHT, DOCTOR—JUST ONCE, CAN WE GO SOMEWHERE THAT DOESN'T TRY TO KILL US?
COME ON, CLARA, LOOK AROUND. NOTHING'S TRIED TO KILL US YET...
ARE YOU INSANE? GET OFF THE STREET BEFORE HE KILLS YOU!
BEFORE WHO KILLS US?
THE MASKED GUNMAN, OF COURSE! KILLED THE SHERIFF NO MORE THAN AN HOUR BACK!
THE TOWNSFOLK THAT HAVEN'T FLED ARE MEETING IN THE NUGGET SALOON RIGHT NOW!
THIS GUNMAN. TELL ME ABOUT HIM.
HE WEARS A MASK, NO PISTOLS. POINTS HIS FINGER AT YOU—BAM! YOU'RE DEAD!
POINTS HIS FINGER? DOES IT SNAP DOWN, LIKE A HINGE?
OF COURSE NOT!
NOT AN AUTON THEN.
SO, THE NUGGET SALOON. SHALL WE GO AND SAY HELLO?
IT'D BE RUDE NOT TO.

THE NUGGET SALOON.

BRADFORD WAS A GOOD MAN—AND OF *COURSE* I WANT TO SEEK JUSTICE— BUT I'M NO LONGER DEADWOOD'S SHERIFF.

WE NEED TO CONTACT *MARSHAL RAYMOND* IN *YANKTON* ON THIS.

THAT'LL TAKE DAYS, *BULLOCK!* WE NEED ACTION *NOW!*

BRADFORD SHOT THE GUNSLINGER *FOUR TIMES*, DEAD CENTRE! HE STAYED STANDING!

THIS AIN'T NO MAN, THIS IS A *DEMON*, SENT TO TEST US!

HE AIN'T NO DEMON, BUT HE AIN'T NO MAN, EITHER. THIS MASKED GUNMAN IS *WILD BILL HIMSELF.*

I LOOKED IN THE *CEMETERY* THIS MORNING— HIS BODY'S BEEN *TAKEN.*

THAT'S *MADNESS!* WILD BILL CAN'T COME BACK FROM THE DEAD!

YOU MET BILL WHEN HE WAS ALIVE, FERRIS! YOU TELLIN' ME IT DIDN'T *LOOK* LIKE HIM?

HE WAS WEARING A *MASK!*

WE NEED TO CALL THE *7TH CAVALRY!* WHO ELSE CAN HELP US?

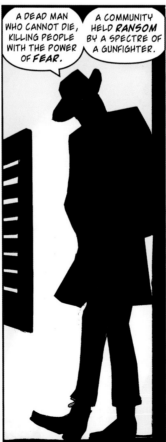

A DEAD MAN WHO CANNOT DIE, KILLING PEOPLE WITH THE POWER OF *FEAR.*

A COMMUNITY HELD *RANSOM* BY A SPECTRE OF A GUNFIGHTER.

SOUNDS LIKE YOU NEED A *NEW SHERIFF* IN TOWN.

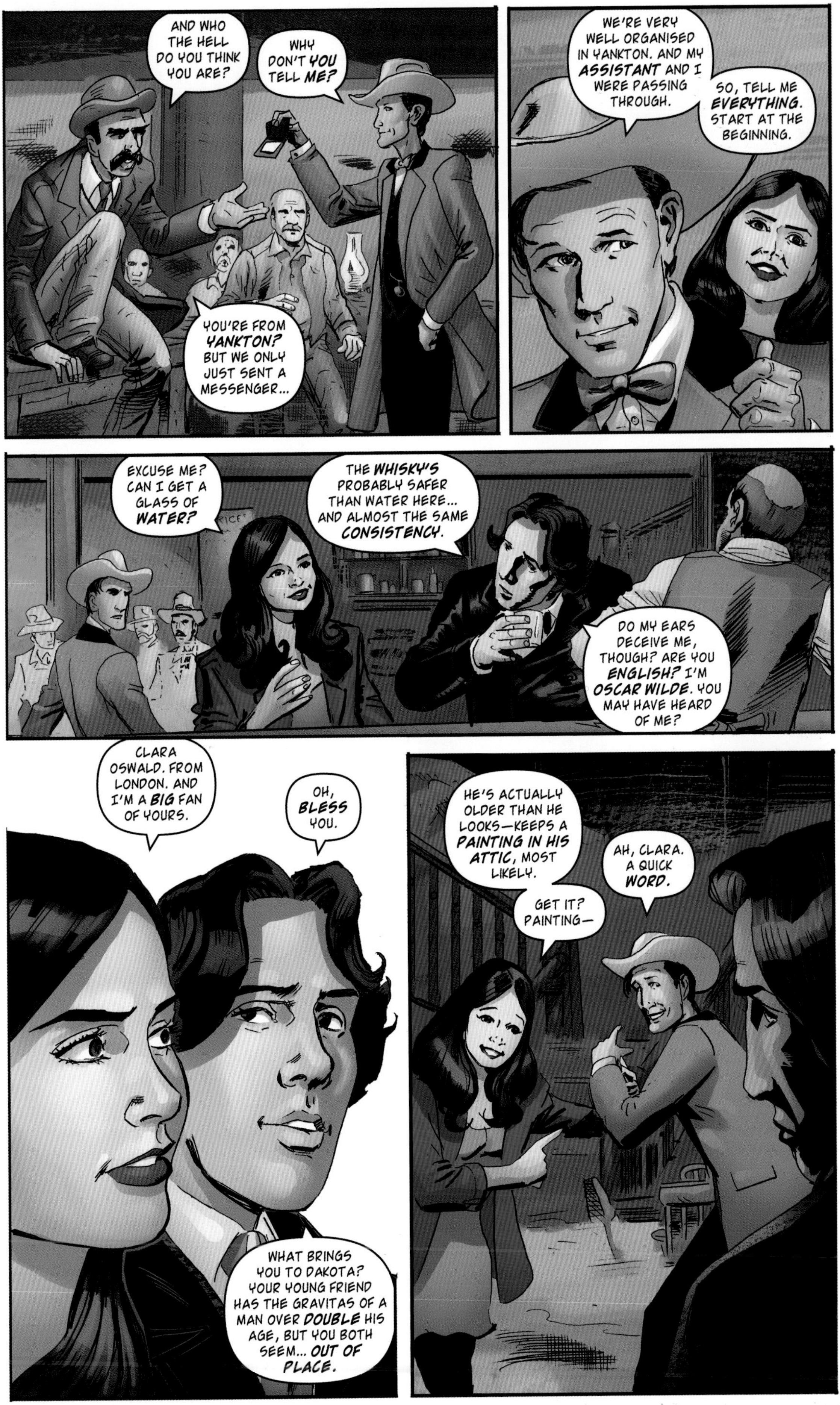
AND WHO THE HELL DO YOU THINK YOU ARE?
WHY DON'T YOU TELL ME?
YOU'RE FROM YANKTON? BUT WE ONLY JUST SENT A MESSENGER...
WE'RE VERY WELL ORGANISED IN YANKTON. AND MY ASSISTANT AND I WERE PASSING THROUGH.
SO, TELL ME EVERYTHING. START AT THE BEGINNING.
EXCUSE ME? CAN I GET A GLASS OF WATER?
THE WHISKY'S PROBABLY SAFER THAN WATER HERE... AND ALMOST THE SAME CONSISTENCY.
DO MY EARS DECEIVE ME, THOUGH? ARE YOU ENGLISH? I'M OSCAR WILDE. YOU MAY HAVE HEARD OF ME?
CLARA OSWALD. FROM LONDON. AND I'M A BIG FAN OF YOURS.
OH, BLESS YOU.
WHAT BRINGS YOU TO DAKOTA? YOUR YOUNG FRIEND HAS THE GRAVITAS OF A MAN OVER DOUBLE HIS AGE, BUT YOU BOTH SEEM... OUT OF PLACE.
HE'S ACTUALLY OLDER THAN HE LOOKS—KEEPS A PAINTING IN HIS ATTIC, MOST LIKELY.
GET IT? PAINTING—
AH, CLARA. A QUICK WORD.

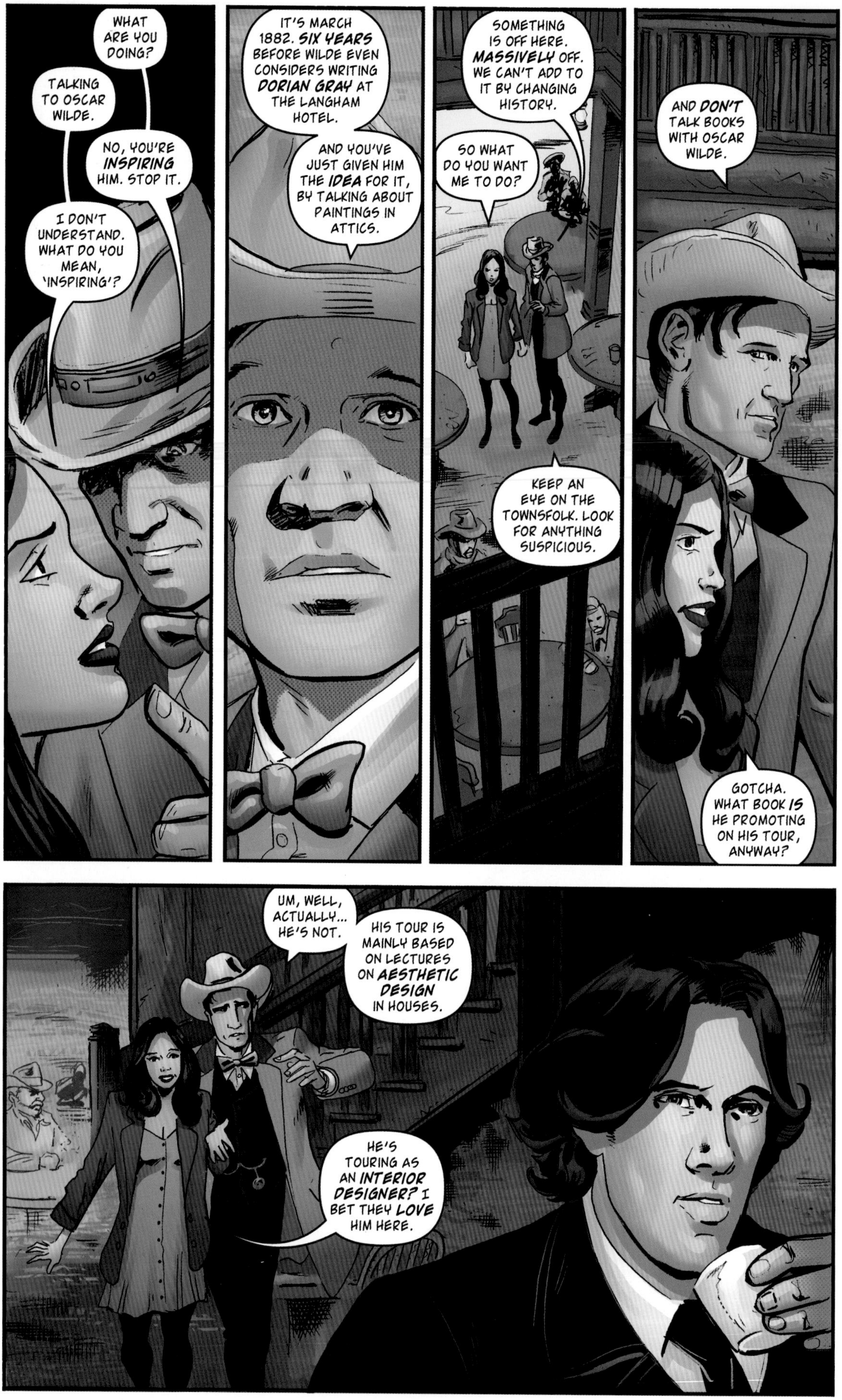
WHAT ARE YOU DOING?
TALKING TO OSCAR WILDE.
NO, YOU'RE INSPIRING HIM. STOP IT.
I DON'T UNDERSTAND. WHAT DO YOU MEAN, 'INSPIRING'?
IT'S MARCH 1882. SIX YEARS BEFORE WILDE EVEN CONSIDERS WRITING DORIAN GRAY AT THE LANGHAM HOTEL.
AND YOU'VE JUST GIVEN HIM THE IDEA FOR IT, BY TALKING ABOUT PAINTINGS IN ATTICS.
SOMETHING IS OFF HERE. MASSIVELY OFF. WE CAN'T ADD TO IT BY CHANGING HISTORY.
SO WHAT DO YOU WANT ME TO DO?
KEEP AN EYE ON THE TOWNSFOLK. LOOK FOR ANYTHING SUSPICIOUS.
AND DON'T TALK BOOKS WITH OSCAR WILDE.
GOTCHA. WHAT BOOK IS HE PROMOTING ON HIS TOUR, ANYWAY?
UM, WELL, ACTUALLY... HE'S NOT.
HIS TOUR IS MAINLY BASED ON LECTURES ON AESTHETIC DESIGN IN HOUSES.
HE'S TOURING AS AN INTERIOR DESIGNER? I BET THEY LOVE HIM HERE.

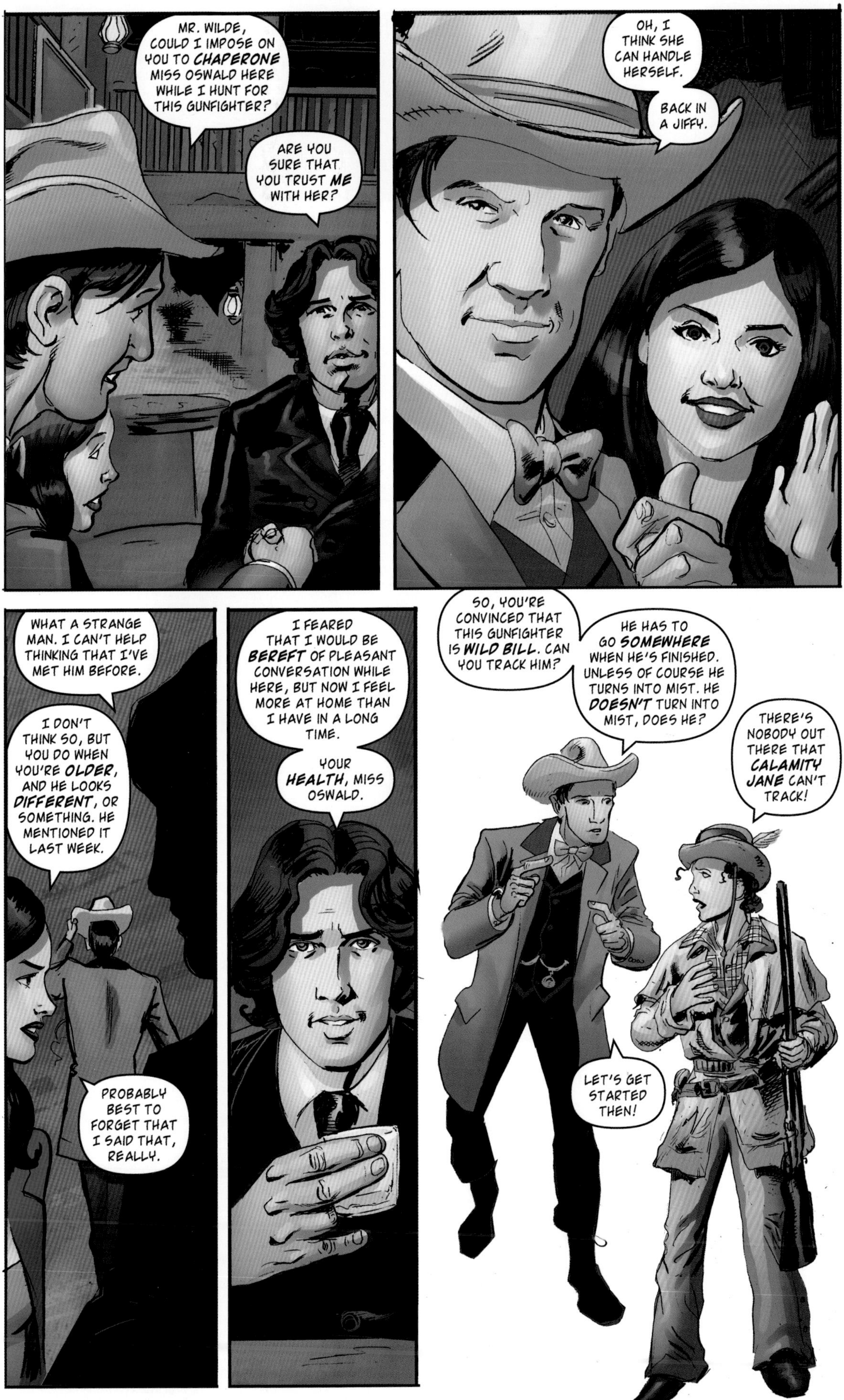
MR. WILDE, COULD I IMPOSE ON YOU TO CHAPERONE MISS OSWALD HERE WHILE I HUNT FOR THIS GUNFIGHTER?
ARE YOU SURE THAT YOU TRUST ME WITH HER?
OH, I THINK SHE CAN HANDLE HERSELF.
BACK IN A JIFFY.
WHAT A STRANGE MAN. I CAN'T HELP THINKING THAT I'VE MET HIM BEFORE.
I DON'T THINK SO, BUT YOU DO WHEN YOU'RE OLDER, AND HE LOOKS DIFFERENT, OR SOMETHING. HE MENTIONED IT LAST WEEK.
PROBABLY BEST TO FORGET THAT I SAID THAT, REALLY.
I FEARED THAT I WOULD BE BEREFT OF PLEASANT CONVERSATION WHILE HERE, BUT NOW I FEEL MORE AT HOME THAN I HAVE IN A LONG TIME.
YOUR HEALTH, MISS OSWALD.
SO, YOU'RE CONVINCED THAT THIS GUNFIGHTER IS WILD BILL. CAN YOU TRACK HIM?
HE HAS TO GO SOMEWHERE WHEN HE'S FINISHED. UNLESS OF COURSE HE TURNS INTO MIST. HE DOESN'T TURN INTO MIST, DOES HE?
THERE'S NOBODY OUT THERE THAT CALAMITY JANE CAN'T TRACK!
LET'S GET STARTED THEN!

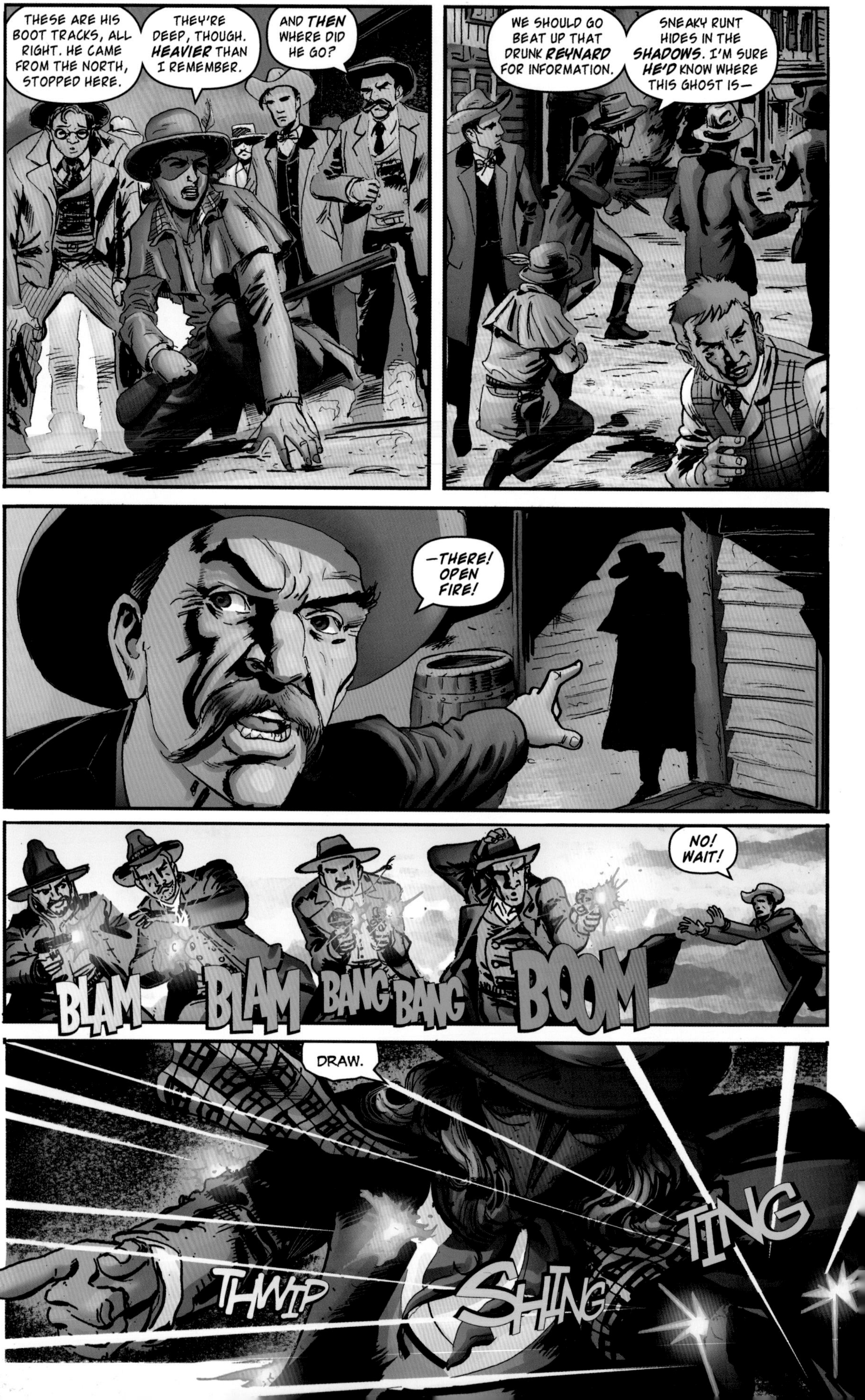
THESE ARE HIS BOOT TRACKS, ALL RIGHT. HE CAME FROM THE NORTH, STOPPED HERE.
THEY'RE DEEP, THOUGH. HEAVIER THAN I REMEMBER.
AND THEN WHERE DID HE GO?
WE SHOULD GO BEAT UP THAT DRUNK REYNARD FOR INFORMATION.
SNEAKY RUNT HIDES IN THE SHADOWS. I'M SURE HE'D KNOW WHERE THIS GHOST IS—
—THERE! OPEN FIRE!
NO! WAIT!
BLAM
BLAM
BANG
BANG
BOOM
DRAW.
THWIP
SHING
TING

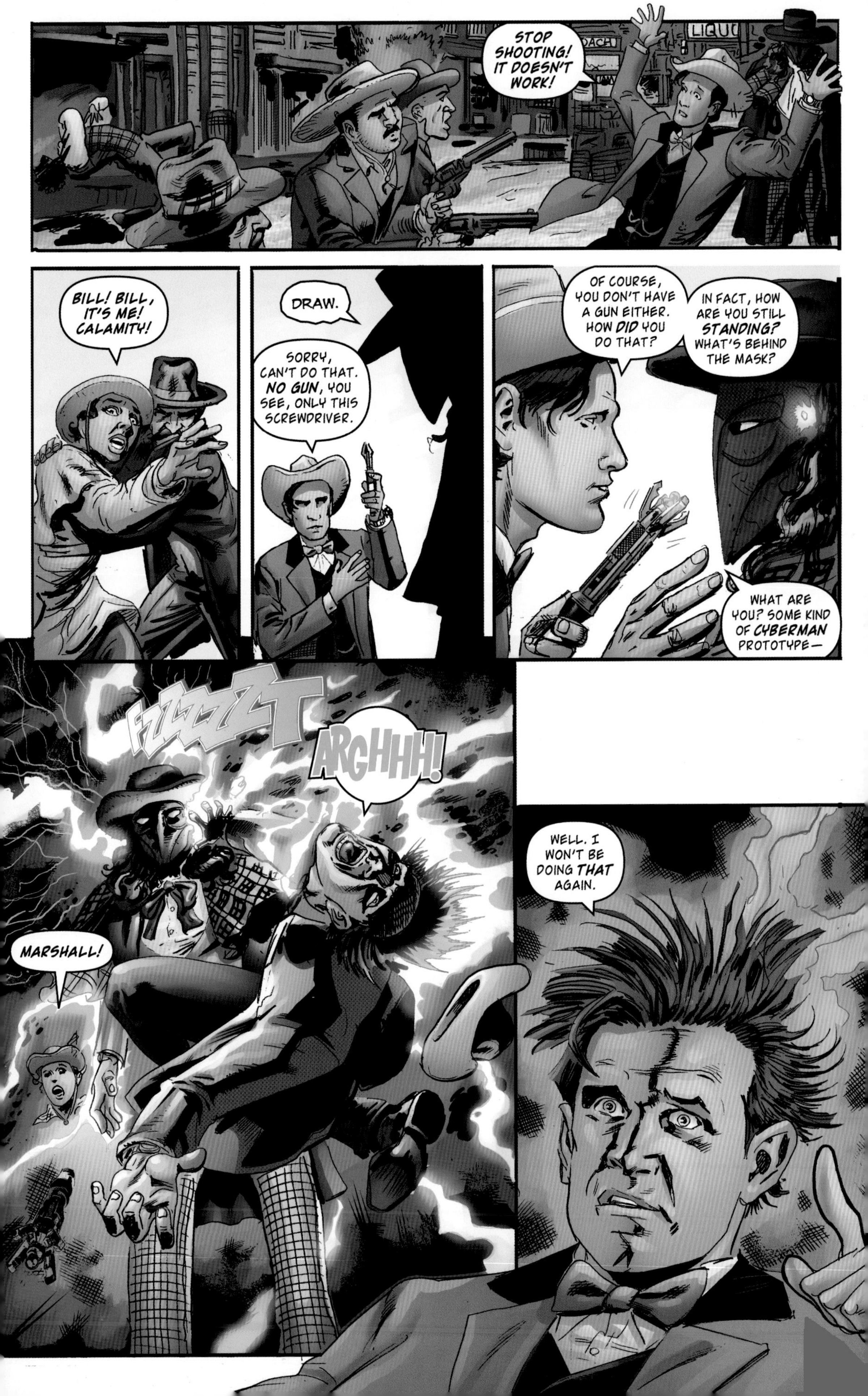
STOP SHOOTING! IT DOESN'T WORK!
LIQU
BILL! BILL, IT'S ME! CALAMITY!
DRAW.
SORRY, CAN'T DO THAT. NO GUN, YOU SEE, ONLY THIS SCREWDRIVER.
OF COURSE, YOU DON'T HAVE A GUN EITHER. HOW DID YOU DO THAT?
IN FACT, HOW ARE YOU STILL STANDING? WHAT'S BEHIND THE MASK?
WHAT ARE YOU? SOME KIND OF CYBERMAN PROTOTYPE—
FZZZZT
ARGHHH!
MARSHALL!
WELL. I WON'T BE DOING THAT AGAIN.

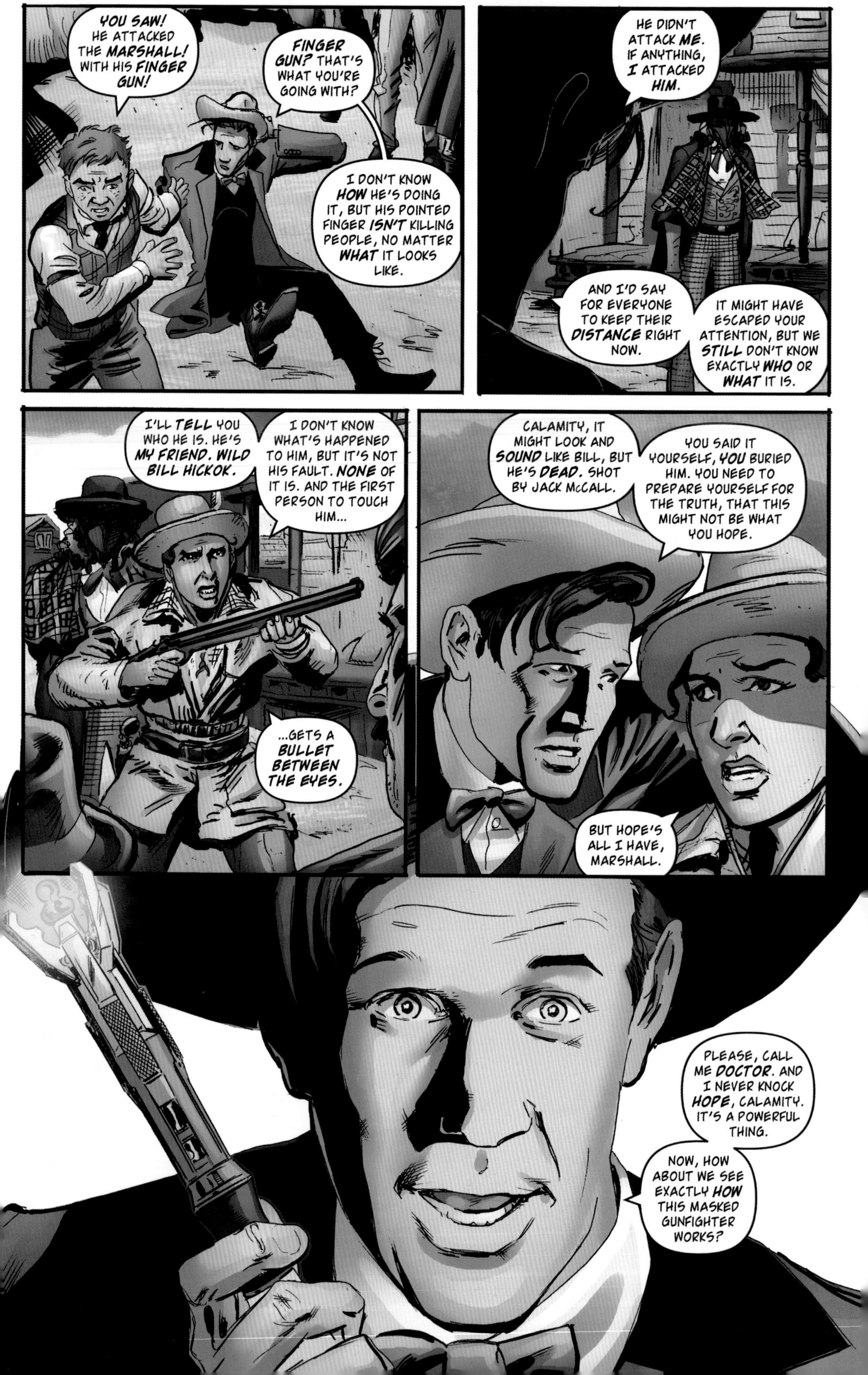
YOU SAW! HE ATTACKED THE MARSHALL! WITH HIS FINGER GUN!
FINGER GUN? THAT'S WHAT YOU'RE GOING WITH?
I DON'T KNOW HOW HE'S DOING IT, BUT HIS POINTED FINGER ISN'T KILLING PEOPLE, NO MATTER WHAT IT LOOKS LIKE.
HE DIDN'T ATTACK ME. IF ANYTHING, I ATTACKED HIM.
AND I'D SAY FOR EVERYONE TO KEEP THEIR DISTANCE RIGHT NOW.
IT MIGHT HAVE ESCAPED YOUR ATTENTION, BUT WE STILL DON'T KNOW EXACTLY WHO OR WHAT IT IS.
I'LL TELL YOU WHO HE IS. HE'S MY FRIEND. WILD BILL HICKOK.
I DON'T KNOW WHAT'S HAPPENED TO HIM, BUT IT'S NOT HIS FAULT. NONE OF IT IS. AND THE FIRST PERSON TO TOUCH HIM...
...GETS A BULLET BETWEEN THE EYES.
CALAMITY, IT MIGHT LOOK AND SOUND LIKE BILL, BUT HE'S DEAD. SHOT BY JACK McCALL.
YOU SAID IT YOURSELF, YOU BURIED HIM. YOU NEED TO PREPARE YOURSELF FOR THE TRUTH, THAT THIS MIGHT NOT BE WHAT YOU HOPE.
BUT HOPE'S ALL I HAVE, MARSHALL.
PLEASE, CALL ME DOCTOR. AND I NEVER KNOCK HOPE, CALAMITY. IT'S A POWERFUL THING.
NOW, HOW ABOUT WE SEE EXACTLY HOW THIS MASKED GUNFIGHTER WORKS?

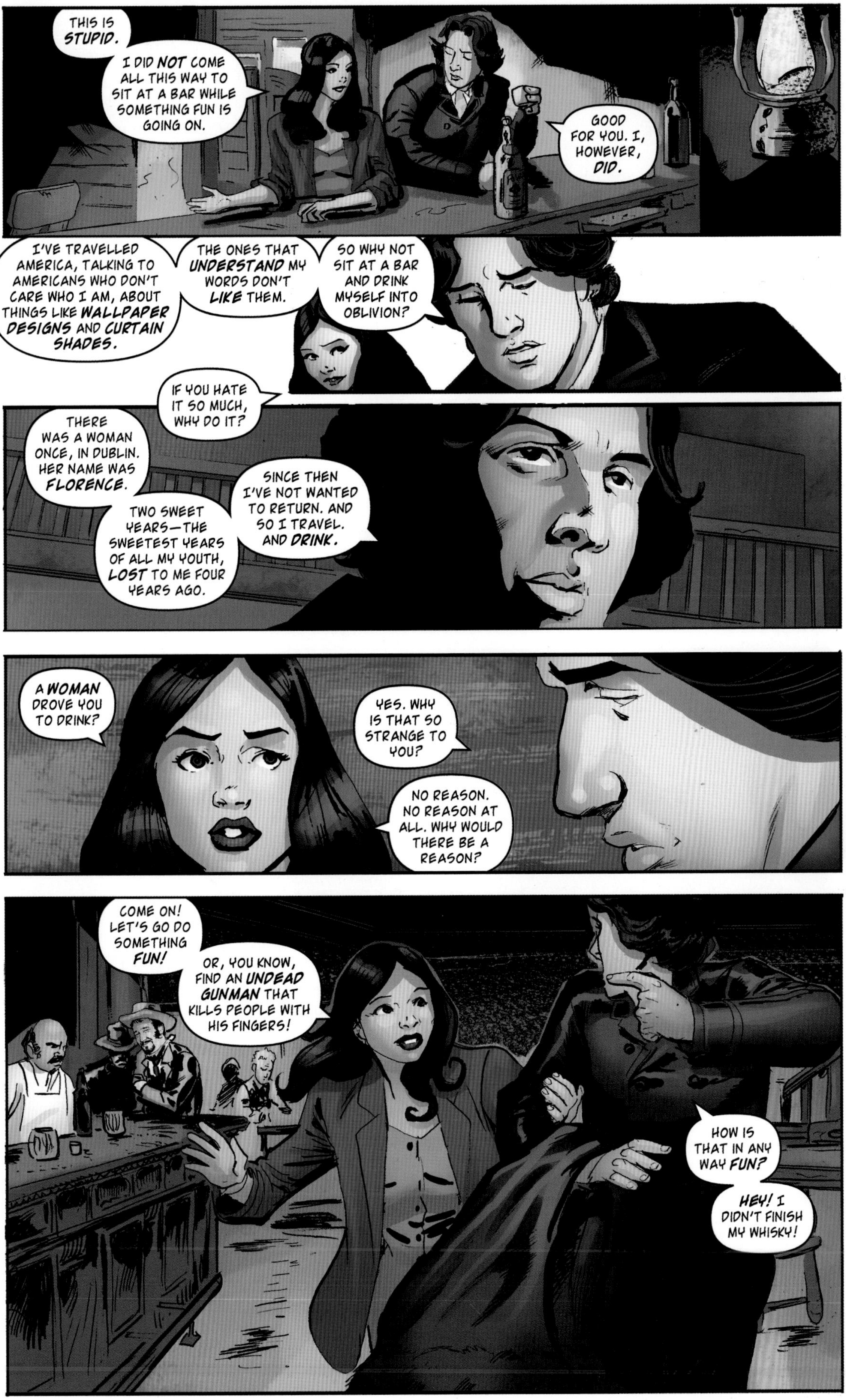
THIS IS STUPID.
I DID NOT COME ALL THIS WAY TO SIT AT A BAR WHILE SOMETHING FUN IS GOING ON.
GOOD FOR YOU. I, HOWEVER, DID.
I'VE TRAVELLED AMERICA, TALKING TO AMERICANS WHO DON'T CARE WHO I AM, ABOUT THINGS LIKE WALLPAPER DESIGNS AND CURTAIN SHADES.
THE ONES THAT UNDERSTAND MY WORDS DON'T LIKE THEM.
SO WHY NOT SIT AT A BAR AND DRINK MYSELF INTO OBLIVION?
IF YOU HATE IT SO MUCH, WHY DO IT?
THERE WAS A WOMAN ONCE, IN DUBLIN. HER NAME WAS FLORENCE.
TWO SWEET YEARS—THE SWEETEST YEARS OF ALL MY YOUTH, LOST TO ME FOUR YEARS AGO.
SINCE THEN I'VE NOT WANTED TO RETURN. AND SO I TRAVEL. AND DRINK.
A WOMAN DROVE YOU TO DRINK?
YES. WHY IS THAT SO STRANGE TO YOU?
NO REASON. NO REASON AT ALL. WHY WOULD THERE BE A REASON?
COME ON! LET'S GO DO SOMETHING FUN!
OR, YOU KNOW, FIND AN UNDEAD GUNMAN THAT KILLS PEOPLE WITH HIS FINGERS!
HOW IS THAT IN ANY WAY FUN?
HEY! I DIDN'T FINISH MY WHISKY!

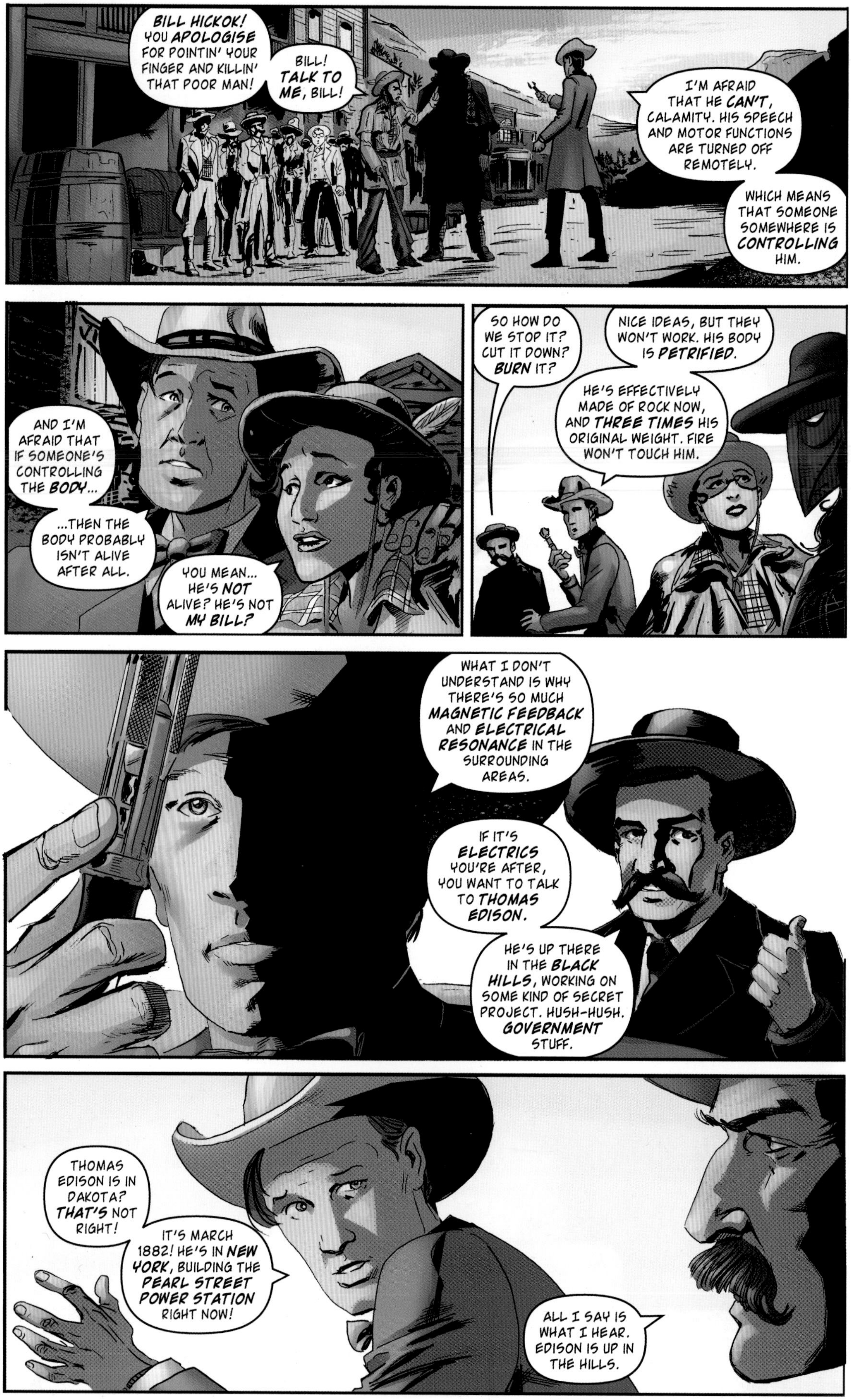
BILL HICKOK! YOU APOLOGISE FOR POINTIN' YOUR FINGER AND KILLIN' THAT POOR MAN!
BILL! TALK TO ME, BILL!
I'M AFRAID THAT HE CAN'T, CALAMITY. HIS SPEECH AND MOTOR FUNCTIONS ARE TURNED OFF REMOTELY.
WHICH MEANS THAT SOMEONE SOMEWHERE IS CONTROLLING HIM.
AND I'M AFRAID THAT IF SOMEONE'S CONTROLLING THE BODY...
...THEN THE BODY PROBABLY ISN'T ALIVE AFTER ALL.
YOU MEAN... HE'S NOT ALIVE? HE'S NOT MY BILL?
SO HOW DO WE STOP IT? CUT IT DOWN? BURN IT?
NICE IDEAS, BUT THEY WON'T WORK. HIS BODY IS PETRIFIED.
HE'S EFFECTIVELY MADE OF ROCK NOW, AND THREE TIMES HIS ORIGINAL WEIGHT. FIRE WON'T TOUCH HIM.
WHAT I DON'T UNDERSTAND IS WHY THERE'S SO MUCH MAGNETIC FEEDBACK AND ELECTRICAL RESONANCE IN THE SURROUNDING AREAS.
IF IT'S ELECTRICS YOU'RE AFTER, YOU WANT TO TALK TO THOMAS EDISON.
HE'S UP THERE IN THE BLACK HILLS, WORKING ON SOME KIND OF SECRET PROJECT. HUSH-HUSH. GOVERNMENT STUFF.
THOMAS EDISON IS IN DAKOTA? THAT'S NOT RIGHT!
IT'S MARCH 1882! HE'S IN NEW YORK, BUILDING THE PEARL STREET POWER STATION RIGHT NOW!
ALL I SAY IS WHAT I HEAR. EDISON IS UP IN THE HILLS.

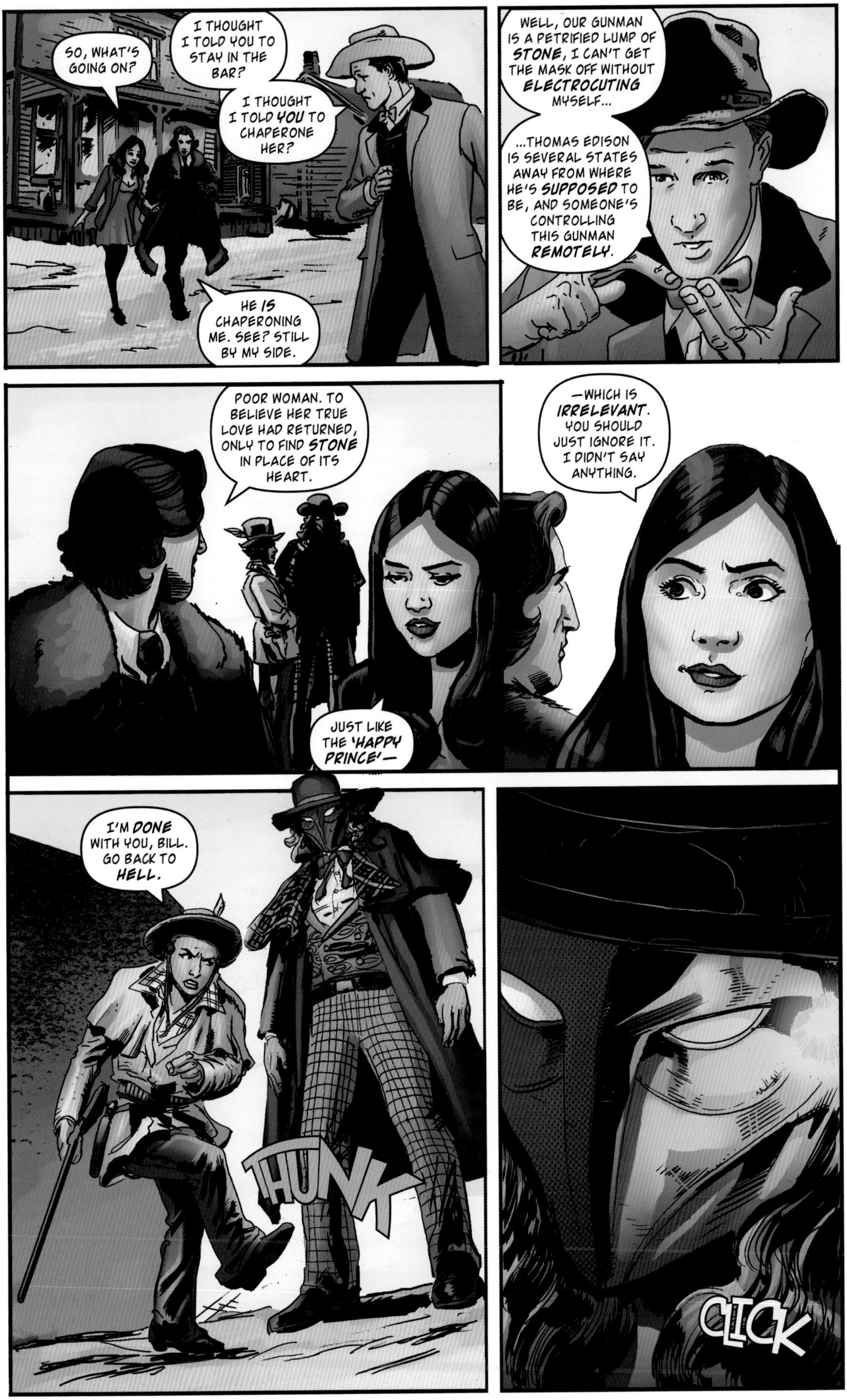

SO, WHAT'S GOING ON?
I THOUGHT I TOLD YOU TO STAY IN THE BAR?
I THOUGHT I TOLD YOU TO CHAPERONE HER?
HE IS CHAPERONING ME. SEE? STILL BY MY SIDE.
WELL, OUR GUNMAN IS A PETRIFIED LUMP OF STONE, I CAN'T GET THE MASK OFF WITHOUT ELECTROCUTING MYSELF...
...THOMAS EDISON IS SEVERAL STATES AWAY FROM WHERE HE'S SUPPOSED TO BE, AND SOMEONE'S CONTROLLING THIS GUNMAN REMOTELY.
POOR WOMAN. TO BELIEVE HER TRUE LOVE HAD RETURNED, ONLY TO FIND STONE IN PLACE OF ITS HEART.
JUST LIKE THE 'HAPPY PRINCE'—
—WHICH IS IRRELEVANT. YOU SHOULD JUST IGNORE IT. I DIDN'T SAY ANYTHING.
I'M DONE WITH YOU, BILL. GO BACK TO HELL.
THUNK
CLICK

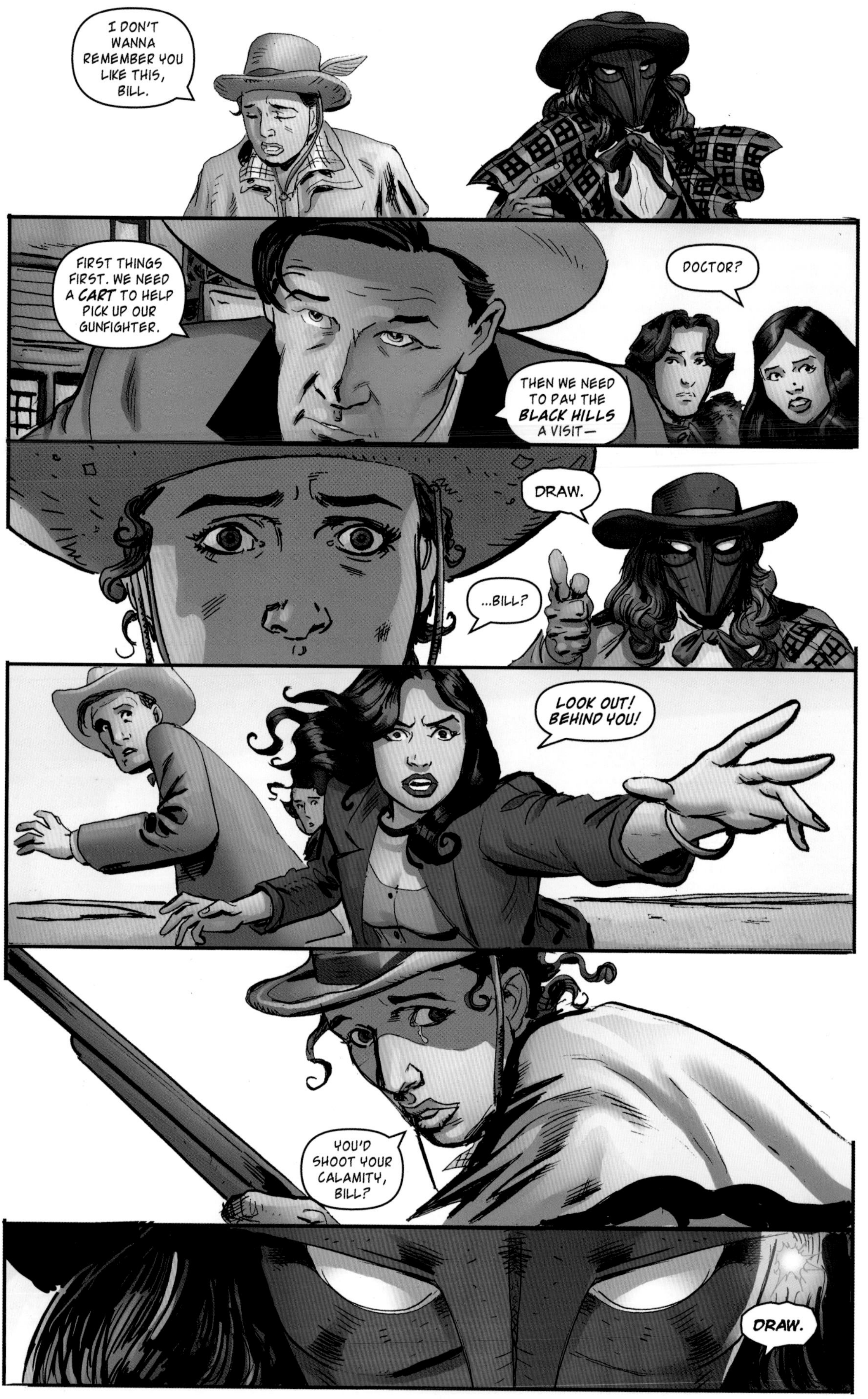
I DON'T WANNA REMEMBER YOU LIKE THIS, BILL.
FIRST THINGS FIRST. WE NEED A CART TO HELP PICK UP OUR GUNFIGHTER.
DOCTOR?
THEN WE NEED TO PAY THE BLACK HILLS A VISIT—
DRAW.
...BILL?
LOOK OUT! BEHIND YOU!
YOU'D SHOOT YOUR CALAMITY, BILL?
DRAW.

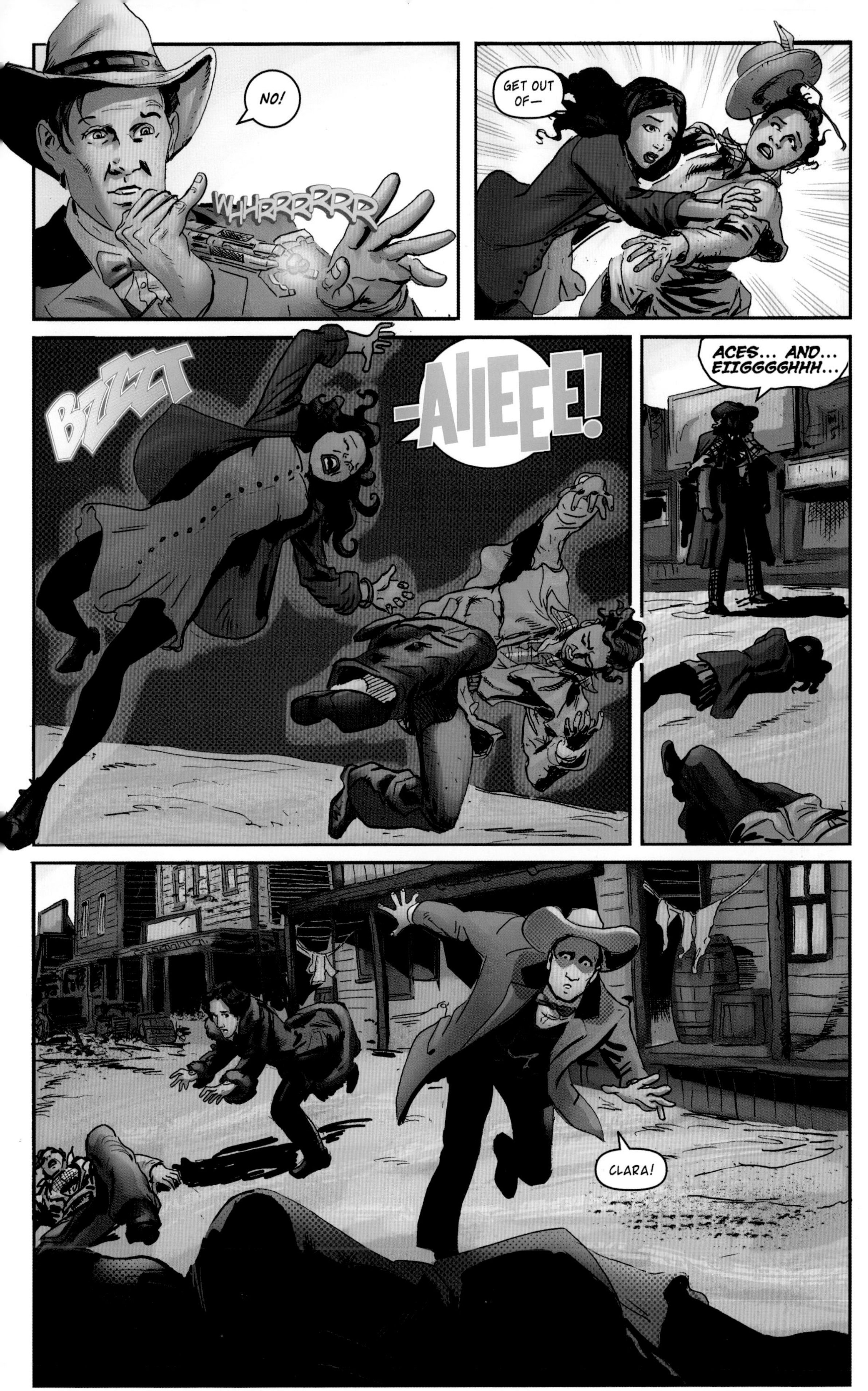
NO!
WHHRRRRRR
GET OUT OF—
BZZZT
-AIIEEE!
ACES... AND... EIIGGGGHHH...
CLARA!

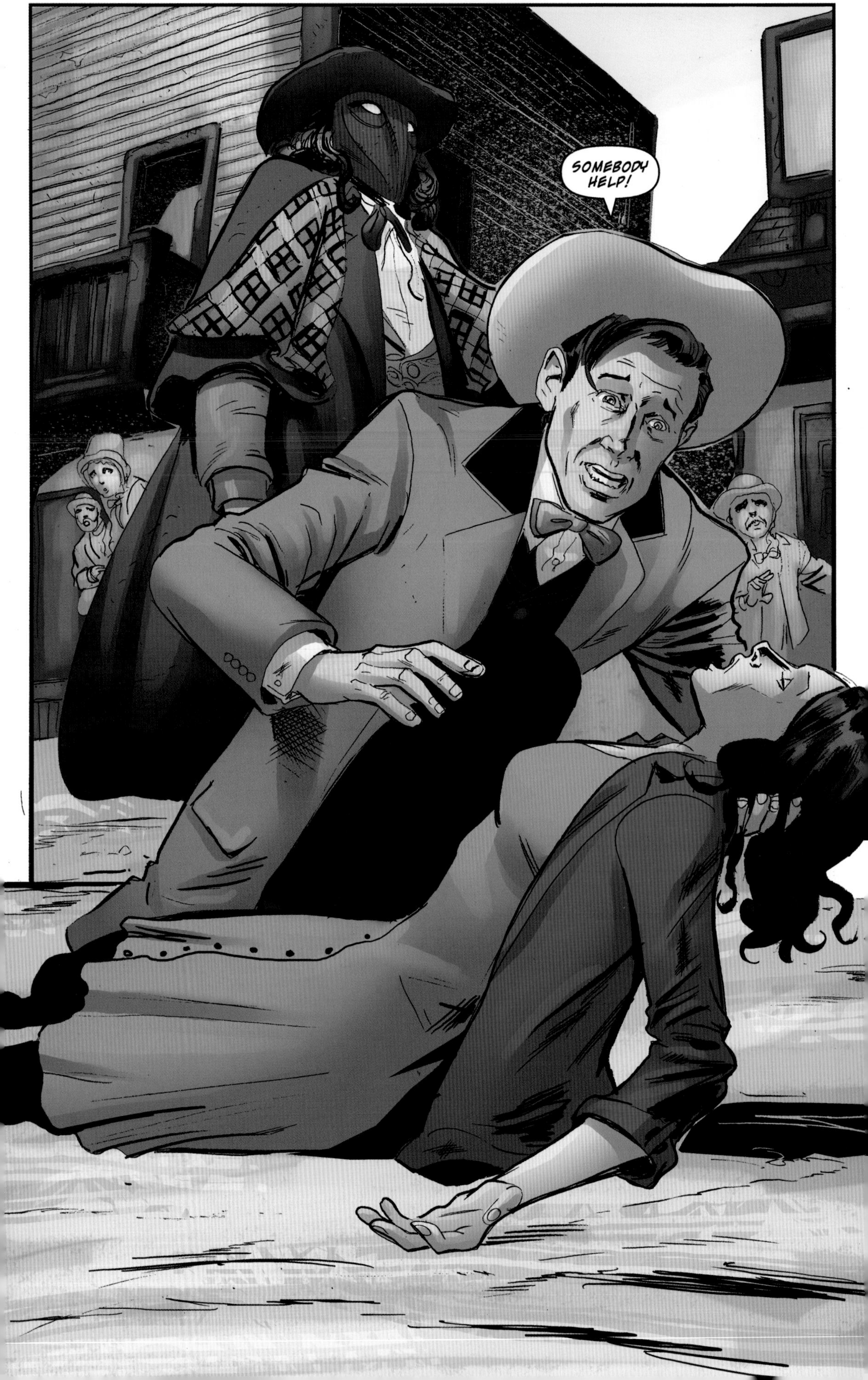
SOMEBODY HELP!

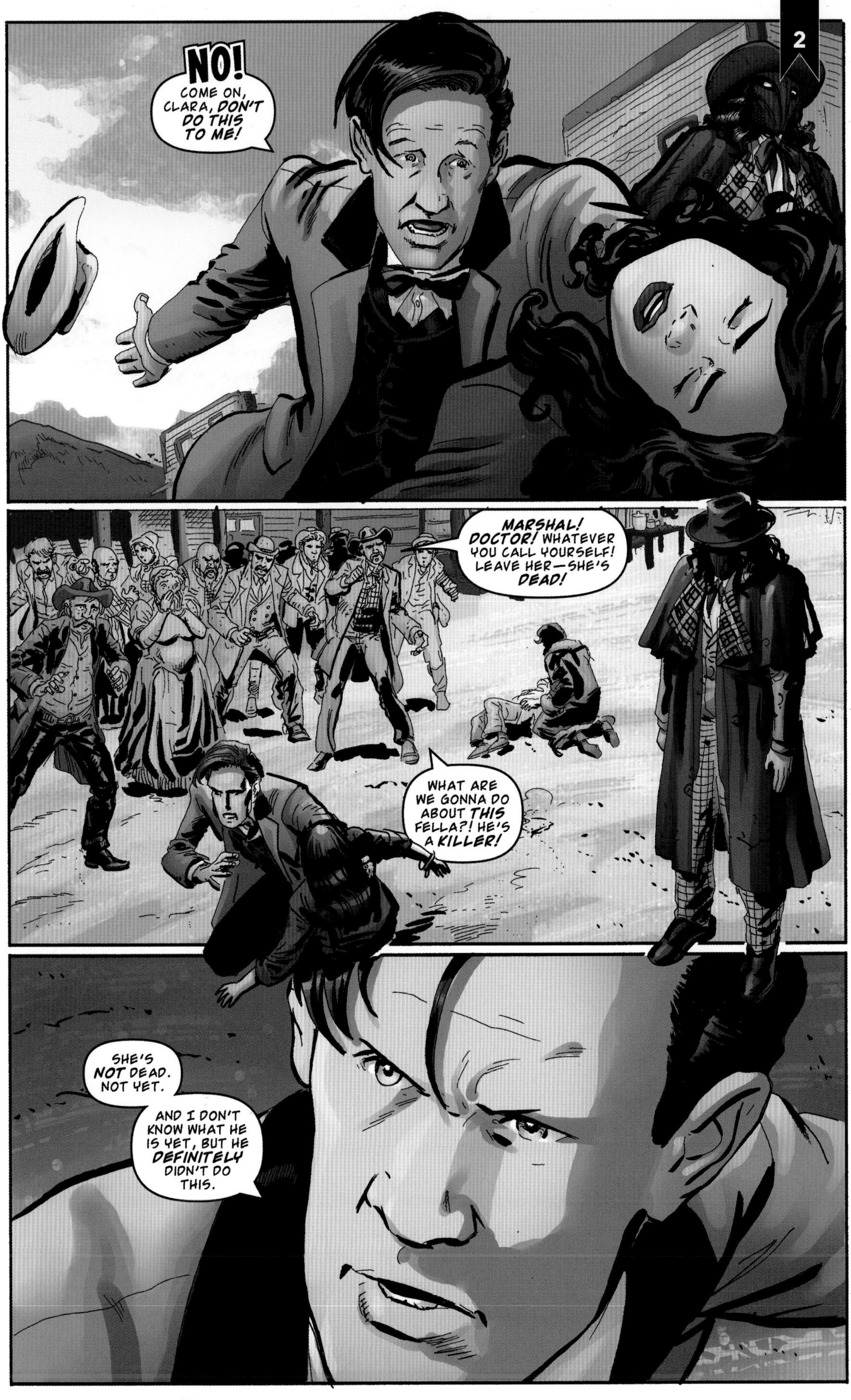
NO!
COME ON, CLARA, DON'T DO THIS TO ME!
MARSHAL! DOCTOR! WHATEVER YOU CALL YOURSELF! LEAVE HER—SHE'S DEAD!
WHAT ARE WE GONNA DO ABOUT THIS FELLA?! HE'S A KILLER!
SHE'S NOT DEAD. NOT YET.
AND I DON'T KNOW WHAT HE IS YET, BUT HE DEFINITELY DIDN'T DO THIS.

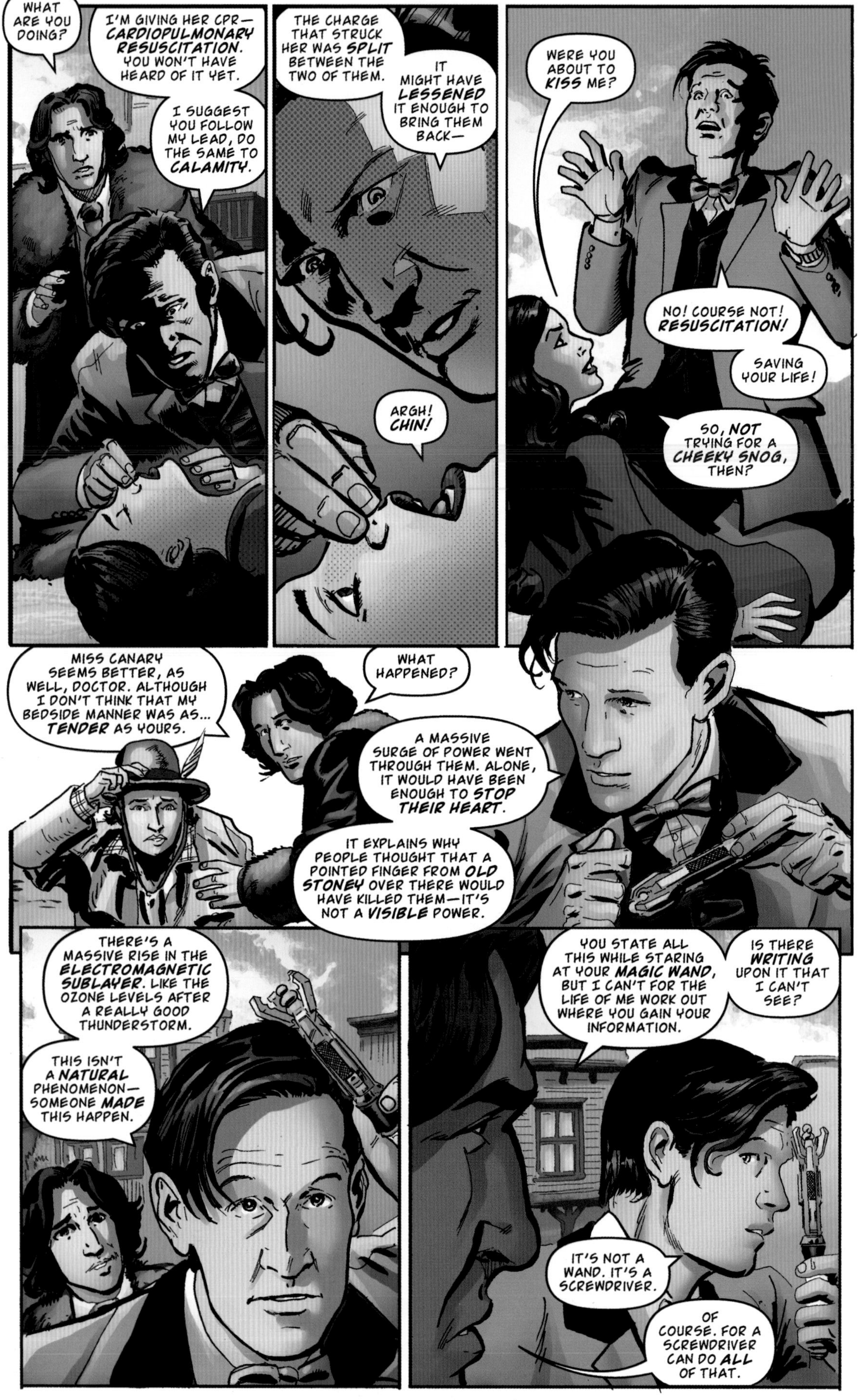
WHAT ARE YOU DOING?
I'M GIVING HER CPR— CARDIOPULMONARY RESUSCITATION. YOU WON'T HAVE HEARD OF IT YET.
I SUGGEST YOU FOLLOW MY LEAD, DO THE SAME TO CALAMITY.
THE CHARGE THAT STRUCK HER WAS SPLIT BETWEEN THE TWO OF THEM.
IT MIGHT HAVE LESSENED IT ENOUGH TO BRING THEM BACK—
ARGH! CHIN!
WERE YOU ABOUT TO KISS ME?
NO! COURSE NOT! RESUSCITATION!
SAVING YOUR LIFE!
SO, NOT TRYING FOR A CHEEKY SNOG, THEN?
MISS CANARY SEEMS BETTER, AS WELL, DOCTOR. ALTHOUGH I DON'T THINK THAT MY BEDSIDE MANNER WAS AS... TENDER AS YOURS.
WHAT HAPPENED?
A MASSIVE SURGE OF POWER WENT THROUGH THEM. ALONE, IT WOULD HAVE BEEN ENOUGH TO STOP THEIR HEART.
IT EXPLAINS WHY PEOPLE THOUGHT THAT A POINTED FINGER FROM OLD STONEY OVER THERE WOULD HAVE KILLED THEM—IT'S NOT A VISIBLE POWER.
THERE'S A MASSIVE RISE IN THE ELECTROMAGNETIC SUBLAYER. LIKE THE OZONE LEVELS AFTER A REALLY GOOD THUNDERSTORM.
THIS ISN'T A NATURAL PHENOMENON— SOMEONE MADE THIS HAPPEN.
YOU STATE ALL THIS WHILE STARING AT YOUR MAGIC WAND, BUT I CAN'T FOR THE LIFE OF ME WORK OUT WHERE YOU GAIN YOUR INFORMATION.
IS THERE WRITING UPON IT THAT I CAN'T SEE?
IT'S NOT A WAND. IT'S A SCREWDRIVER.
OF COURSE. FOR A SCREWDRIVER CAN DO ALL OF THAT.

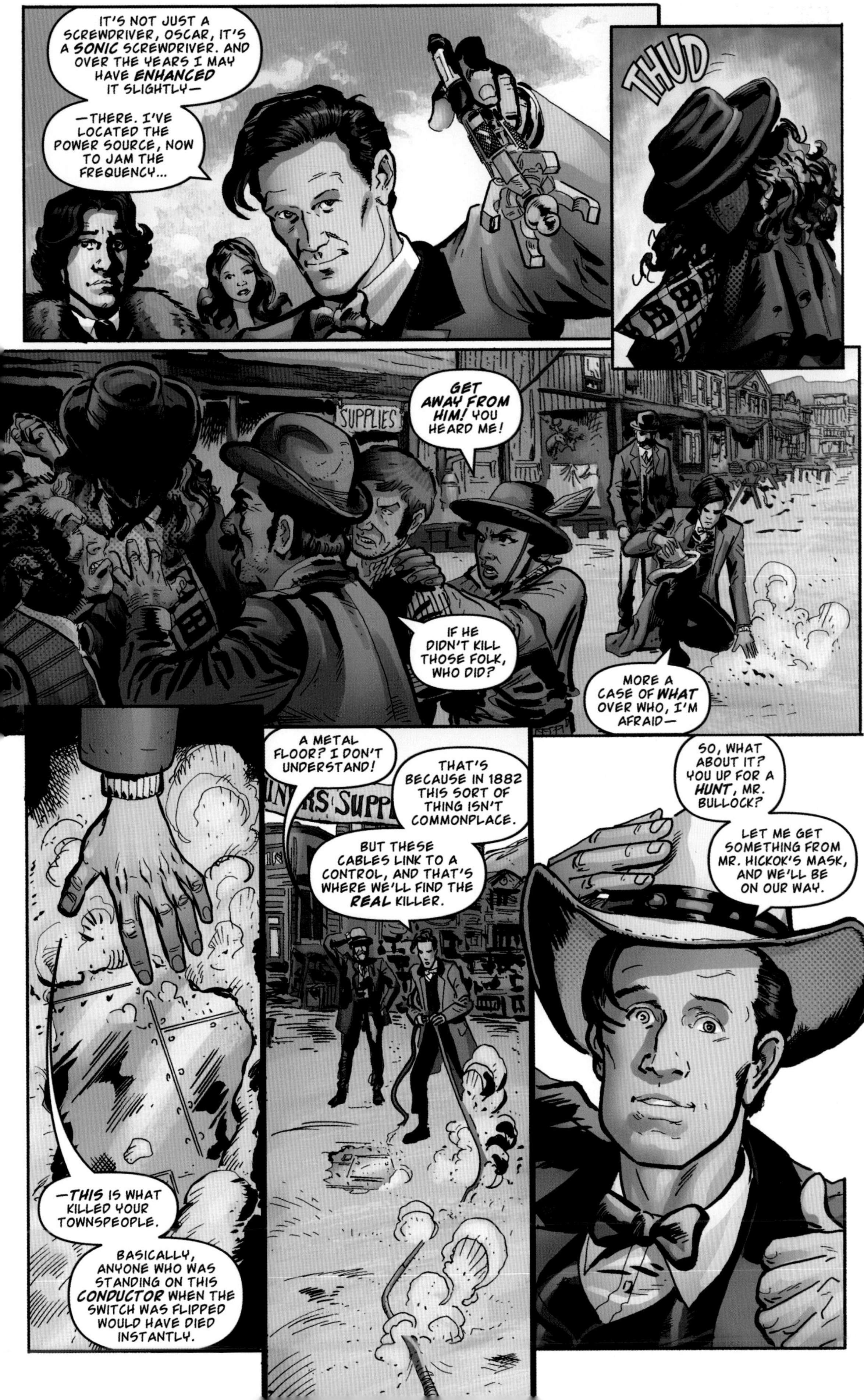

IT'S NOT JUST A SCREWDRIVER, OSCAR, IT'S A SONIC SCREWDRIVER. AND OVER THE YEARS I MAY HAVE ENHANCED IT SLIGHTLY—
—THERE. I'VE LOCATED THE POWER SOURCE, NOW TO JAM THE FREQUENCY...
THUD
SUPPLIES
GET AWAY FROM HIM! YOU HEARD ME!
IF HE DIDN'T KILL THOSE FOLK, WHO DID?
MORE A CASE OF WHAT OVER WHO, I'M AFRAID—
—THIS IS WHAT KILLED YOUR TOWNSPEOPLE.
BASICALLY, ANYONE WHO WAS STANDING ON THIS CONDUCTOR WHEN THE SWITCH WAS FLIPPED WOULD HAVE DIED INSTANTLY.
A METAL FLOOR? I DON'T UNDERSTAND!
THAT'S BECAUSE IN 1882 THIS SORT OF THING ISN'T COMMONPLACE.
BUT THESE CABLES LINK TO A CONTROL, AND THAT'S WHERE WE'LL FIND THE REAL KILLER.
SO, WHAT ABOUT IT? YOU UP FOR A HUNT, MR. BULLOCK?
LET ME GET SOMETHING FROM MR. HICKOK'S MASK, AND WE'LL BE ON OUR WAY.

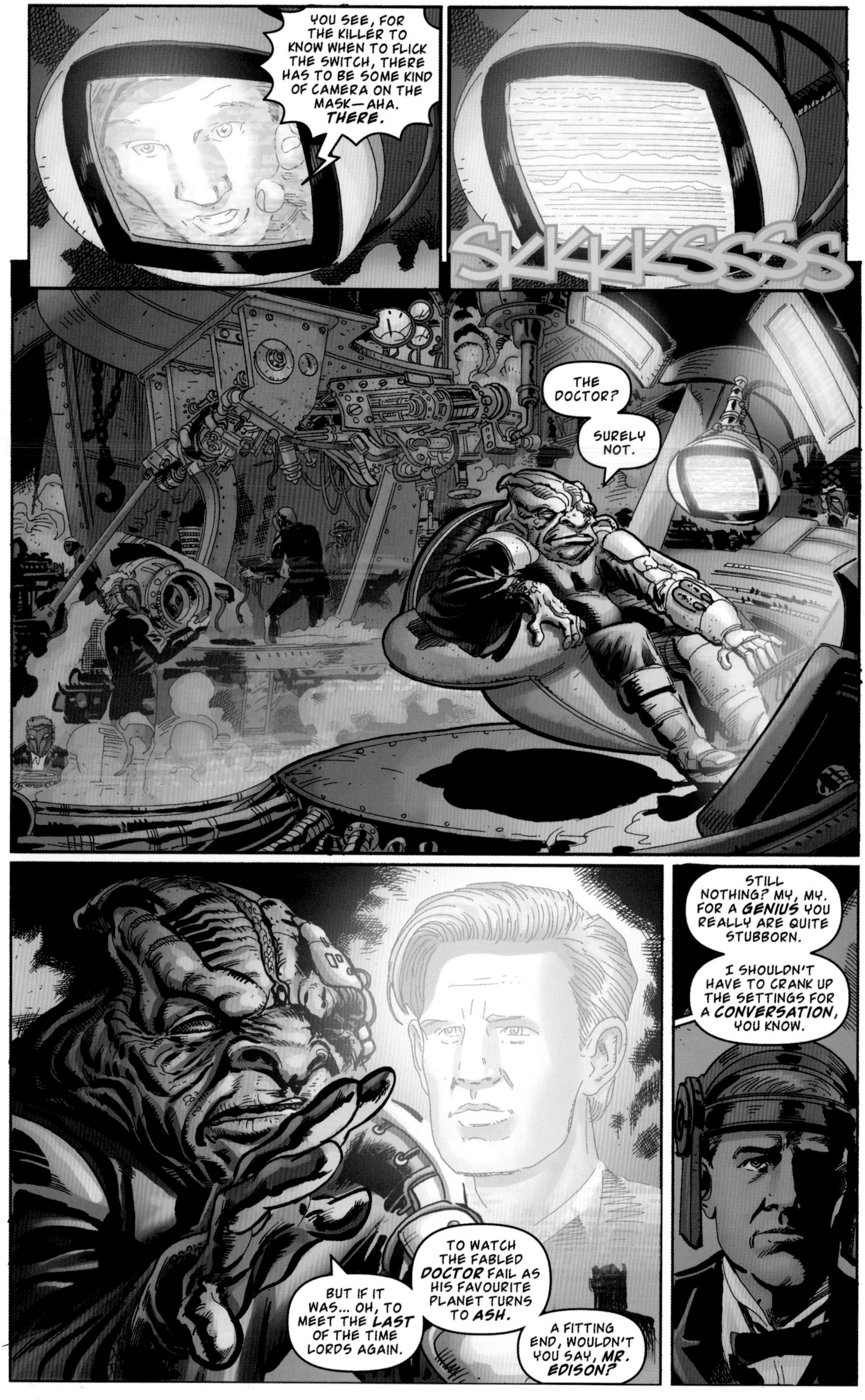

YOU SEE, FOR THE KILLER TO KNOW WHEN TO FLICK THE SWITCH, THERE HAS TO BE SOME KIND OF CAMERA ON THE MASK—AHA. THERE.
SKKKSSSS
THE DOCTOR?
SURELY NOT.
BUT IF IT WAS... OH, TO MEET THE LAST OF THE TIME LORDS AGAIN.
TO WATCH THE FABLED DOCTOR FAIL AS HIS FAVOURITE PLANET TURNS TO ASH.
A FITTING END, WOULDN'T YOU SAY, MR. EDISON?
STILL NOTHING? MY, MY. FOR A GENIUS YOU REALLY ARE QUITE STUBBORN.
I SHOULDN'T HAVE TO CRANK UP THE SETTINGS FOR A CONVERSATION, YOU KNOW.

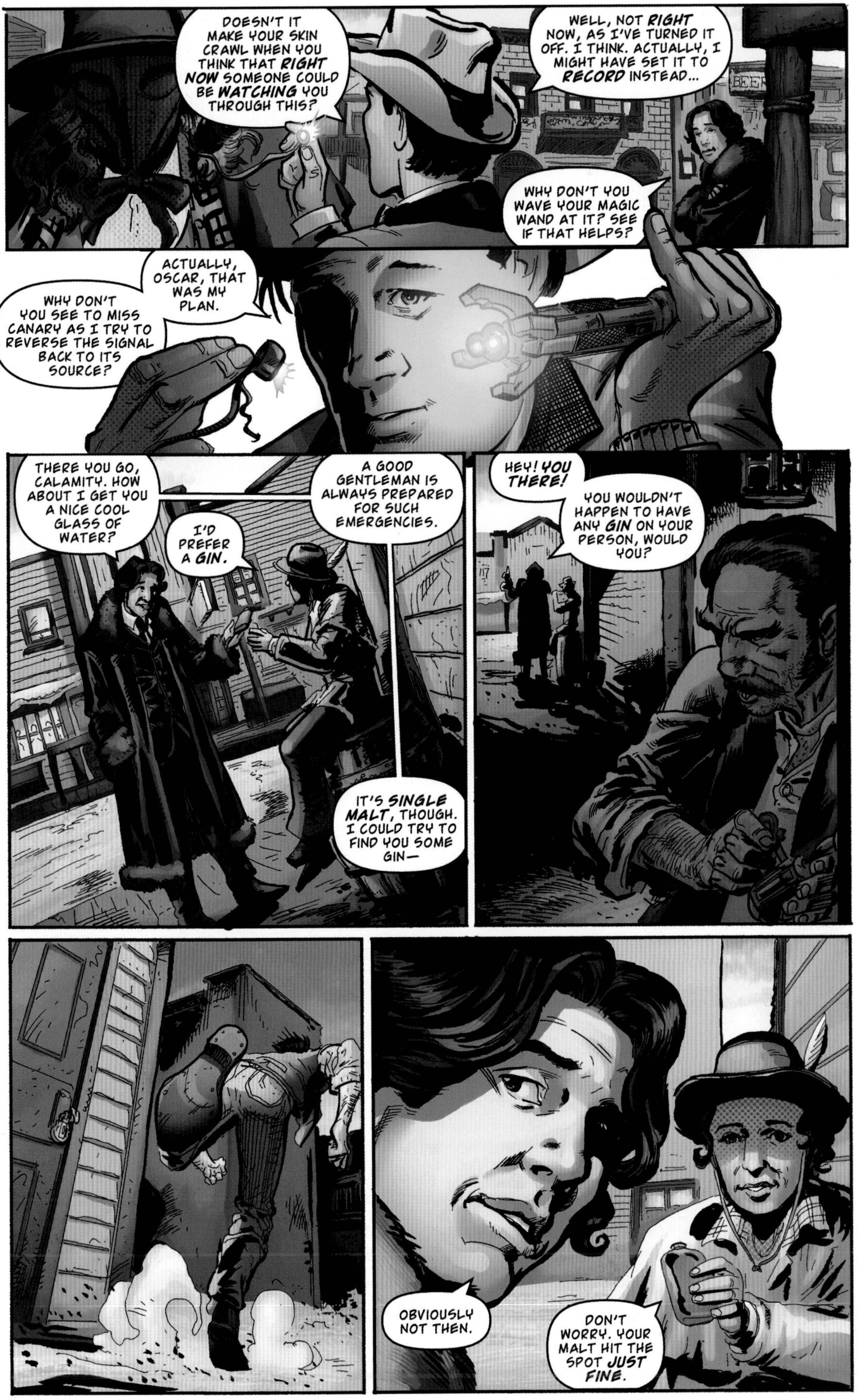
DOESN'T IT MAKE YOUR SKIN CRAWL WHEN YOU THINK THAT *RIGHT NOW* SOMEONE COULD BE *WATCHING* YOU THROUGH THIS?
WELL, NOT *RIGHT* NOW, AS I'VE TURNED IT OFF. I THINK. ACTUALLY, I MIGHT HAVE SET IT TO *RECORD* INSTEAD...
BEER
WHY DON'T YOU WAVE YOUR MAGIC WAND AT IT? SEE IF THAT HELPS?
ACTUALLY, OSCAR, THAT WAS MY PLAN.
WHY DON'T YOU SEE TO MISS CANARY AS I TRY TO REVERSE THE SIGNAL BACK TO ITS SOURCE?
THERE YOU GO, CALAMITY. HOW ABOUT I GET YOU A NICE COOL GLASS OF WATER?
I'D PREFER A *GIN*.
A GOOD GENTLEMAN IS ALWAYS PREPARED FOR SUCH EMERGENCIES.
IT'S *SINGLE MALT*, THOUGH. I COULD TRY TO FIND YOU SOME GIN—
HEY! *YOU THERE!*
YOU WOULDN'T HAPPEN TO HAVE ANY *GIN* ON YOUR PERSON, WOULD YOU?
OBVIOUSLY NOT THEN.
DON'T WORRY. YOUR MALT HIT THE SPOT *JUST FINE*.

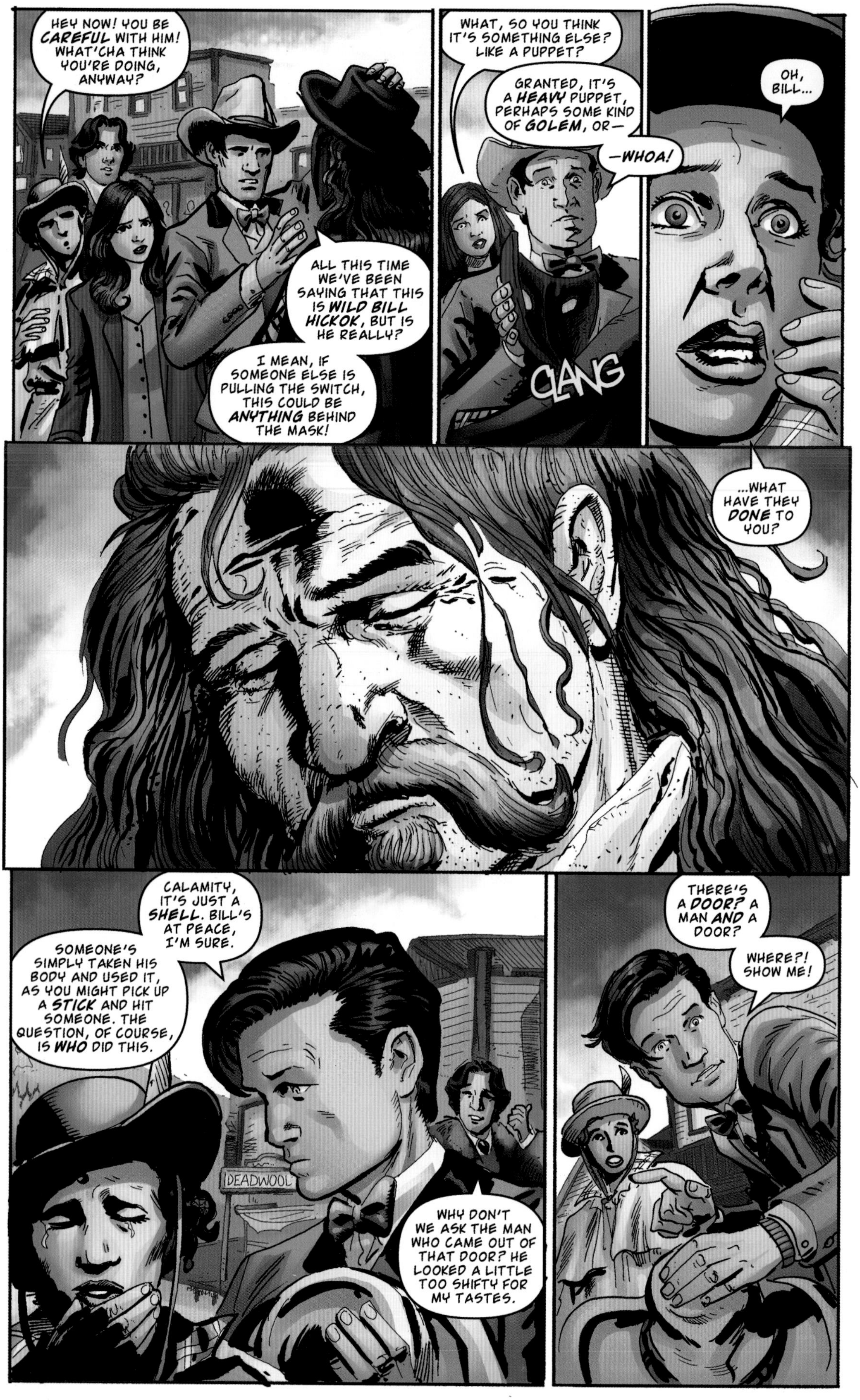
HEY NOW! YOU BE CAREFUL WITH HIM! WHAT'CHA THINK YOU'RE DOING, ANYWAY?
ALL THIS TIME WE'VE BEEN SAYING THAT THIS IS WILD BILL HICKOK, BUT IS HE REALLY?
I MEAN, IF SOMEONE ELSE IS PULLING THE SWITCH, THIS COULD BE ANYTHING BEHIND THE MASK!
WHAT, SO YOU THINK IT'S SOMETHING ELSE? LIKE A PUPPET?
GRANTED, IT'S A HEAVY PUPPET, PERHAPS SOME KIND OF GOLEM, OR—
—WHOA!
CLANG
OH, BILL...
...WHAT HAVE THEY DONE TO YOU?
CALAMITY, IT'S JUST A SHELL. BILL'S AT PEACE, I'M SURE.
SOMEONE'S SIMPLY TAKEN HIS BODY AND USED IT, AS YOU MIGHT PICK UP A STICK AND HIT SOMEONE. THE QUESTION, OF COURSE, IS WHO DID THIS.
DEADWOOD
WHY DON'T WE ASK THE MAN WHO CAME OUT OF THAT DOOR? HE LOOKED A LITTLE TOO SHIFTY FOR MY TASTES.
THERE'S A DOOR? A MAN AND A DOOR?
WHERE?! SHOW ME!

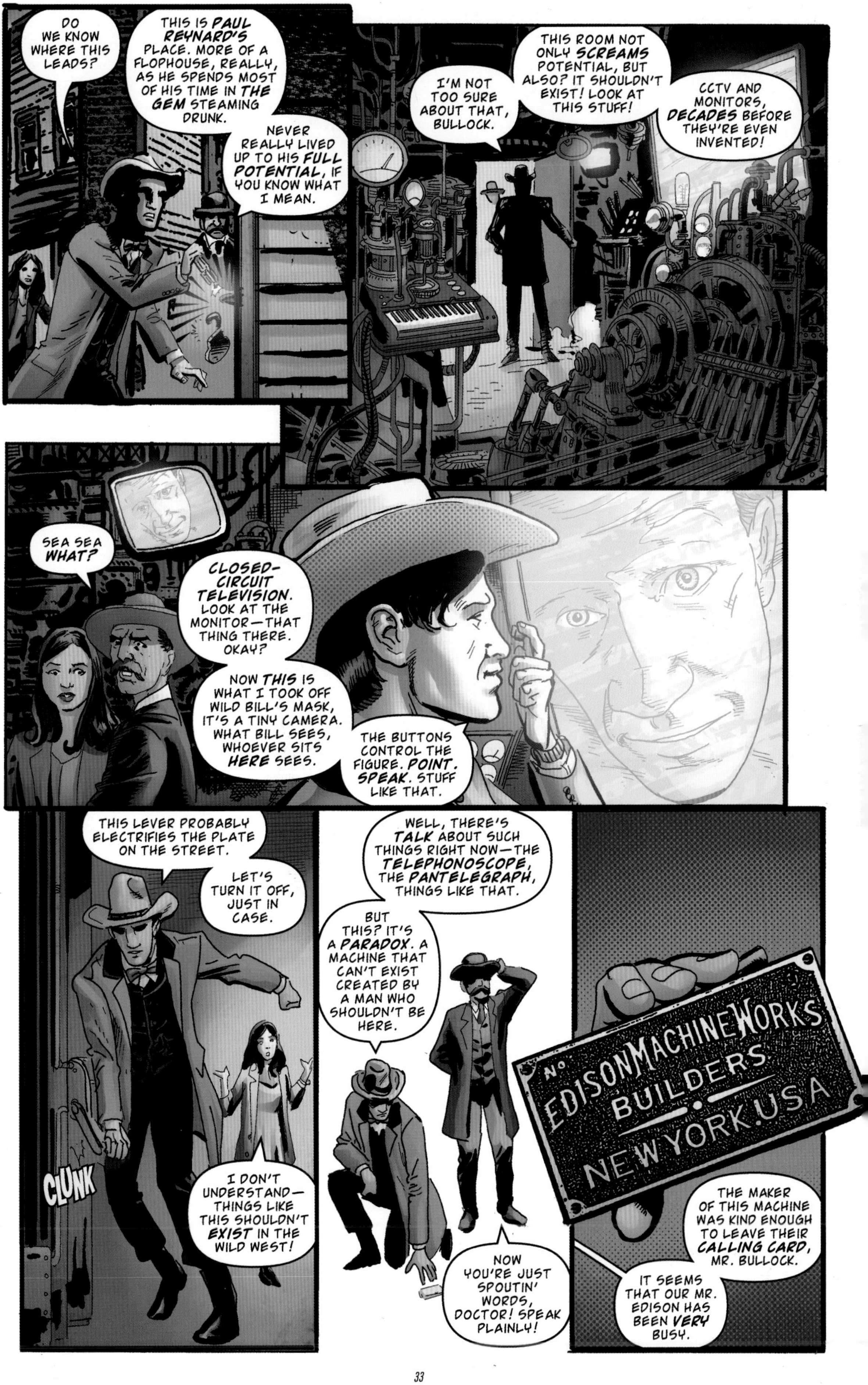
DO WE KNOW WHERE THIS LEADS?
THIS IS PAUL REYNARD'S PLACE. MORE OF A FLOPHOUSE, REALLY, AS HE SPENDS MOST OF HIS TIME IN THE GEM STEAMING DRUNK.
NEVER REALLY LIVED UP TO HIS FULL POTENTIAL, IF YOU KNOW WHAT I MEAN.
I'M NOT TOO SURE ABOUT THAT, BULLOCK.
THIS ROOM NOT ONLY SCREAMS POTENTIAL, BUT ALSO? IT SHOULDN'T EXIST! LOOK AT THIS STUFF!
CCTV AND MONITORS, DECADES BEFORE THEY'RE EVEN INVENTED!
SEA SEA WHAT?
CLOSED-CIRCUIT TELEVISION. LOOK AT THE MONITOR—THAT THING THERE. OKAY?
NOW THIS IS WHAT I TOOK OFF WILD BILL'S MASK, IT'S A TINY CAMERA. WHAT BILL SEES, WHOEVER SITS HERE SEES.
THE BUTTONS CONTROL THE FIGURE. POINT. SPEAK. STUFF LIKE THAT.
THIS LEVER PROBABLY ELECTRIFIES THE PLATE ON THE STREET.
LET'S TURN IT OFF, JUST IN CASE.
CLUNK
I DON'T UNDERSTAND—THINGS LIKE THIS SHOULDN'T EXIST IN THE WILD WEST!
WELL, THERE'S TALK ABOUT SUCH THINGS RIGHT NOW—THE TELEPHONOSCOPE, THE PANTELEGRAPH, THINGS LIKE THAT.
BUT THIS? IT'S A PARADOX. A MACHINE THAT CAN'T EXIST CREATED BY A MAN WHO SHOULDN'T BE HERE.
NOW YOU'RE JUST SPOUTIN' WORDS, DOCTOR! SPEAK PLAINLY!
No
EDISON MACHINE WORKS
BUILDERS
NEW YORK. USA
THE MAKER OF THIS MACHINE WAS KIND ENOUGH TO LEAVE THEIR CALLING CARD, MR. BULLOCK.
IT SEEMS THAT OUR MR. EDISON HAS BEEN VERY BUSY.

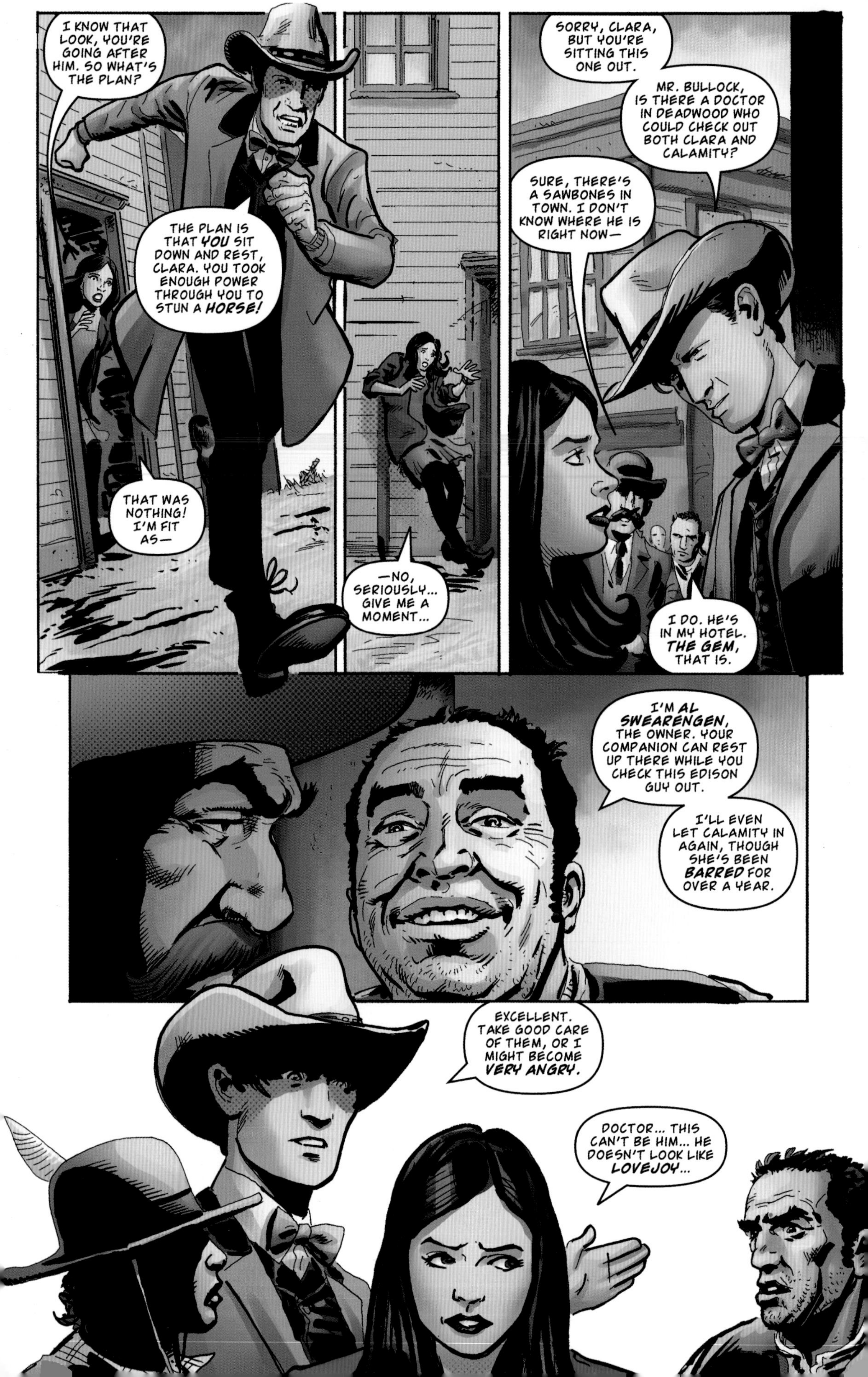
I KNOW THAT LOOK, YOU'RE GOING AFTER HIM. SO WHAT'S THE PLAN?
THE PLAN IS THAT YOU SIT DOWN AND REST, CLARA. YOU TOOK ENOUGH POWER THROUGH YOU TO STUN A HORSE!
THAT WAS NOTHING! I'M FIT AS—
—NO, SERIOUSLY... GIVE ME A MOMENT...
SORRY, CLARA, BUT YOU'RE SITTING THIS ONE OUT.
MR. BULLOCK, IS THERE A DOCTOR IN DEADWOOD WHO COULD CHECK OUT BOTH CLARA AND CALAMITY?
SURE, THERE'S A SAWBONES IN TOWN. I DON'T KNOW WHERE HE IS RIGHT NOW—
I DO. HE'S IN MY HOTEL. THE GEM, THAT IS.
I'M AL SWEARENGEN, THE OWNER. YOUR COMPANION CAN REST UP THERE WHILE YOU CHECK THIS EDISON GUY OUT.
I'LL EVEN LET CALAMITY IN AGAIN, THOUGH SHE'S BEEN BARRED FOR OVER A YEAR.
EXCELLENT. TAKE GOOD CARE OF THEM, OR I MIGHT BECOME VERY ANGRY.
DOCTOR... THIS CAN'T BE HIM... HE DOESN'T LOOK LIKE LOVEJOY...

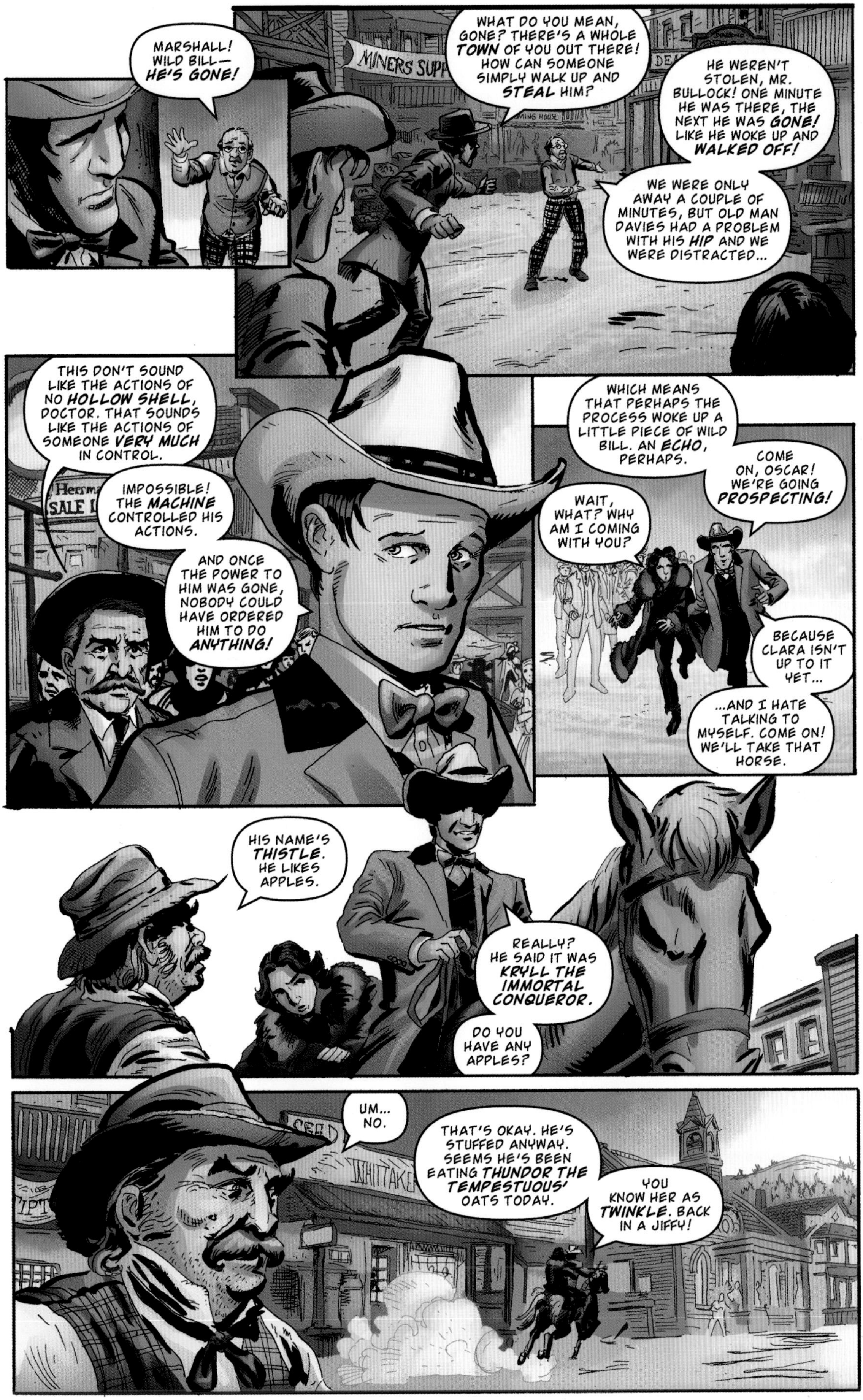
MARSHALL! WILD BILL— HE'S GONE!
WHAT DO YOU MEAN, GONE? THERE'S A WHOLE TOWN OF YOU OUT THERE! HOW CAN SOMEONE SIMPLY WALK UP AND STEAL HIM?
HE WEREN'T STOLEN, MR. BULLOCK! ONE MINUTE HE WAS THERE, THE NEXT HE WAS GONE! LIKE HE WOKE UP AND WALKED OFF!
WE WERE ONLY AWAY A COUPLE OF MINUTES, BUT OLD MAN DAVIES HAD A PROBLEM WITH HIS HIP AND WE WERE DISTRACTED...
THIS DON'T SOUND LIKE THE ACTIONS OF NO HOLLOW SHELL, DOCTOR. THAT SOUNDS LIKE THE ACTIONS OF SOMEONE VERY MUCH IN CONTROL.
IMPOSSIBLE! THE MACHINE CONTROLLED HIS ACTIONS.
AND ONCE THE POWER TO HIM WAS GONE, NOBODY COULD HAVE ORDERED HIM TO DO ANYTHING!
WHICH MEANS THAT PERHAPS THE PROCESS WOKE UP A LITTLE PIECE OF WILD BILL. AN ECHO, PERHAPS.
COME ON, OSCAR! WE'RE GOING PROSPECTING!
WAIT, WHAT? WHY AM I COMING WITH YOU?
BECAUSE CLARA ISN'T UP TO IT YET...
...AND I HATE TALKING TO MYSELF. COME ON! WE'LL TAKE THAT HORSE.
HIS NAME'S THISTLE. HE LIKES APPLES.
REALLY? HE SAID IT WAS KRYLL THE IMMORTAL CONQUEROR.
DO YOU HAVE ANY APPLES?
UM... NO.
THAT'S OKAY. HE'S STUFFED ANYWAY. SEEMS HE'S BEEN EATING THUNDOR THE TEMPESTUOUS' OATS TODAY.
YOU KNOW HER AS TWINKLE. BACK IN A JIFFY!

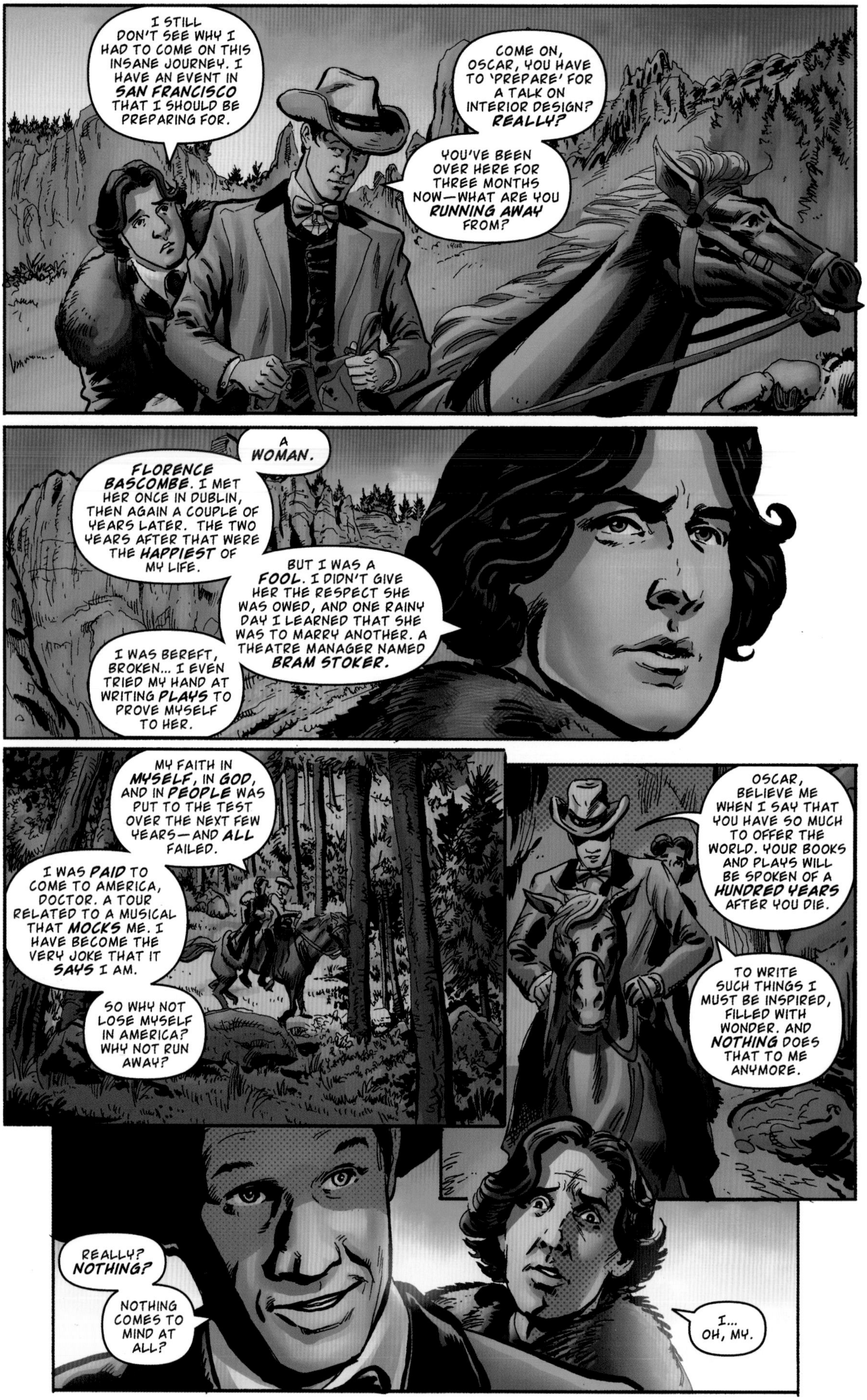
I STILL DON'T SEE WHY I HAD TO COME ON THIS INSANE JOURNEY. I HAVE AN EVENT IN SAN FRANCISCO THAT I SHOULD BE PREPARING FOR.
COME ON, OSCAR, YOU HAVE TO 'PREPARE' FOR A TALK ON INTERIOR DESIGN? REALLY?
YOU'VE BEEN OVER HERE FOR THREE MONTHS NOW—WHAT ARE YOU RUNNING AWAY FROM?
A WOMAN.
FLORENCE BASCOMBE. I MET HER ONCE IN DUBLIN, THEN AGAIN A COUPLE OF YEARS LATER. THE TWO YEARS AFTER THAT WERE THE HAPPIEST OF MY LIFE.
BUT I WAS A FOOL. I DIDN'T GIVE HER THE RESPECT SHE WAS OWED, AND ONE RAINY DAY I LEARNED THAT SHE WAS TO MARRY ANOTHER. A THEATRE MANAGER NAMED BRAM STOKER.
I WAS BEREFT, BROKEN... I EVEN TRIED MY HAND AT WRITING PLAYS TO PROVE MYSELF TO HER.
MY FAITH IN MYSELF, IN GOD, AND IN PEOPLE WAS PUT TO THE TEST OVER THE NEXT FEW YEARS—AND ALL FAILED.
I WAS PAID TO COME TO AMERICA, DOCTOR. A TOUR RELATED TO A MUSICAL THAT MOCKS ME. I HAVE BECOME THE VERY JOKE THAT IT SAYS I AM.
SO WHY NOT LOSE MYSELF IN AMERICA? WHY NOT RUN AWAY?
OSCAR, BELIEVE ME WHEN I SAY THAT YOU HAVE SO MUCH TO OFFER THE WORLD. YOUR BOOKS AND PLAYS WILL BE SPOKEN OF A HUNDRED YEARS AFTER YOU DIE.
TO WRITE SUCH THINGS I MUST BE INSPIRED, FILLED WITH WONDER. AND NOTHING DOES THAT TO ME ANYMORE.
REALLY? NOTHING?
NOTHING COMES TO MIND AT ALL?
I... OH, MY.

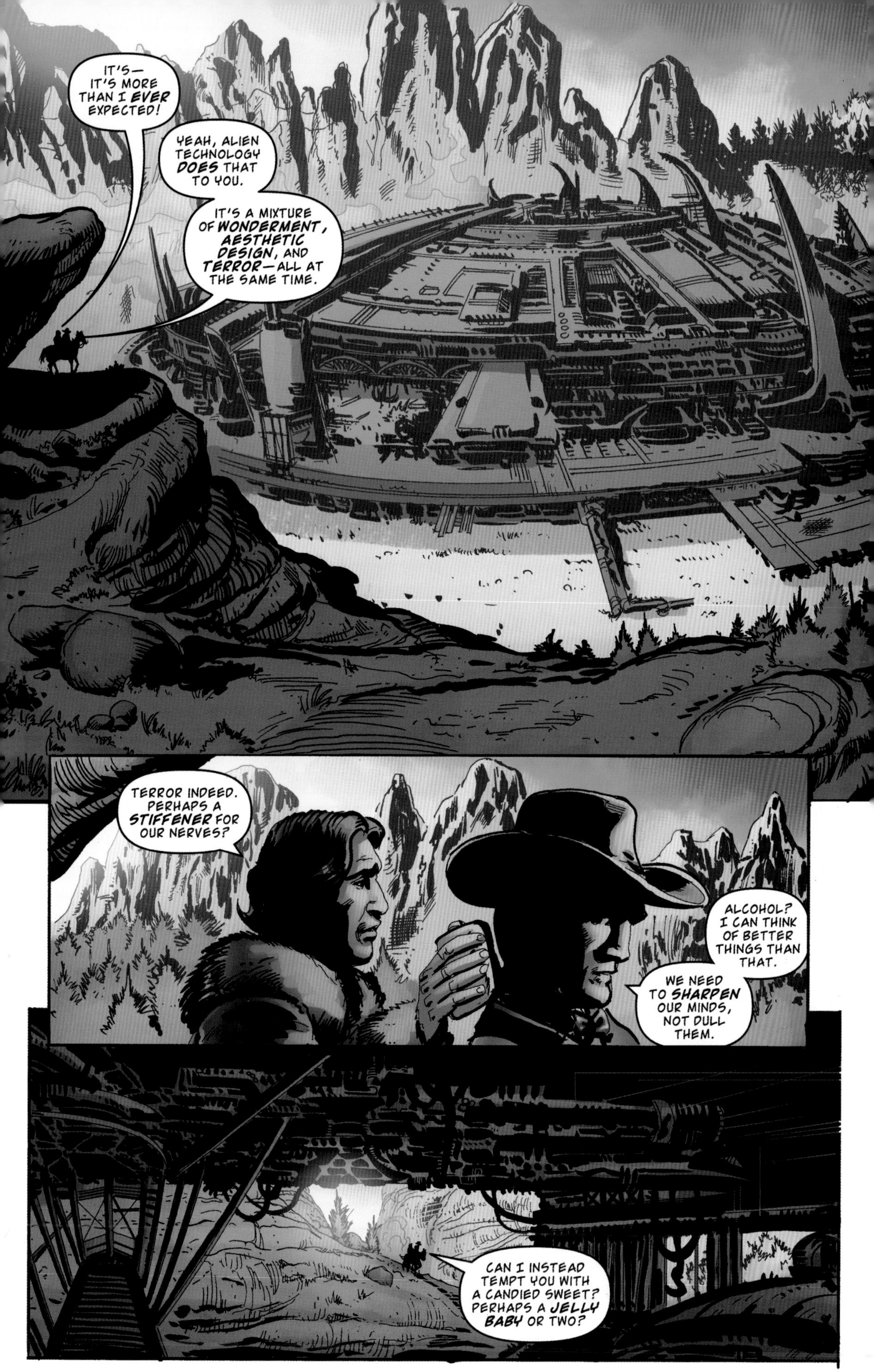
IT'S— IT'S MORE THAN I EVER EXPECTED!
YEAH, ALIEN TECHNOLOGY DOES THAT TO YOU.
IT'S A MIXTURE OF WONDERMENT, AESTHETIC DESIGN, AND TERROR—ALL AT THE SAME TIME.
TERROR INDEED. PERHAPS A STIFFENER FOR OUR NERVES?
ALCOHOL? I CAN THINK OF BETTER THINGS THAN THAT.
WE NEED TO SHARPEN OUR MINDS, NOT DULL THEM.
CAN I INSTEAD TEMPT YOU WITH A CANDIED SWEET? PERHAPS A JELLY BABY OR TWO?

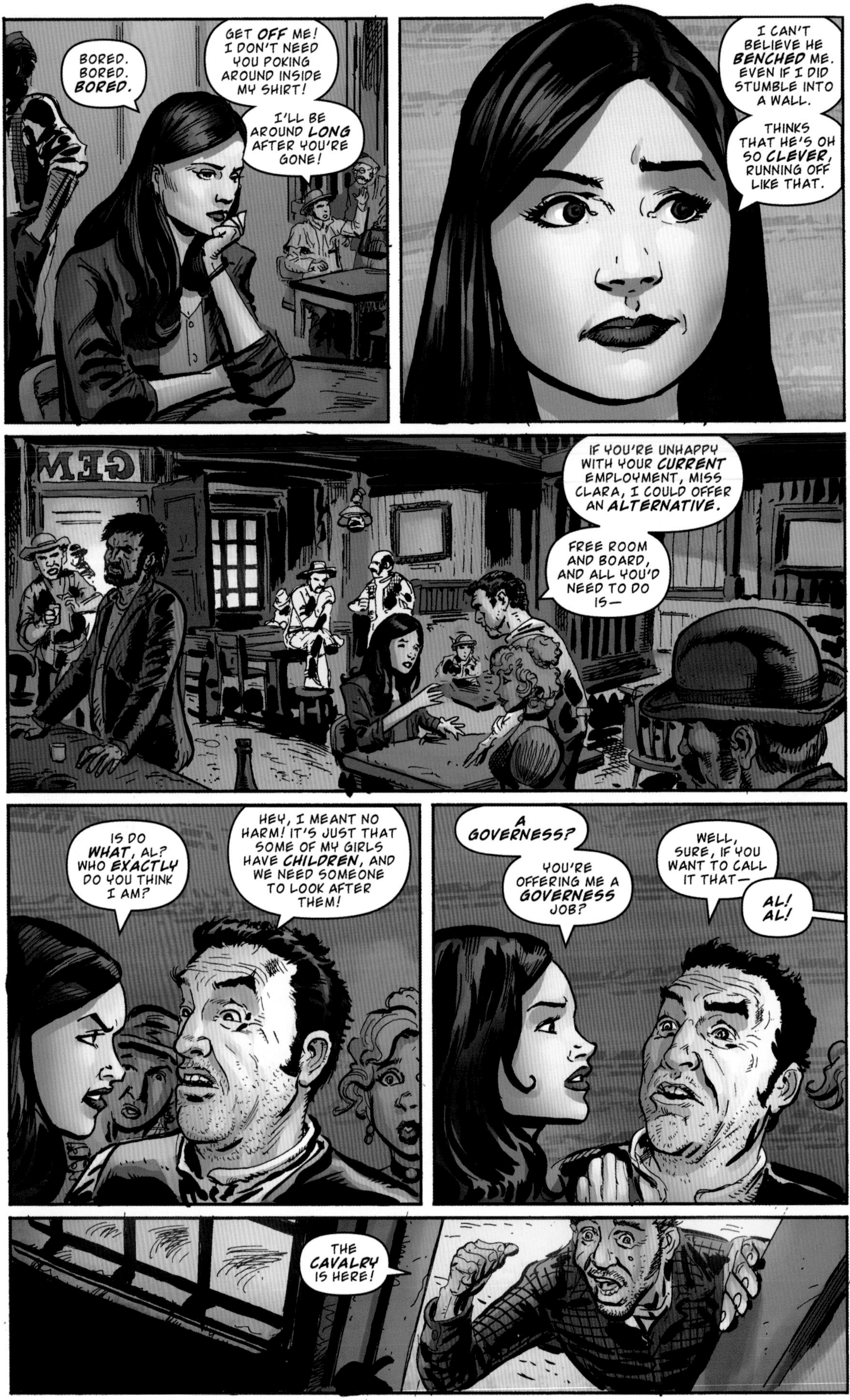
BORED. BORED. BORED.
GET OFF ME! I DON'T NEED YOU POKING AROUND INSIDE MY SHIRT!
I'LL BE AROUND LONG AFTER YOU'RE GONE!
I CAN'T BELIEVE HE BENCHED ME. EVEN IF I DID STUMBLE INTO A WALL.
THINKS THAT HE'S OH SO CLEVER, RUNNING OFF LIKE THAT.
IF YOU'RE UNHAPPY WITH YOUR CURRENT EMPLOYMENT, MISS CLARA, I COULD OFFER AN ALTERNATIVE.
FREE ROOM AND BOARD, AND ALL YOU'D NEED TO DO IS—
IS DO WHAT, AL? WHO EXACTLY DO YOU THINK I AM?
HEY, I MEANT NO HARM! IT'S JUST THAT SOME OF MY GIRLS HAVE CHILDREN, AND WE NEED SOMEONE TO LOOK AFTER THEM!
A GOVERNESS?
YOU'RE OFFERING ME A GOVERNESS JOB?
WELL, SURE, IF YOU WANT TO CALL IT THAT—
AL! AL!
THE CAVALRY IS HERE!

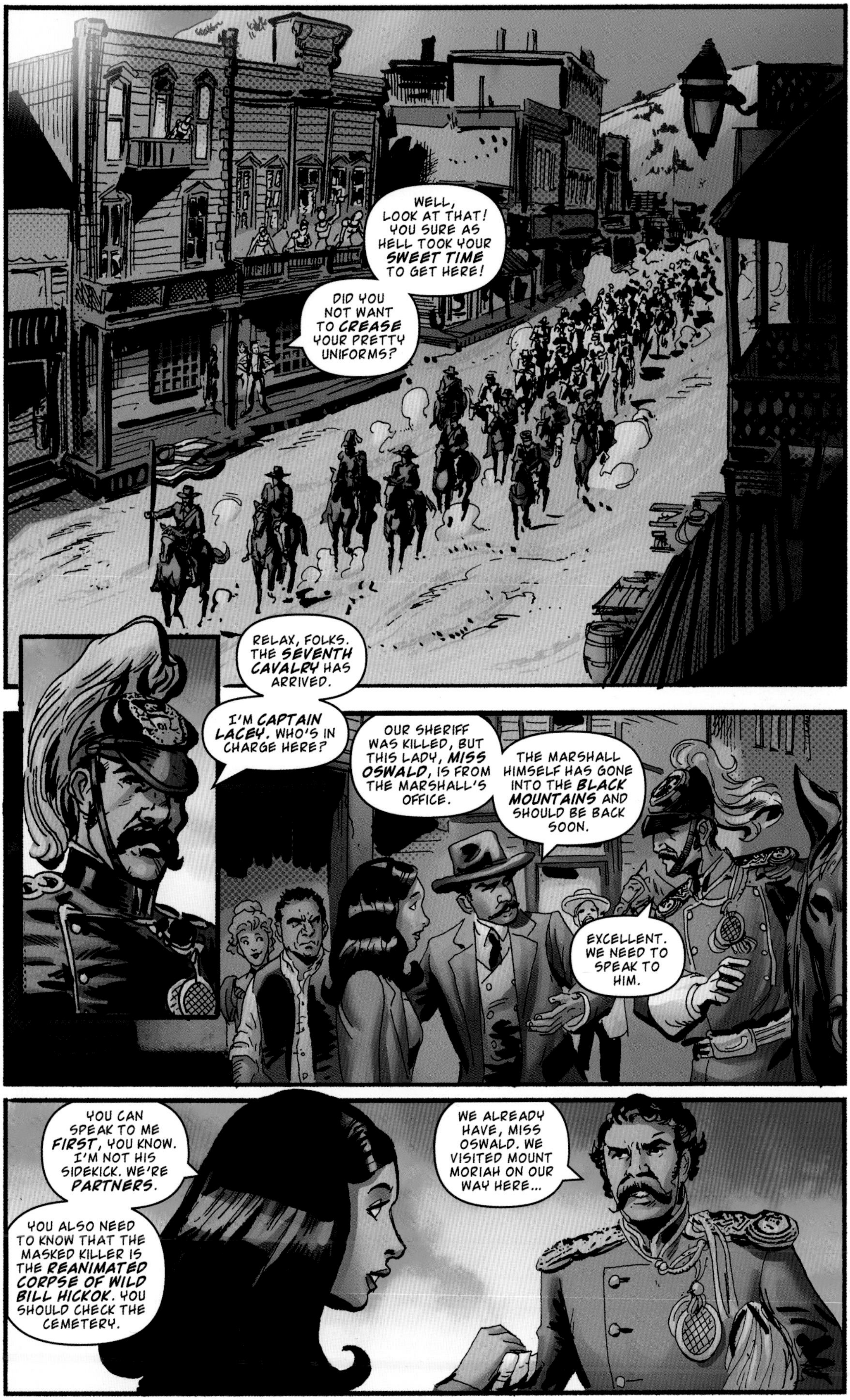

WELL, LOOK AT THAT! YOU SURE AS HELL TOOK YOUR SWEET TIME TO GET HERE!
DID YOU NOT WANT TO CREASE YOUR PRETTY UNIFORMS?
RELAX, FOLKS. THE SEVENTH CAVALRY HAS ARRIVED.
I'M CAPTAIN LACEY. WHO'S IN CHARGE HERE?
OUR SHERIFF WAS KILLED, BUT THIS LADY, MISS OSWALD, IS FROM THE MARSHALL'S OFFICE.
THE MARSHALL HIMSELF HAS GONE INTO THE BLACK MOUNTAINS AND SHOULD BE BACK SOON.
EXCELLENT. WE NEED TO SPEAK TO HIM.
YOU CAN SPEAK TO ME FIRST, YOU KNOW. I'M NOT HIS SIDEKICK. WE'RE PARTNERS.
YOU ALSO NEED TO KNOW THAT THE MASKED KILLER IS THE REANIMATED CORPSE OF WILD BILL HICKOK. YOU SHOULD CHECK THE CEMETERY.
WE ALREADY HAVE, MISS OSWALD. WE VISITED MOUNT MORIAH ON OUR WAY HERE...

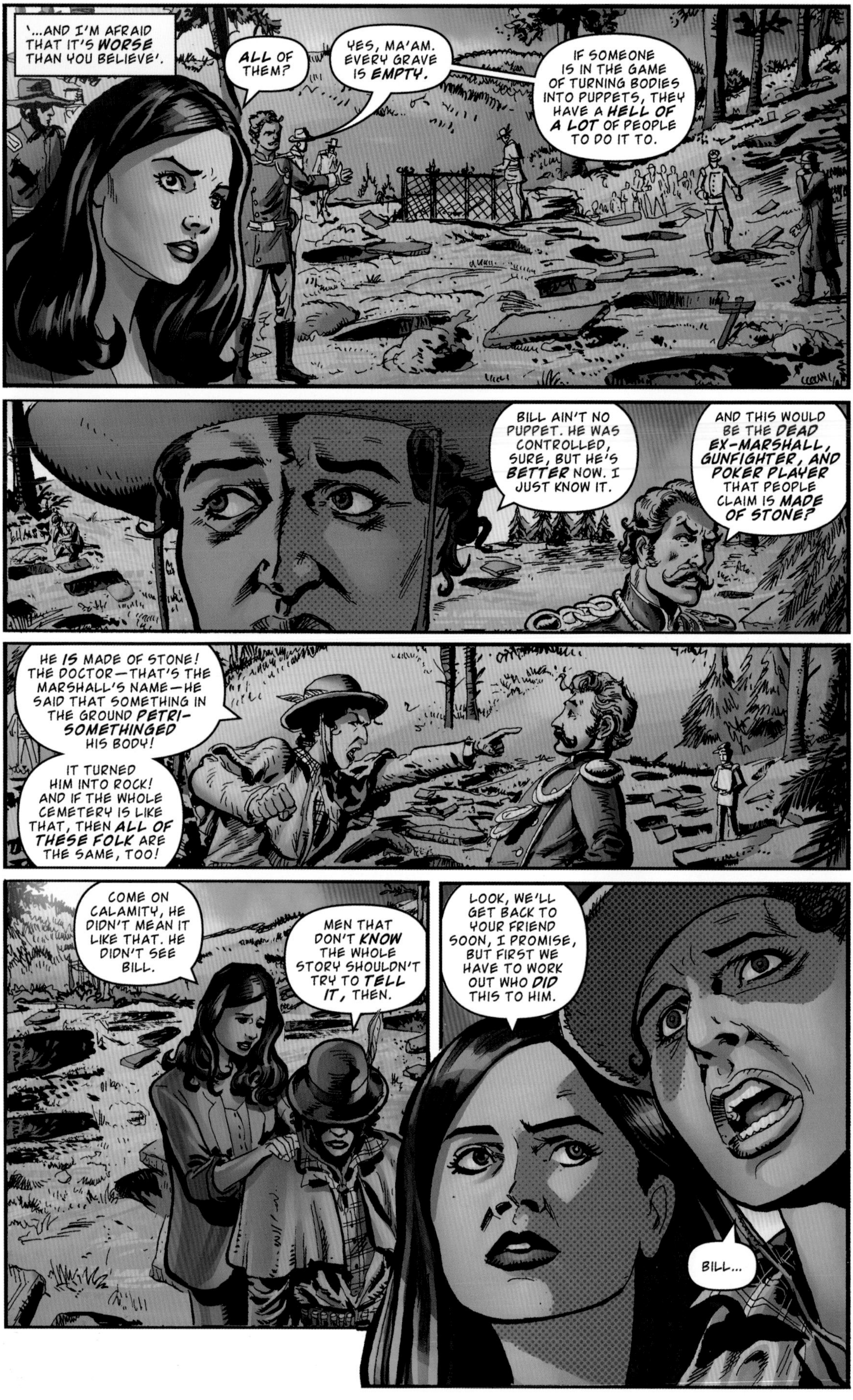
'...AND I'M AFRAID THAT IT'S WORSE THAN YOU BELIEVE'.
ALL OF THEM?
YES, MA'AM. EVERY GRAVE IS EMPTY.
IF SOMEONE IS IN THE GAME OF TURNING BODIES INTO PUPPETS, THEY HAVE A HELL OF A LOT OF PEOPLE TO DO IT TO.
BILL AIN'T NO PUPPET. HE WAS CONTROLLED, SURE, BUT HE'S BETTER NOW. I JUST KNOW IT.
AND THIS WOULD BE THE DEAD EX-MARSHALL, GUNFIGHTER, AND POKER PLAYER THAT PEOPLE CLAIM IS MADE OF STONE?
HE IS MADE OF STONE! THE DOCTOR—THAT'S THE MARSHALL'S NAME—HE SAID THAT SOMETHING IN THE GROUND PETRI-SOMETHINGED HIS BODY!
IT TURNED HIM INTO ROCK! AND IF THE WHOLE CEMETERY IS LIKE THAT, THEN ALL OF THESE FOLK ARE THE SAME, TOO!
COME ON CALAMITY, HE DIDN'T MEAN IT LIKE THAT. HE DIDN'T SEE BILL.
MEN THAT DON'T KNOW THE WHOLE STORY SHOULDN'T TRY TO TELL IT, THEN.
LOOK, WE'LL GET BACK TO YOUR FRIEND SOON, I PROMISE, BUT FIRST WE HAVE TO WORK OUT WHO DID THIS TO HIM.
BILL...

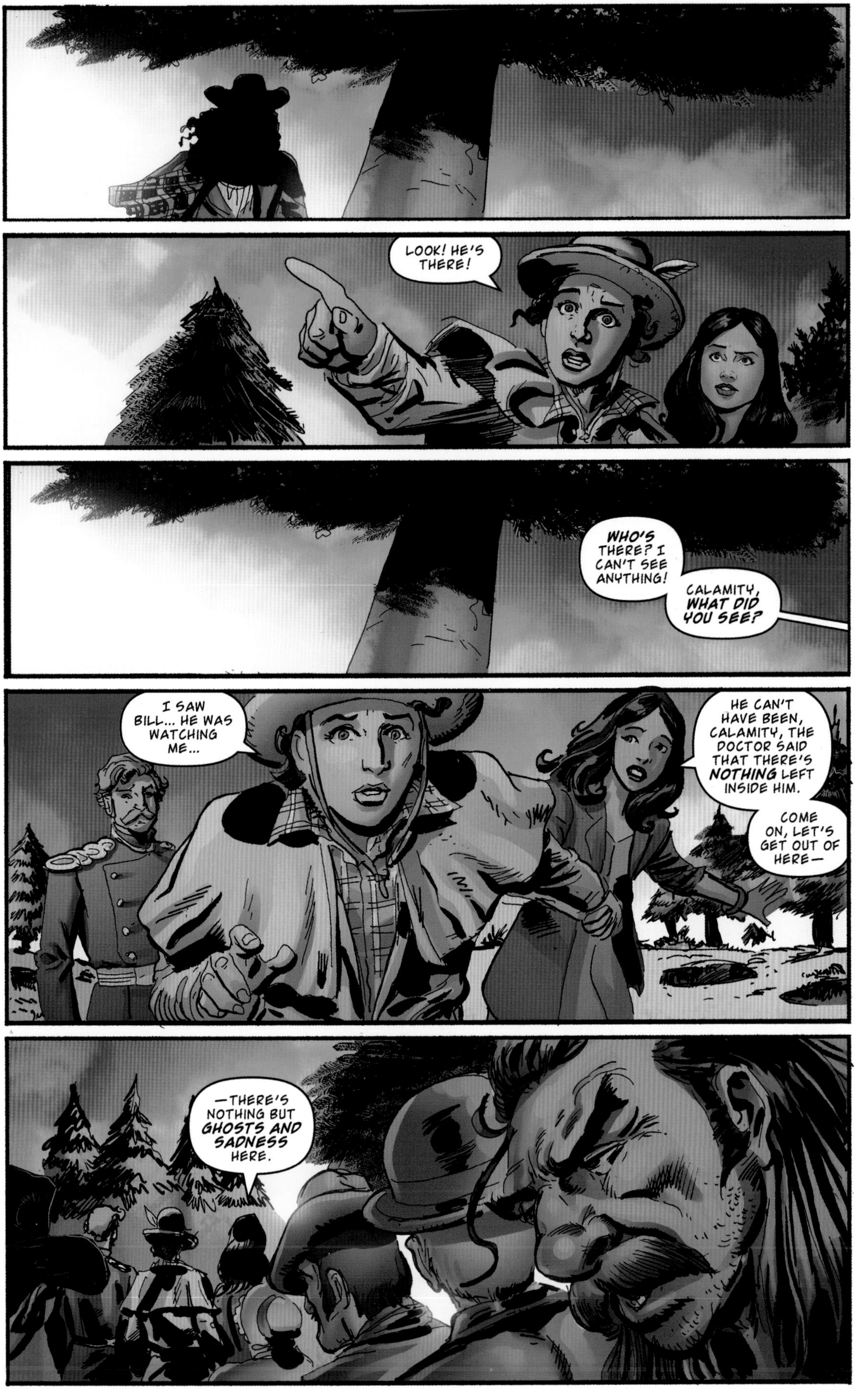
LOOK! HE'S THERE!
WHO'S THERE? I CAN'T SEE ANYTHING!
CALAMITY, WHAT DID YOU SEE?
I SAW BILL... HE WAS WATCHING ME...
HE CAN'T HAVE BEEN, CALAMITY, THE DOCTOR SAID THAT THERE'S NOTHING LEFT INSIDE HIM.
COME ON, LET'S GET OUT OF HERE—
—THERE'S NOTHING BUT GHOSTS AND SADNESS HERE.

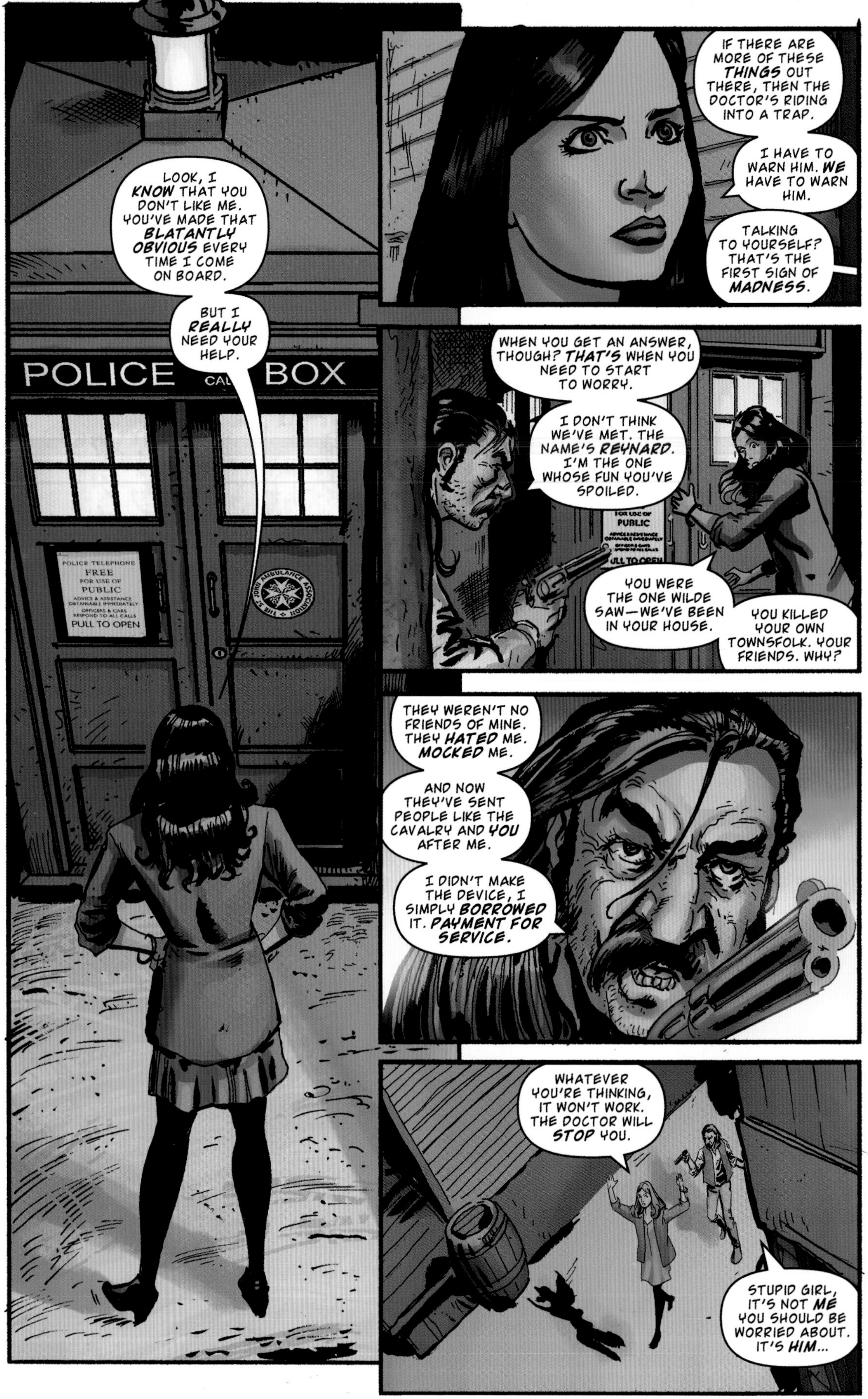
LOOK, I KNOW THAT YOU DON'T LIKE ME. YOU'VE MADE THAT BLATANTLY OBVIOUS EVERY TIME I COME ON BOARD.
BUT I REALLY NEED YOUR HELP.
POLICE BOX
POLICE TELEPHONE FREE FOR USE OF PUBLIC ADVICE & ASSISTANCE OBTAINABLE IMMEDIATELY OFFICERS & CARS RESPOND TO ALL CALLS PULL TO OPEN
IF THERE ARE MORE OF THESE THINGS OUT THERE, THEN THE DOCTOR'S RIDING INTO A TRAP.
I HAVE TO WARN HIM. WE HAVE TO WARN HIM.
TALKING TO YOURSELF? THAT'S THE FIRST SIGN OF MADNESS.
WHEN YOU GET AN ANSWER, THOUGH? THAT'S WHEN YOU NEED TO START TO WORRY.
I DON'T THINK WE'VE MET. THE NAME'S REYNARD. I'M THE ONE WHOSE FUN YOU'VE SPOILED.
YOU WERE THE ONE WILDE SAW—WE'VE BEEN IN YOUR HOUSE.
YOU KILLED YOUR OWN TOWNSFOLK. YOUR FRIENDS. WHY?
THEY WEREN'T NO FRIENDS OF MINE. THEY HATED ME. MOCKED ME.
AND NOW THEY'VE SENT PEOPLE LIKE THE CAVALRY AND YOU AFTER ME.
I DIDN'T MAKE THE DEVICE, I SIMPLY BORROWED IT. PAYMENT FOR SERVICE.
WHATEVER YOU'RE THINKING, IT WON'T WORK. THE DOCTOR WILL STOP YOU.
STUPID GIRL, IT'S NOT ME YOU SHOULD BE WORRIED ABOUT. IT'S HIM...

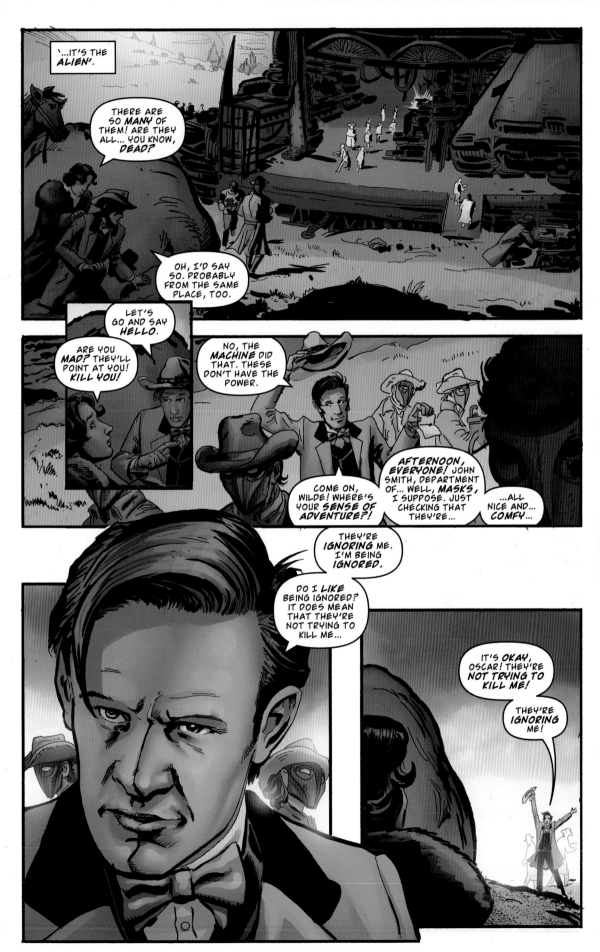

'...IT'S THE ALIEN'.

THERE ARE SO *MANY* OF THEM! ARE THEY ALL... YOU KNOW, *DEAD?*

OH, I'D SAY SO. PROBABLY FROM THE SAME PLACE, TOO.

LET'S GO AND SAY *HELLO.*

ARE YOU *MAD?* THEY'LL POINT AT YOU! *KILL YOU!*

NO, THE *MACHINE* DID THAT. THESE DON'T HAVE THE POWER.

AFTERNOON, EVERYONE! JOHN SMITH, DEPARTMENT OF... WELL, *MASKS,* I SUPPOSE. JUST CHECKING THAT THEY'RE...

...ALL NICE AND... *COMFY...*

COME ON, WILDE! WHERE'S YOUR *SENSE OF ADVENTURE?!*

THEY'RE *IGNORING* ME. I'M BEING *IGNORED.*

DO I *LIKE* BEING IGNORED? IT DOES MEAN THAT THEY'RE NOT TRYING TO KILL ME...

IT'S *OKAY,* OSCAR! THEY'RE *NOT TRYING TO KILL ME!*

THEY'RE *IGNORING ME!*

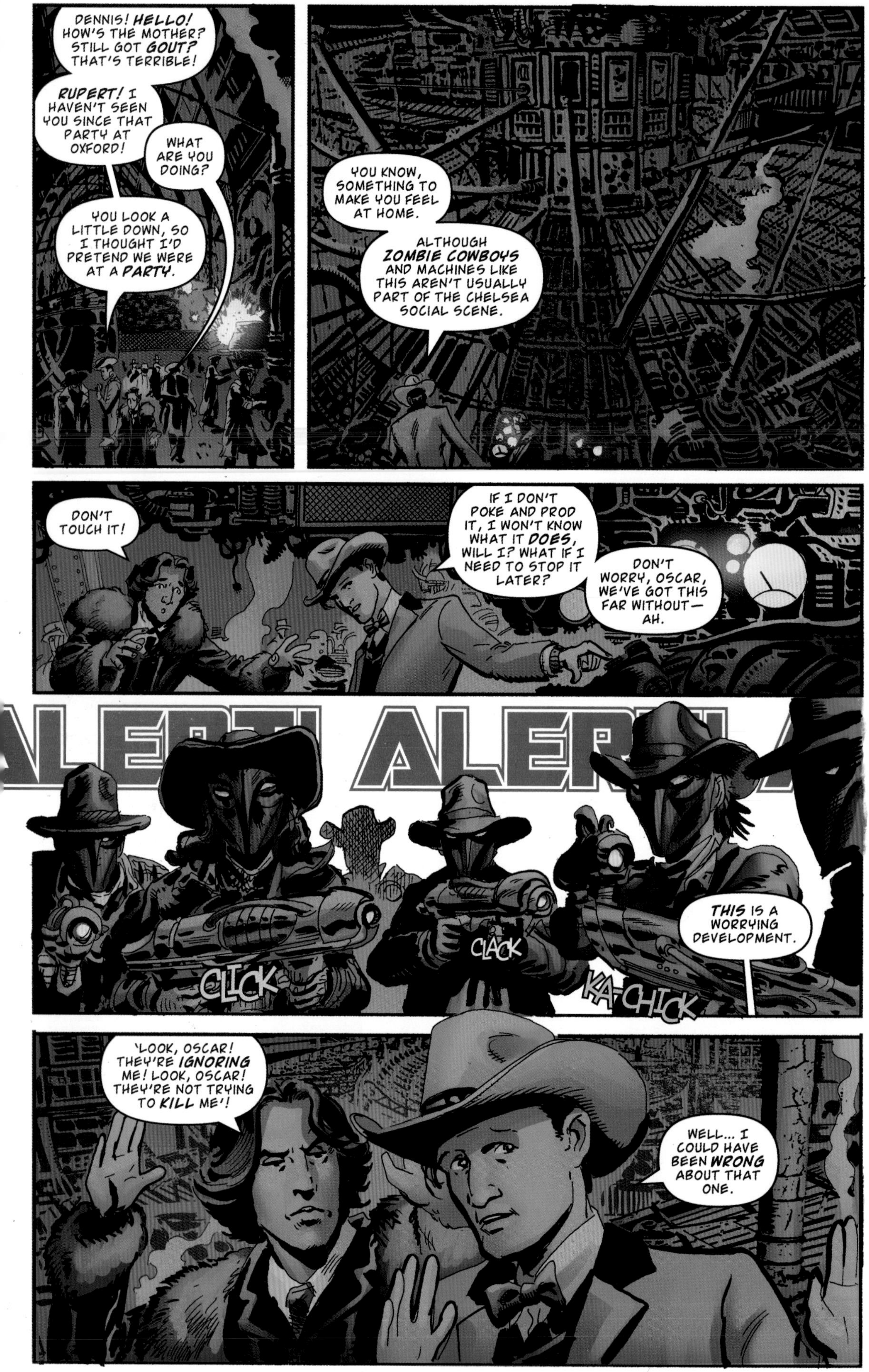
DENNIS! HELLO! HOW'S THE MOTHER? STILL GOT GOUT? THAT'S TERRIBLE!
RUPERT! I HAVEN'T SEEN YOU SINCE THAT PARTY AT OXFORD!
WHAT ARE YOU DOING?
YOU LOOK A LITTLE DOWN, SO I THOUGHT I'D PRETEND WE WERE AT A PARTY.
YOU KNOW, SOMETHING TO MAKE YOU FEEL AT HOME.
ALTHOUGH ZOMBIE COWBOYS AND MACHINES LIKE THIS AREN'T USUALLY PART OF THE CHELSEA SOCIAL SCENE.
DON'T TOUCH IT!
IF I DON'T POKE AND PROD IT, I WON'T KNOW WHAT IT DOES, WILL I? WHAT IF I NEED TO STOP IT LATER?
DON'T WORRY, OSCAR, WE'VE GOT THIS FAR WITHOUT— AH.
ALERT! ALERT!
THIS IS A WORRYING DEVELOPMENT.
CLICK
CLACK
KA-CHICK
'LOOK, OSCAR! THEY'RE IGNORING ME! LOOK, OSCAR! THEY'RE NOT TRYING TO KILL ME'!
WELL... I COULD HAVE BEEN WRONG ABOUT THAT ONE.

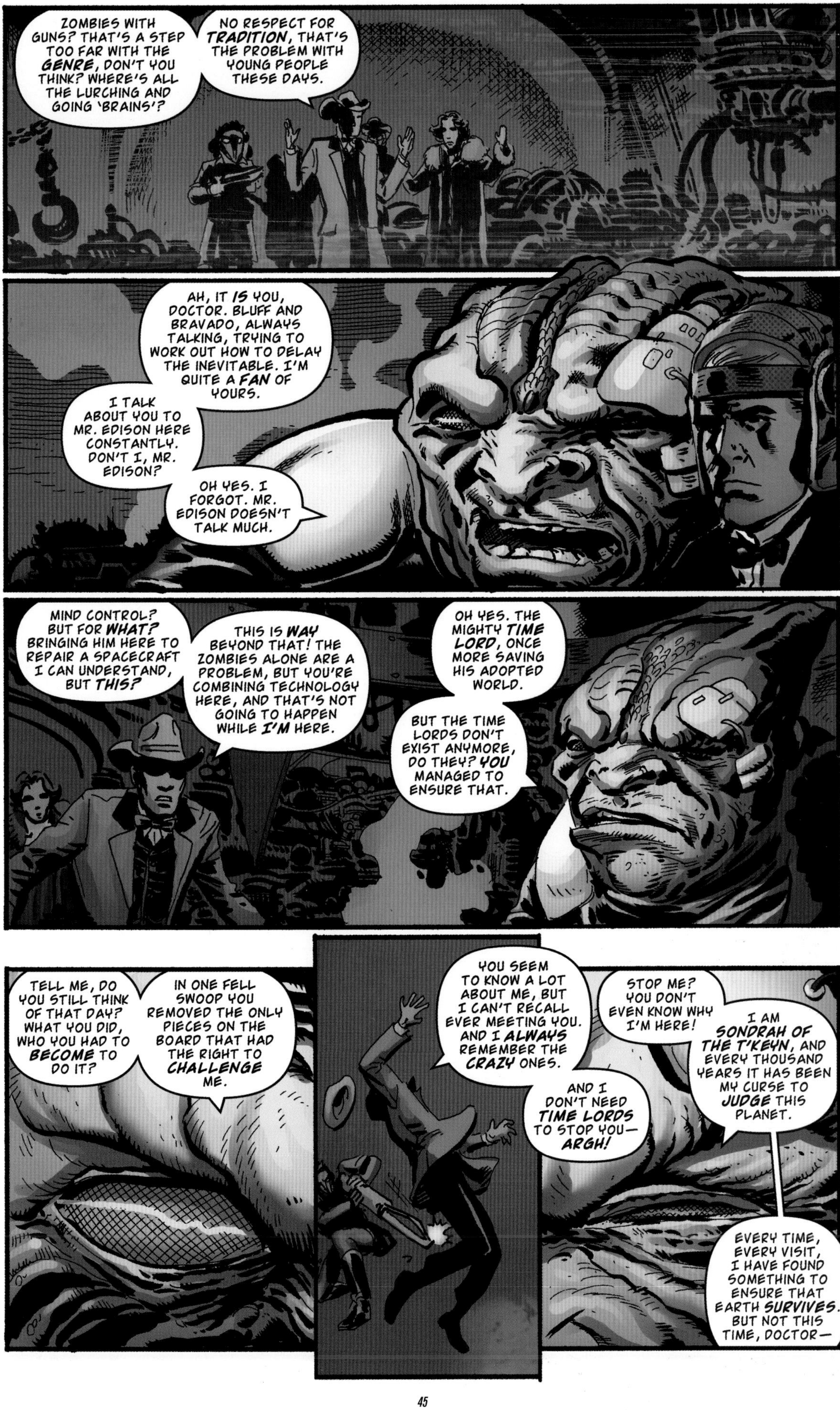
ZOMBIES WITH GUNS? THAT'S A STEP TOO FAR WITH THE GENRE, DON'T YOU THINK? WHERE'S ALL THE LURCHING AND GOING 'BRAINS'?
NO RESPECT FOR TRADITION, THAT'S THE PROBLEM WITH YOUNG PEOPLE THESE DAYS.
AH, IT IS YOU, DOCTOR. BLUFF AND BRAVADO, ALWAYS TALKING, TRYING TO WORK OUT HOW TO DELAY THE INEVITABLE. I'M QUITE A FAN OF YOURS.
I TALK ABOUT YOU TO MR. EDISON HERE CONSTANTLY. DON'T I, MR. EDISON?
OH YES. I FORGOT. MR. EDISON DOESN'T TALK MUCH.
MIND CONTROL? BUT FOR WHAT? BRINGING HIM HERE TO REPAIR A SPACECRAFT I CAN UNDERSTAND, BUT THIS?
THIS IS WAY BEYOND THAT! THE ZOMBIES ALONE ARE A PROBLEM, BUT YOU'RE COMBINING TECHNOLOGY HERE, AND THAT'S NOT GOING TO HAPPEN WHILE I'M HERE.
OH YES. THE MIGHTY TIME LORD, ONCE MORE SAVING HIS ADOPTED WORLD.
BUT THE TIME LORDS DON'T EXIST ANYMORE, DO THEY? YOU MANAGED TO ENSURE THAT.
TELL ME, DO YOU STILL THINK OF THAT DAY? WHAT YOU DID, WHO YOU HAD TO BECOME TO DO IT?
IN ONE FELL SWOOP YOU REMOVED THE ONLY PIECES ON THE BOARD THAT HAD THE RIGHT TO CHALLENGE ME.
YOU SEEM TO KNOW A LOT ABOUT ME, BUT I CAN'T RECALL EVER MEETING YOU. AND I ALWAYS REMEMBER THE CRAZY ONES.
AND I DON'T NEED TIME LORDS TO STOP YOU— ARGH!
STOP ME? YOU DON'T EVEN KNOW WHY I'M HERE!
I AM SONDRAH OF THE T'KEYN, AND EVERY THOUSAND YEARS IT HAS BEEN MY CURSE TO JUDGE THIS PLANET.
EVERY TIME, EVERY VISIT, I HAVE FOUND SOMETHING TO ENSURE THAT EARTH SURVIVES. BUT NOT THIS TIME, DOCTOR—

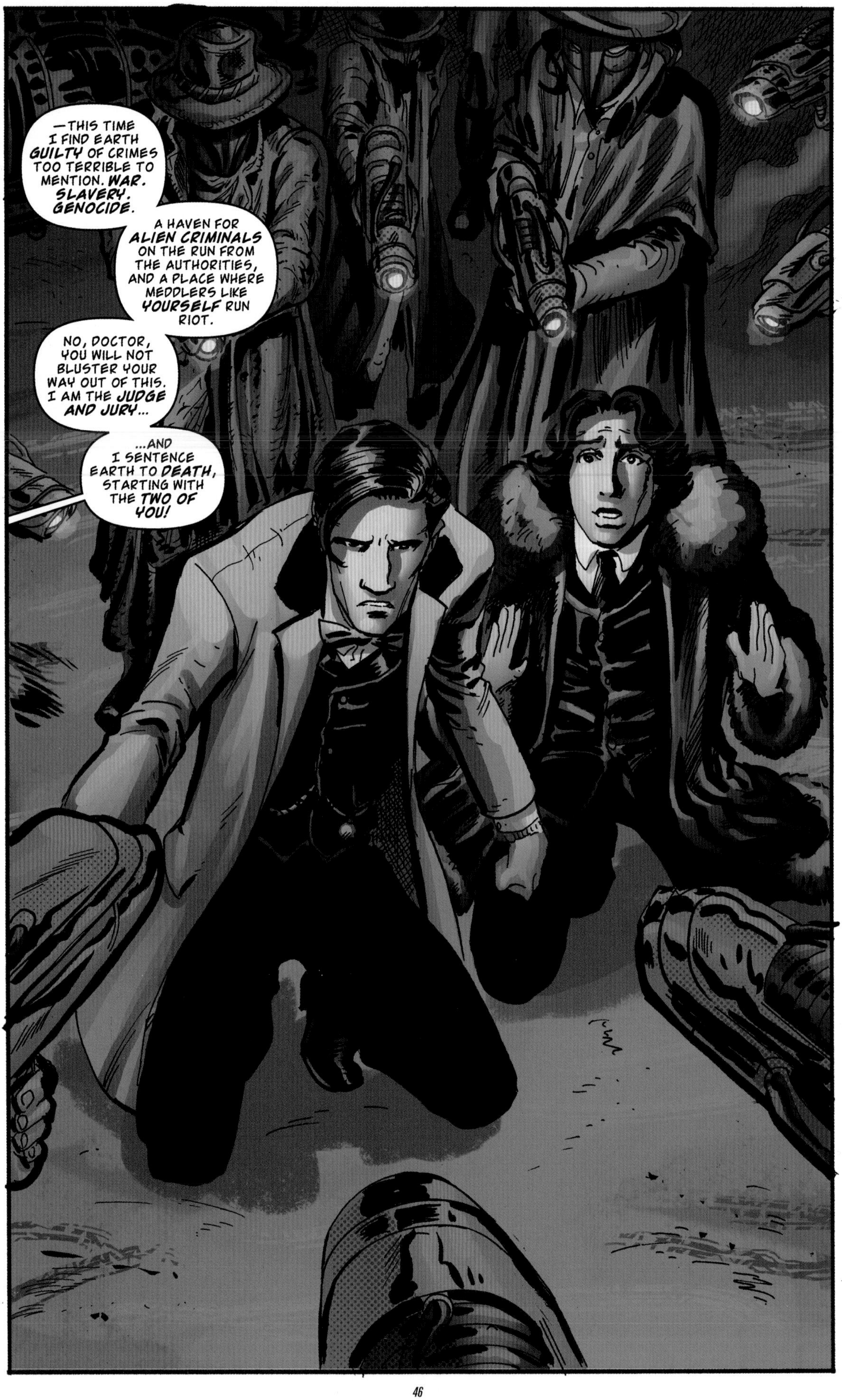
—THIS TIME I FIND EARTH GUILTY OF CRIMES TOO TERRIBLE TO MENTION. WAR. SLAVERY. GENOCIDE.
A HAVEN FOR ALIEN CRIMINALS ON THE RUN FROM THE AUTHORITIES, AND A PLACE WHERE MEDDLERS LIKE YOURSELF RUN RIOT.
NO, DOCTOR, YOU WILL NOT BLUSTER YOUR WAY OUT OF THIS. I AM THE JUDGE AND JURY...
...AND I SENTENCE EARTH TO DEATH, STARTING WITH THE TWO OF YOU!

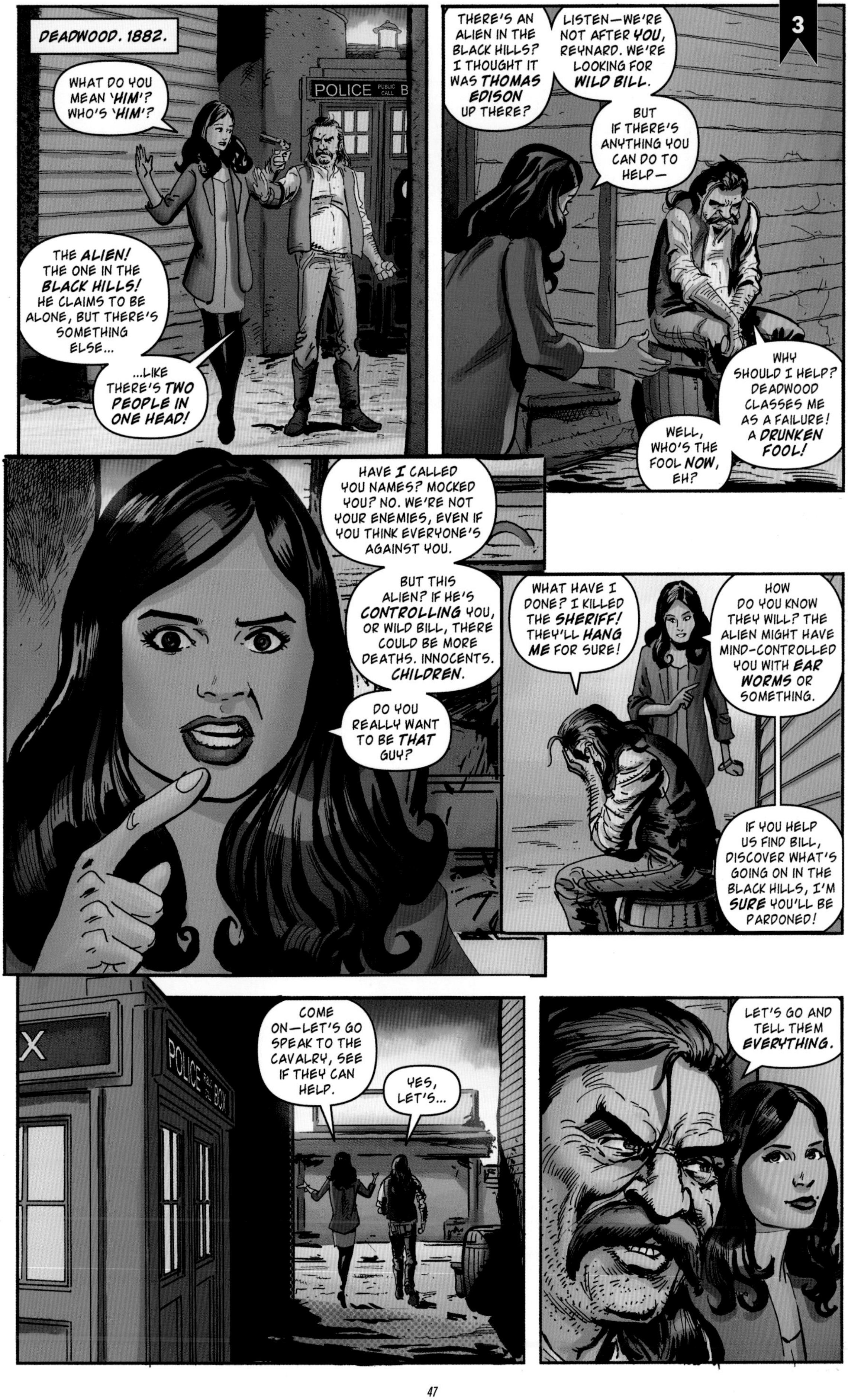
3
DEADWOOD. 1882.
WHAT DO YOU MEAN 'HIM'? WHO'S 'HIM'?
POLICE PUBLIC CALL B
THE ALIEN! THE ONE IN THE BLACK HILLS! HE CLAIMS TO BE ALONE, BUT THERE'S SOMETHING ELSE...
...LIKE THERE'S TWO PEOPLE IN ONE HEAD!
THERE'S AN ALIEN IN THE BLACK HILLS? I THOUGHT IT WAS THOMAS EDISON UP THERE?
LISTEN—WE'RE NOT AFTER YOU, REYNARD. WE'RE LOOKING FOR WILD BILL.
BUT IF THERE'S ANYTHING YOU CAN DO TO HELP—
WHY SHOULD I HELP? DEADWOOD CLASSES ME AS A FAILURE! A DRUNKEN FOOL!
WELL, WHO'S THE FOOL NOW, EH?
HAVE I CALLED YOU NAMES? MOCKED YOU? NO. WE'RE NOT YOUR ENEMIES, EVEN IF YOU THINK EVERYONE'S AGAINST YOU.
BUT THIS ALIEN? IF HE'S CONTROLLING YOU, OR WILD BILL, THERE COULD BE MORE DEATHS. INNOCENTS. CHILDREN.
DO YOU REALLY WANT TO BE THAT GUY?
WHAT HAVE I DONE? I KILLED THE SHERIFF! THEY'LL HANG ME FOR SURE!
HOW DO YOU KNOW THEY WILL? THE ALIEN MIGHT HAVE MIND-CONTROLLED YOU WITH EAR WORMS OR SOMETHING.
IF YOU HELP US FIND BILL, DISCOVER WHAT'S GOING ON IN THE BLACK HILLS, I'M SURE YOU'LL BE PARDONED!
X
POLICE BOX
COME ON—LET'S GO SPEAK TO THE CAVALRY, SEE IF THEY CAN HELP.
YES, LET'S...
LET'S GO AND TELL THEM EVERYTHING.

THE BLACK HILLS.

FOR *CENTURIES* I HAVE WAITED FOR YOU TO MEDDLE IN ONE OF MY *AUDITS*, DOCTOR!

AND NOW, BEFORE I PASS SENTENCE ON THE EARTH, I GET TO *EXECUTE YOU!*

SONDRAH! *WAIT!* YOU SAID YOU'RE OF THE *T'KEYN*, RIGHT?

THEN BY THE *T'KEYN BYLAWS OF THE SHADOW PROCLAMATION'S CONVENTION 15,* I GET TO DEFEND MYSELF IN THE *T'KEYN NEXUS!*

YOU'RE NOT A CONDEMNED *RACE!* YOU'RE JUST A *TIME LORD!*

AH, BUT AS YOU SAID, I'M THE *LAST* OF THE TIME LORDS. WHICH MEANS THAT IF YOU KILL ME, YOU *END MY RACE.*

WHICH MEANS THAT I GET MY RIGHT TO REPLY, OR THE SHADOW PROCLAMATION WILL *REVOKE* YOUR RIGHT TO AUDIT.

AND BY REVOKE, I MEAN *TERMINATE WITH FORCE.*

THE T'KEYN AND THE TIME LORDS *IGNORED* EACH OTHER PRETTY MUCH, BUT HE KNOWS FAR TOO MUCH ABOUT ME, AND SOMETHING ABOUT HIM IS *FAMILIAR.*

OSCAR, WHILE I'M IN THE NEXUS, I HAVE A SMALL FAVOUR TO ASK OF YOU. AND IT MIGHT JUST SAVE US ALL.

WELL, A *COUPLE* OF SMALL FAVOURS, ACTUALLY.

PERHAPS *BIG* ONES.

HERE, TAKE IT. LET US END THIS. THE T'KEYN NEXUS IS—

—IS A VIRTUAL REALITY LIKE THE *TIME LORD MATRIX,* SONDRAH. I KNOW. I'M NOT AN AMATEUR TO THIS.

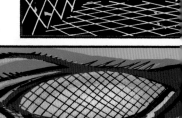

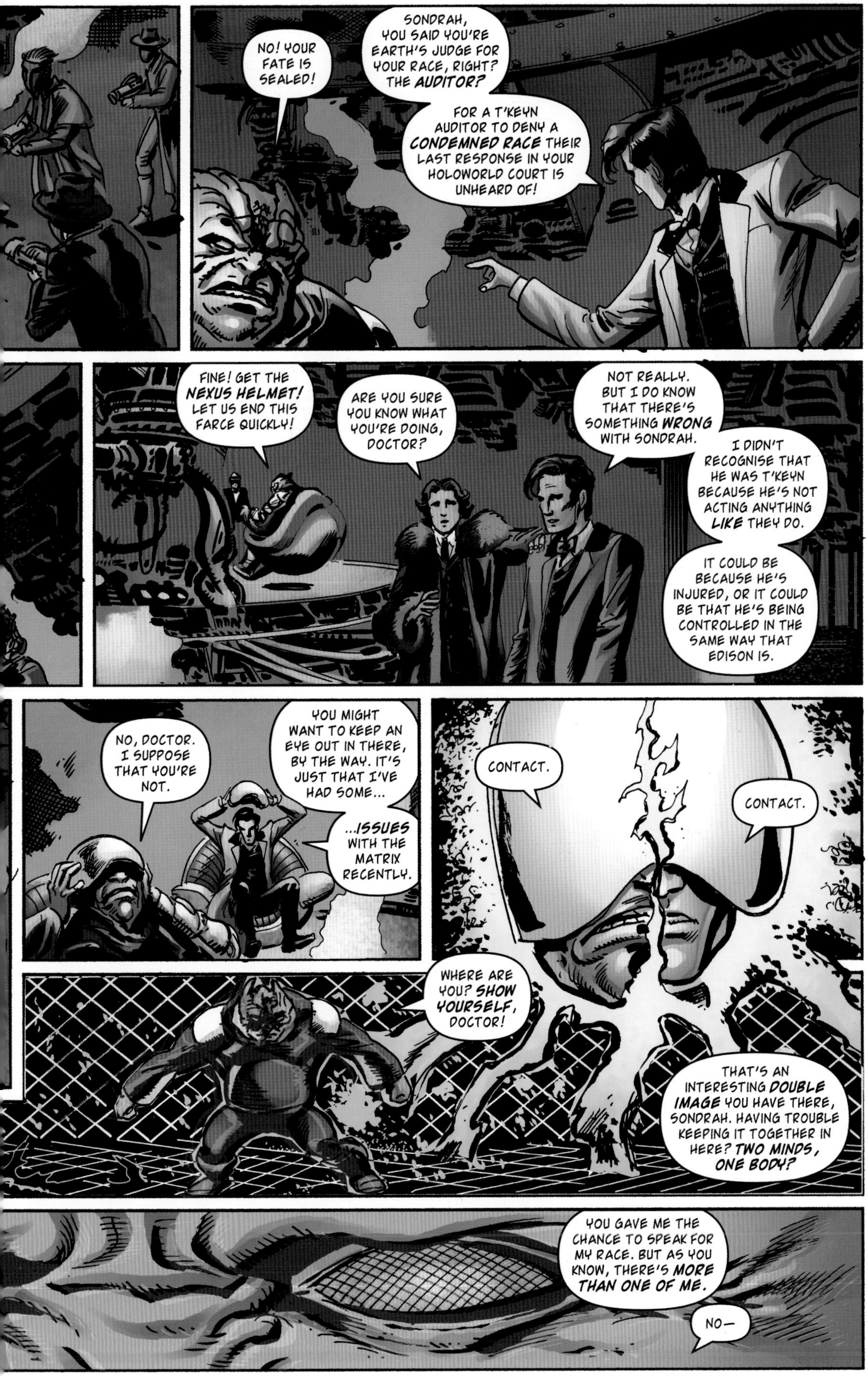
NO! YOUR FATE IS SEALED!
SONDRAH, YOU SAID YOU'RE EARTH'S JUDGE FOR YOUR RACE, RIGHT? THE AUDITOR?
FOR A T'KEYN AUDITOR TO DENY A CONDEMNED RACE THEIR LAST RESPONSE IN YOUR HOLOWORLD COURT IS UNHEARD OF!
FINE! GET THE NEXUS HELMET! LET US END THIS FARCE QUICKLY!
ARE YOU SURE YOU KNOW WHAT YOU'RE DOING, DOCTOR?
NOT REALLY. BUT I DO KNOW THAT THERE'S SOMETHING WRONG WITH SONDRAH.
I DIDN'T RECOGNISE THAT HE WAS T'KEYN BECAUSE HE'S NOT ACTING ANYTHING LIKE THEY DO.
IT COULD BE BECAUSE HE'S INJURED, OR IT COULD BE THAT HE'S BEING CONTROLLED IN THE SAME WAY THAT EDISON IS.
NO, DOCTOR. I SUPPOSE THAT YOU'RE NOT.
YOU MIGHT WANT TO KEEP AN EYE OUT IN THERE, BY THE WAY. IT'S JUST THAT I'VE HAD SOME...
...ISSUES WITH THE MATRIX RECENTLY.
CONTACT.
CONTACT.
WHERE ARE YOU? SHOW YOURSELF, DOCTOR!
THAT'S AN INTERESTING DOUBLE IMAGE YOU HAVE THERE, SONDRAH. HAVING TROUBLE KEEPING IT TOGETHER IN HERE? TWO MINDS, ONE BODY?
YOU GAVE ME THE CHANCE TO SPEAK FOR MY RACE. BUT AS YOU KNOW, THERE'S MORE THAN ONE OF ME.
NO—

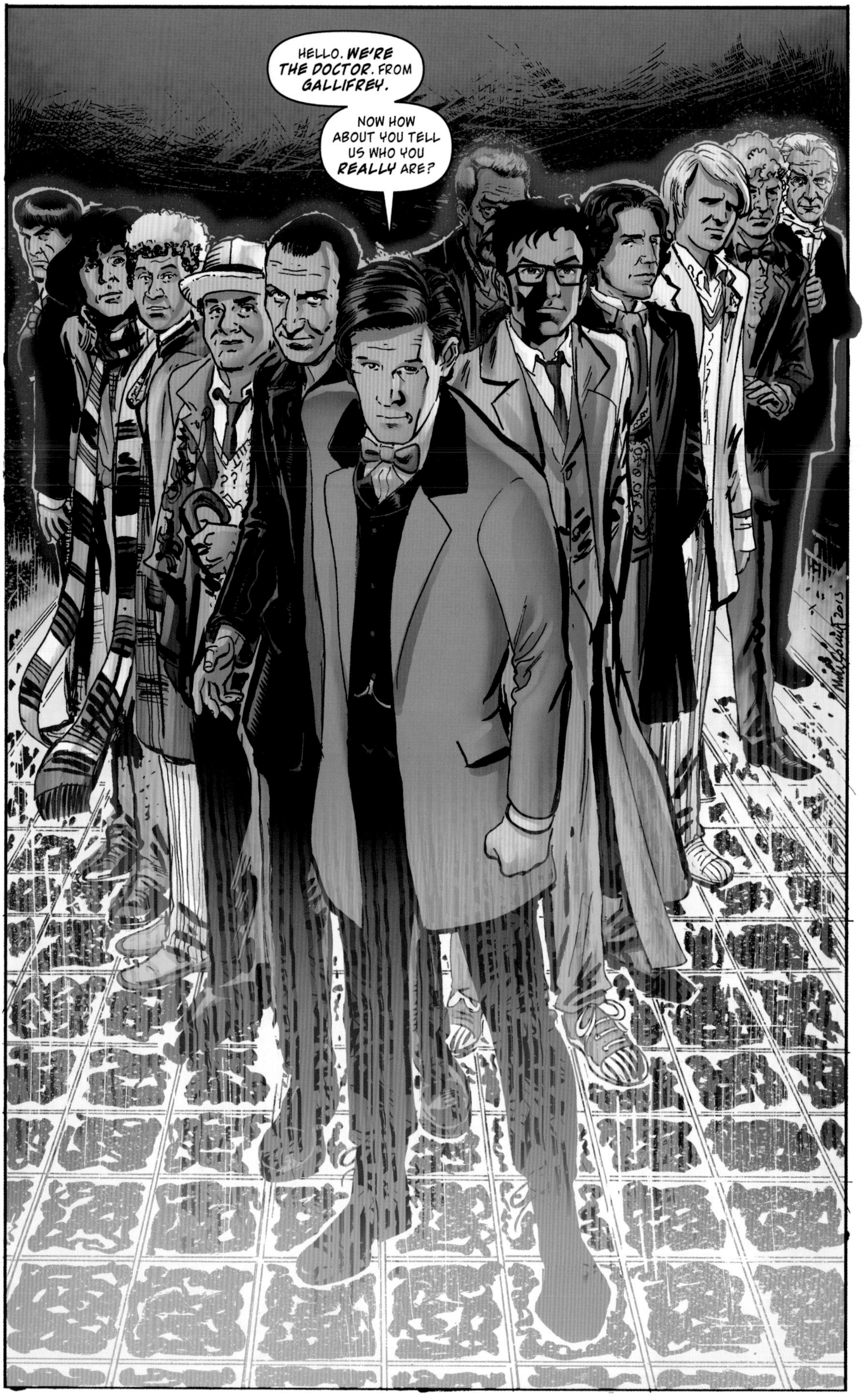
HELLO. WE'RE THE DOCTOR. FROM GALLIFREY.
NOW HOW ABOUT YOU TELL US WHO YOU REALLY ARE?

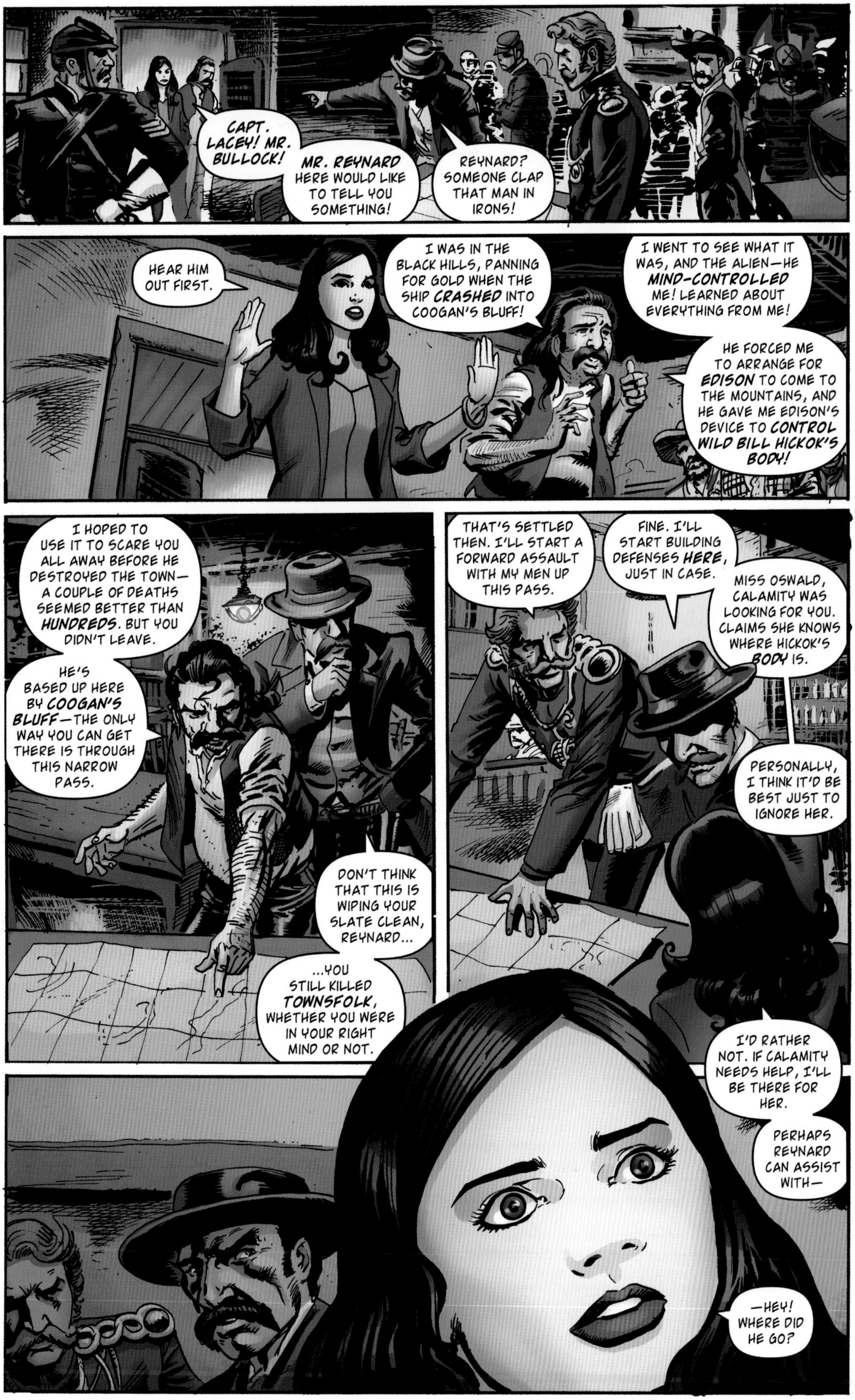
CAPT. LACEY! MR. BULLOCK!
MR. REYNARD HERE WOULD LIKE TO TELL YOU SOMETHING!
REYNARD? SOMEONE CLAP THAT MAN IN IRONS!
HEAR HIM OUT FIRST.
I WAS IN THE BLACK HILLS, PANNING FOR GOLD WHEN THE SHIP CRASHED INTO COOGAN'S BLUFF!
I WENT TO SEE WHAT IT WAS, AND THE ALIEN—HE MIND-CONTROLLED ME! LEARNED ABOUT EVERYTHING FROM ME!
HE FORCED ME TO ARRANGE FOR EDISON TO COME TO THE MOUNTAINS, AND HE GAVE ME EDISON'S DEVICE TO CONTROL WILD BILL HICKOK'S BODY!
I HOPED TO USE IT TO SCARE YOU ALL AWAY BEFORE HE DESTROYED THE TOWN—A COUPLE OF DEATHS SEEMED BETTER THAN HUNDREDS. BUT YOU DIDN'T LEAVE.
HE'S BASED UP HERE BY COOGAN'S BLUFF—THE ONLY WAY YOU CAN GET THERE IS THROUGH THIS NARROW PASS.
DON'T THINK THAT THIS IS WIPING YOUR SLATE CLEAN, REYNARD...
...YOU STILL KILLED TOWNSFOLK, WHETHER YOU WERE IN YOUR RIGHT MIND OR NOT.
THAT'S SETTLED THEN. I'LL START A FORWARD ASSAULT WITH MY MEN UP THIS PASS.
FINE. I'LL START BUILDING DEFENSES HERE, JUST IN CASE.
MISS OSWALD, CALAMITY WAS LOOKING FOR YOU. CLAIMS SHE KNOWS WHERE HICKOK'S BODY IS.
PERSONALLY, I THINK IT'D BE BEST JUST TO IGNORE HER.
I'D RATHER NOT. IF CALAMITY NEEDS HELP, I'LL BE THERE FOR HER.
PERHAPS REYNARD CAN ASSIST WITH—
—HEY! WHERE DID HE GO?

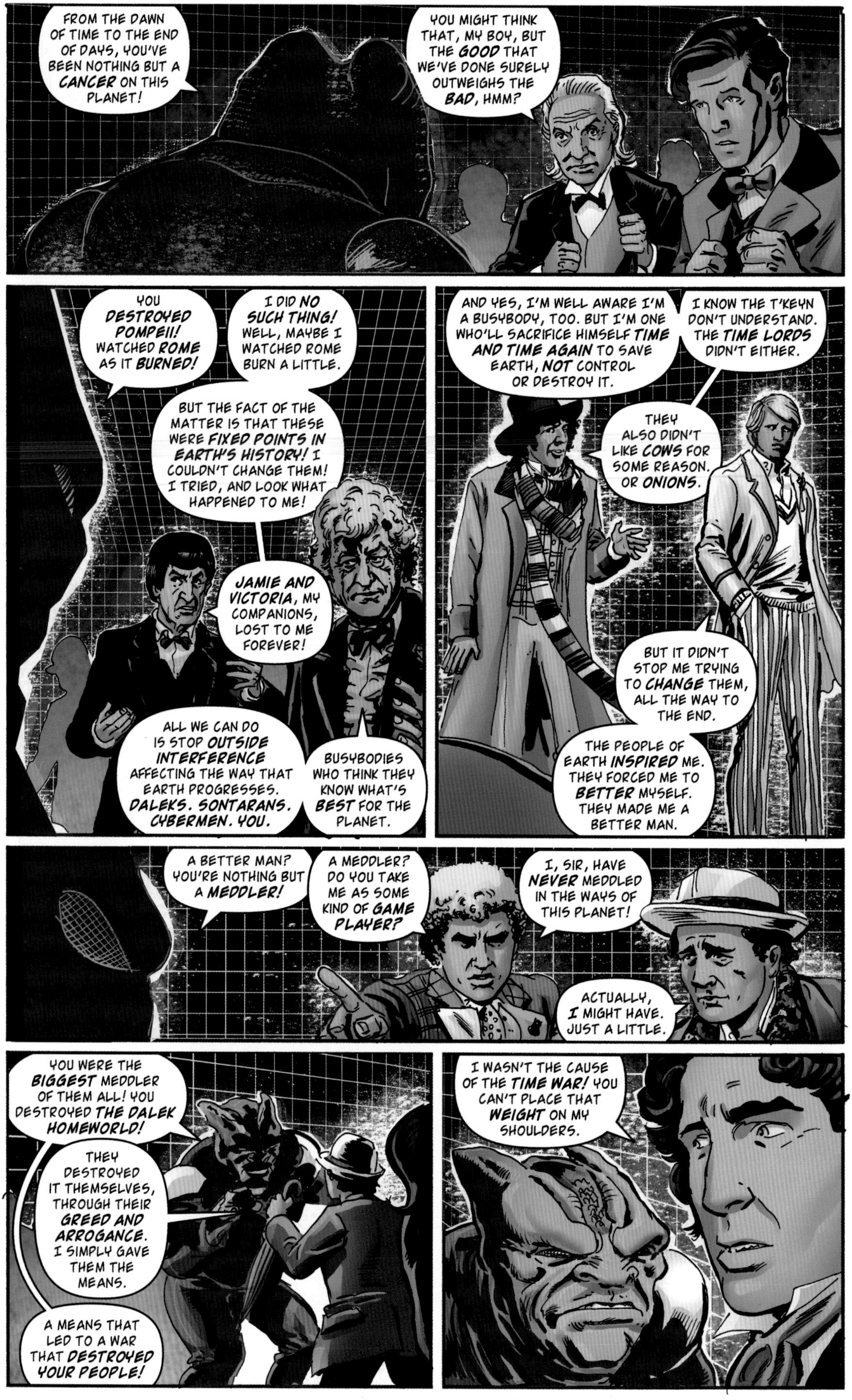
FROM THE DAWN OF TIME TO THE END OF DAYS, YOU'VE BEEN NOTHING BUT A CANCER ON THIS PLANET!
YOU MIGHT THINK THAT, MY BOY, BUT THE GOOD THAT WE'VE DONE SURELY OUTWEIGHS THE BAD, HMM?
YOU DESTROYED POMPEII! WATCHED ROME AS IT BURNED!
I DID NO SUCH THING! WELL, MAYBE I WATCHED ROME BURN A LITTLE.
BUT THE FACT OF THE MATTER IS THAT THESE WERE FIXED POINTS IN EARTH'S HISTORY! I COULDN'T CHANGE THEM! I TRIED, AND LOOK WHAT HAPPENED TO ME!
JAMIE AND VICTORIA, MY COMPANIONS, LOST TO ME FOREVER!
ALL WE CAN DO IS STOP OUTSIDE INTERFERENCE AFFECTING THE WAY THAT EARTH PROGRESSES. DALEKS. SONTARANS. CYBERMEN. YOU.
BUSYBODIES WHO THINK THEY KNOW WHAT'S BEST FOR THE PLANET.
AND YES, I'M WELL AWARE I'M A BUSYBODY, TOO. BUT I'M ONE WHO'LL SACRIFICE HIMSELF TIME AND TIME AGAIN TO SAVE EARTH, NOT CONTROL OR DESTROY IT.
I KNOW THE T'KEYN DON'T UNDERSTAND. THE TIME LORDS DIDN'T EITHER.
THEY ALSO DIDN'T LIKE COWS FOR SOME REASON. OR ONIONS.
BUT IT DIDN'T STOP ME TRYING TO CHANGE THEM, ALL THE WAY TO THE END.
THE PEOPLE OF EARTH INSPIRED ME. THEY FORCED ME TO BETTER MYSELF. THEY MADE ME A BETTER MAN.
A BETTER MAN? YOU'RE NOTHING BUT A MEDDLER!
A MEDDLER? DO YOU TAKE ME AS SOME KIND OF GAME PLAYER?
I, SIR, HAVE NEVER MEDDLED IN THE WAYS OF THIS PLANET!
ACTUALLY, I MIGHT HAVE. JUST A LITTLE.
YOU WERE THE BIGGEST MEDDLER OF THEM ALL! YOU DESTROYED THE DALEK HOMEWORLD!
THEY DESTROYED IT THEMSELVES, THROUGH THEIR GREED AND ARROGANCE. I SIMPLY GAVE THEM THE MEANS.
A MEANS THAT LED TO A WAR THAT DESTROYED YOUR PEOPLE!
I WASN'T THE CAUSE OF THE TIME WAR! YOU CAN'T PLACE THAT WEIGHT ON MY SHOULDERS.

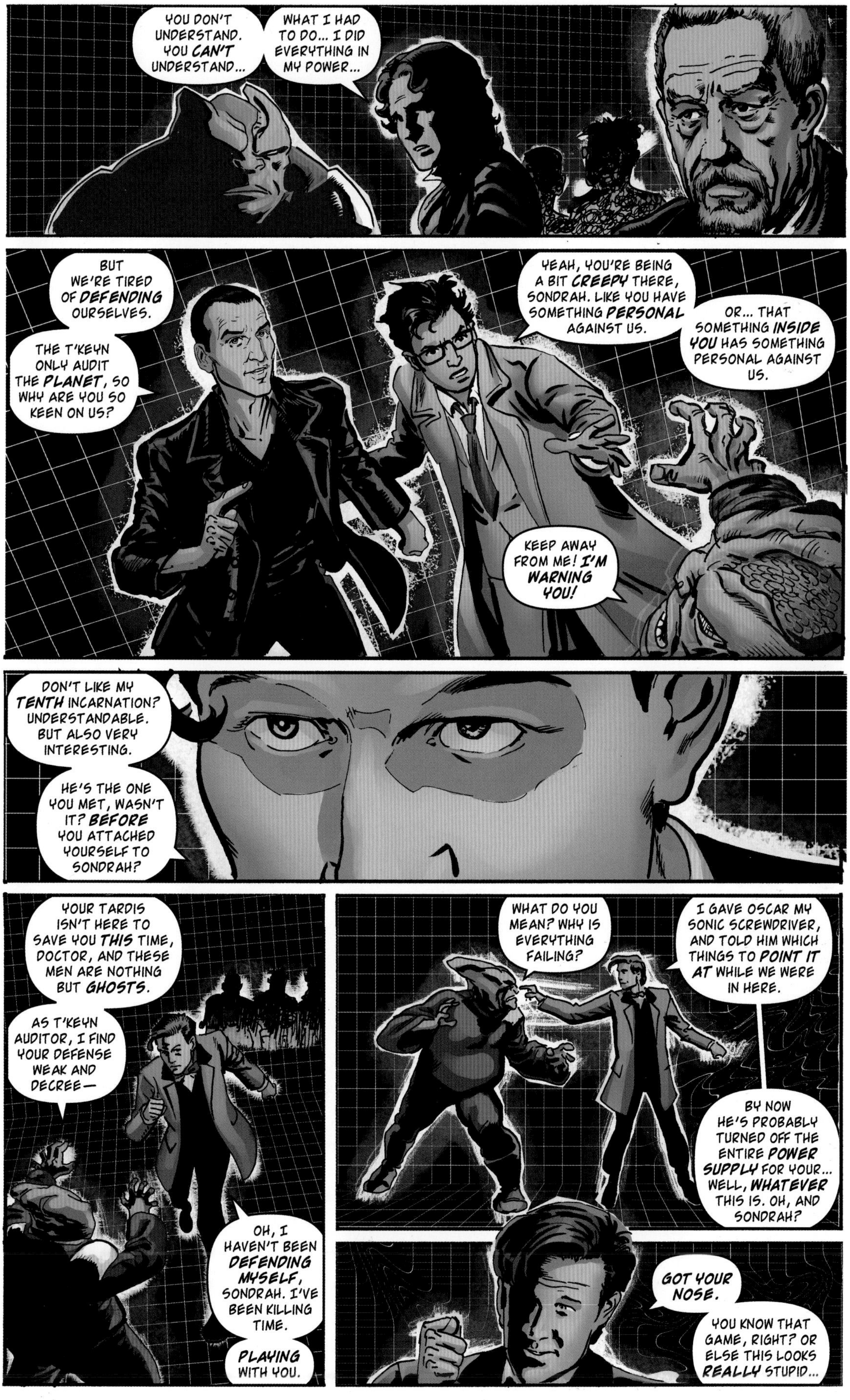

YOU DON'T UNDERSTAND. YOU CAN'T UNDERSTAND...
WHAT I HAD TO DO... I DID EVERYTHING IN MY POWER...
BUT WE'RE TIRED OF DEFENDING OURSELVES.
THE T'KEYN ONLY AUDIT THE PLANET, SO WHY ARE YOU SO KEEN ON US?
YEAH, YOU'RE BEING A BIT CREEPY THERE, SONDRAH. LIKE YOU HAVE SOMETHING PERSONAL AGAINST US.
OR... THAT SOMETHING INSIDE YOU HAS SOMETHING PERSONAL AGAINST US.
KEEP AWAY FROM ME! I'M WARNING YOU!
DON'T LIKE MY TENTH INCARNATION? UNDERSTANDABLE. BUT ALSO VERY INTERESTING.
HE'S THE ONE YOU MET, WASN'T IT? BEFORE YOU ATTACHED YOURSELF TO SONDRAH?
YOUR TARDIS ISN'T HERE TO SAVE YOU THIS TIME, DOCTOR, AND THESE MEN ARE NOTHING BUT GHOSTS.
AS T'KEYN AUDITOR, I FIND YOUR DEFENSE WEAK AND DECREE—
OH, I HAVEN'T BEEN DEFENDING MYSELF, SONDRAH. I'VE BEEN KILLING TIME.
PLAYING WITH YOU.
WHAT DO YOU MEAN? WHY IS EVERYTHING FAILING?
I GAVE OSCAR MY SONIC SCREWDRIVER, AND TOLD HIM WHICH THINGS TO POINT IT AT WHILE WE WERE IN HERE.
BY NOW HE'S PROBABLY TURNED OFF THE ENTIRE POWER SUPPLY FOR YOUR... WELL, WHATEVER THIS IS. OH, AND SONDRAH?
GOT YOUR NOSE.
YOU KNOW THAT GAME, RIGHT? OR ELSE THIS LOOKS REALLY STUPID...

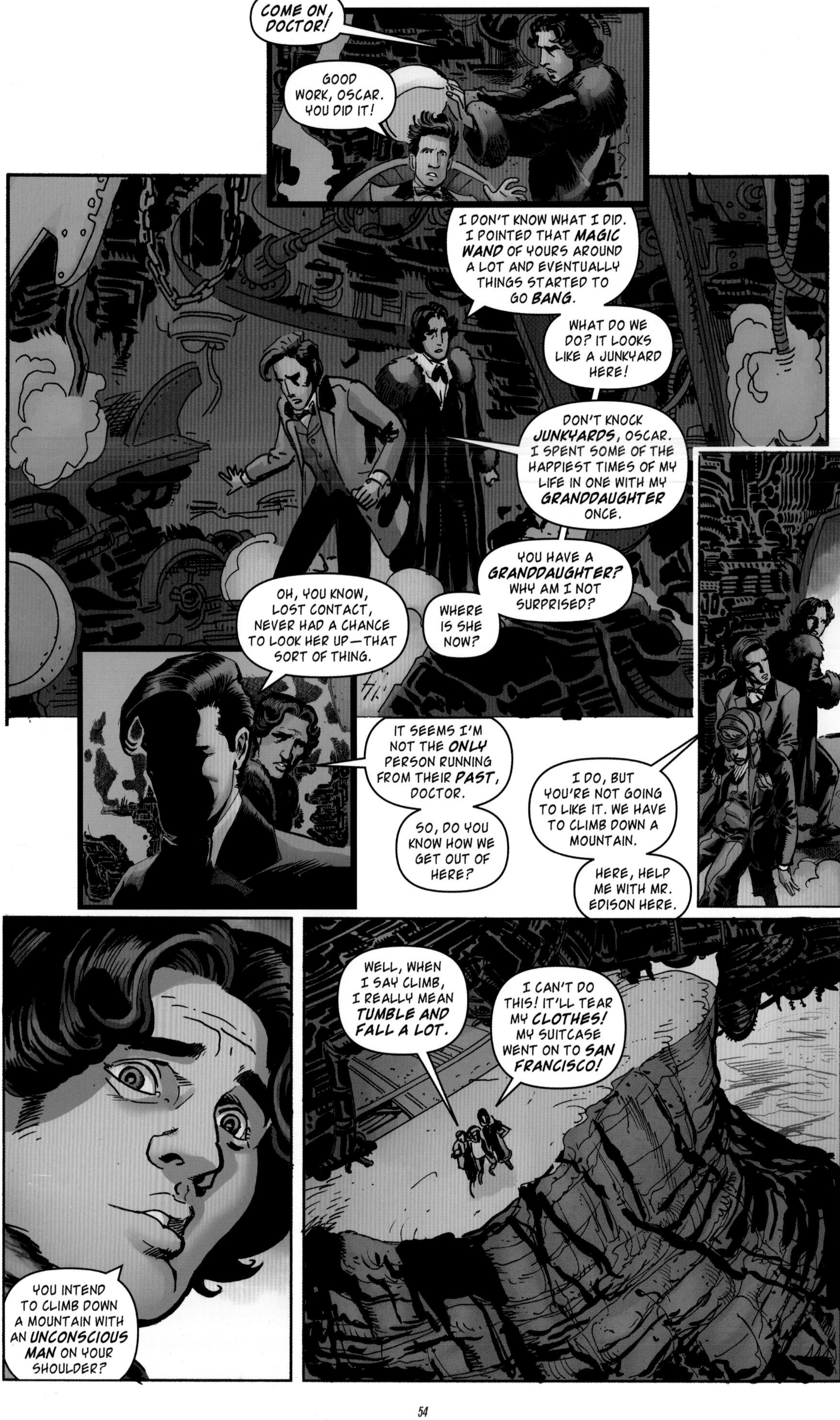
COME ON, DOCTOR!
GOOD WORK, OSCAR. YOU DID IT!
I DON'T KNOW WHAT I DID. I POINTED THAT MAGIC WAND OF YOURS AROUND A LOT AND EVENTUALLY THINGS STARTED TO GO BANG.
WHAT DO WE DO? IT LOOKS LIKE A JUNKYARD HERE!
DON'T KNOCK JUNKYARDS, OSCAR. I SPENT SOME OF THE HAPPIEST TIMES OF MY LIFE IN ONE WITH MY GRANDDAUGHTER ONCE.
YOU HAVE A GRANDDAUGHTER? WHY AM I NOT SURPRISED?
WHERE IS SHE NOW?
OH, YOU KNOW, LOST CONTACT, NEVER HAD A CHANCE TO LOOK HER UP—THAT SORT OF THING.
IT SEEMS I'M NOT THE ONLY PERSON RUNNING FROM THEIR PAST, DOCTOR.
SO, DO YOU KNOW HOW WE GET OUT OF HERE?
I DO, BUT YOU'RE NOT GOING TO LIKE IT. WE HAVE TO CLIMB DOWN A MOUNTAIN.
HERE, HELP ME WITH MR. EDISON HERE.
YOU INTEND TO CLIMB DOWN A MOUNTAIN WITH AN UNCONSCIOUS MAN ON YOUR SHOULDER?
WELL, WHEN I SAY CLIMB, I REALLY MEAN TUMBLE AND FALL A LOT.
I CAN'T DO THIS! IT'LL TEAR MY CLOTHES! MY SUITCASE WENT ON TO SAN FRANCISCO!

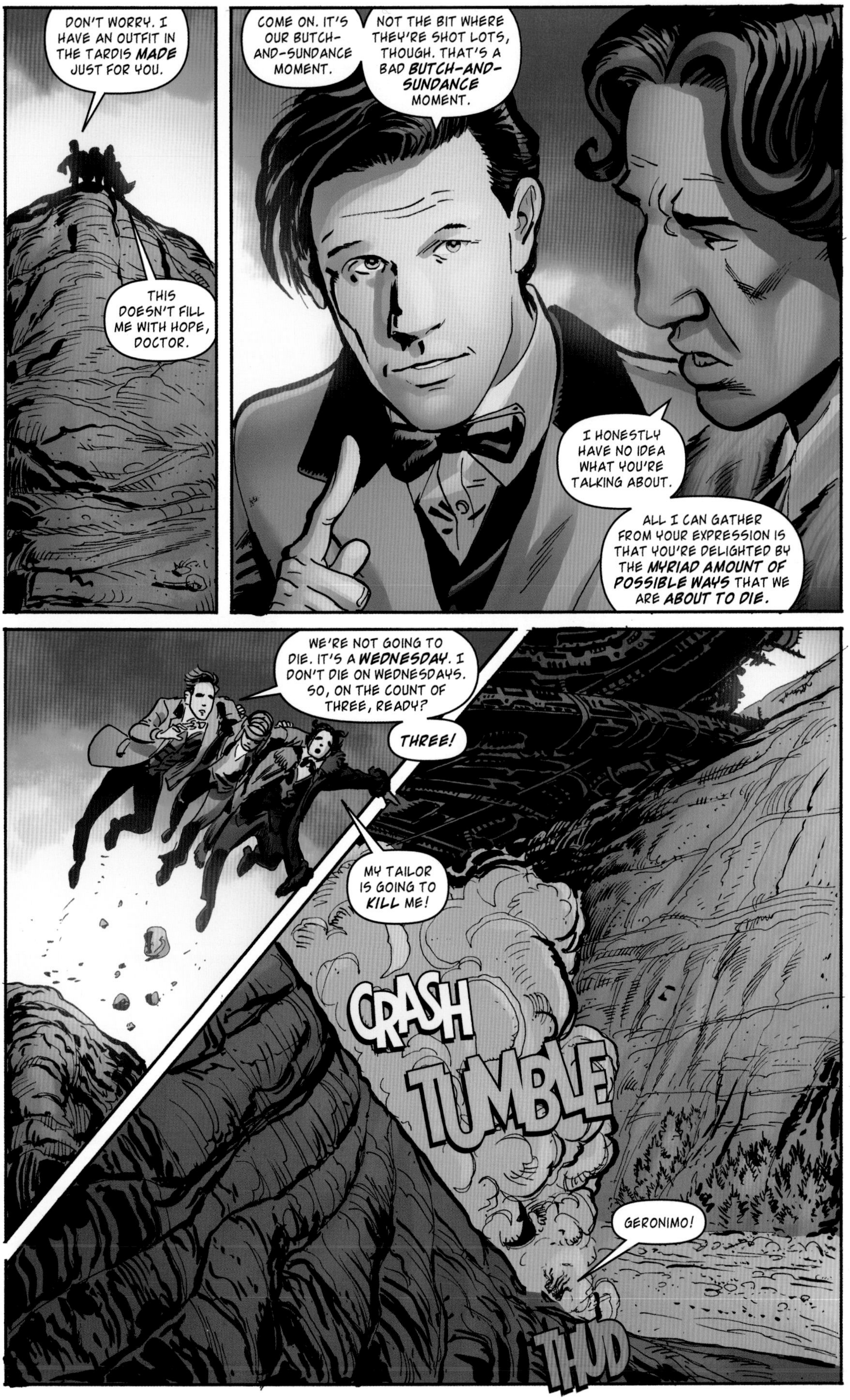
DON'T WORRY. I HAVE AN OUTFIT IN THE TARDIS MADE JUST FOR YOU.
THIS DOESN'T FILL ME WITH HOPE, DOCTOR.
COME ON. IT'S OUR BUTCH-AND-SUNDANCE MOMENT.
NOT THE BIT WHERE THEY'RE SHOT LOTS, THOUGH. THAT'S A BAD BUTCH-AND-SUNDANCE MOMENT.
I HONESTLY HAVE NO IDEA WHAT YOU'RE TALKING ABOUT.
ALL I CAN GATHER FROM YOUR EXPRESSION IS THAT YOU'RE DELIGHTED BY THE MYRIAD AMOUNT OF POSSIBLE WAYS THAT WE ARE ABOUT TO DIE.
WE'RE NOT GOING TO DIE. IT'S A WEDNESDAY. I DON'T DIE ON WEDNESDAYS. SO, ON THE COUNT OF THREE, READY?
THREE!
MY TAILOR IS GOING TO KILL ME!
CRASH
TUMBLE
GERONIMO!
THUD

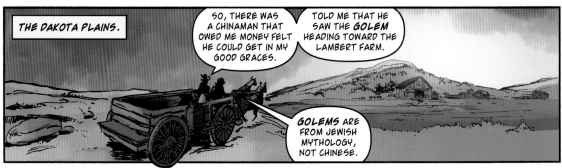

THE DAKOTA PLAINS.

SO, THERE WAS A CHINAMAN THAT OWED ME MONEY FELT HE COULD GET IN MY GOOD GRACES.

TOLD ME THAT HE SAW THE *GOLEM* HEADING TOWARD THE LAMBERT FARM.

GOLEMS ARE FROM JEWISH MYTHOLOGY, NOT CHINESE.

WELL, MAYBE THE CHINAMAN WAS JEWISH?

WILL YOU STOP SQUIRMIN' ABOUT? YOU'RE ACTING LIKE YOU'VE GOT *ANTS IN YOUR BREECHES!*

I CAN'T HELP IT—IT'S THIS *CART!* I'M USED TO THINGS WITH, WELL, MORE *SUSPENSION,* YOU KNOW?

ANY SUSPENSION WOULD BE NICE!

WELL, *EXCUSE ME,* PRINCESS CLARA! NEXT TIME I'LL MAKE SURE TO STEAL A CART WITH *BETTER SUSPENSINING,* OR WHATEVER YOU CALL IT!

HERE, LET ME HELP YOUR *LADYSHIP* DOWN FROM HER SEAT.

AND NOW YOU'RE JUST BEING ANNOYING.

IF BILL IS HERE, WHAT DO YOU INTEND TO DO?

WHY, TAKE HIM HOME, OF COURSE! I'LL *LOOK AFTER* HIM, LIKE HE LOOKED AFTER ME.

WHAT, YOU'LL *LOVE HIM, AND PET HIM, AND NAME HIM GEORGE?*

NEVER MIND. LOOK, I'M WORRIED ABOUT YOU, CALAMITY. THE DOCTOR SAID BILL WAS NOTHING BUT A *SHELL* OPERATED BY REYNARD—

—OH.

THEN YOUR DOCTOR IS *WRONG...*

56

...FOR *NOBODY* CONTROLS ME.

HOW DO YOU EXPLAIN... *THIS?*

THE DOCTOR THINKS THAT YOU MIGHT BE SOME KIND OF *ECHO* OF BILL, WOKEN UP WHEN THE MASK TOOK YOU OVER.

BILL! OH, BILL, *YOU'RE* ALIVE!

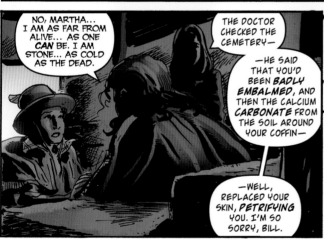

NO, MARTHA... I AM AS FAR FROM ALIVE... AS ONE *CAN* BE. I AM STONE... AS COLD AS THE DEAD.

THE DOCTOR CHECKED THE CEMETERY—

—HE SAID THAT YOU'D BEEN *BADLY EMBALMED*, AND THEN THE CALCIUM *CARBONATE* FROM THE SOIL AROUND YOUR COFFIN—

—WELL, REPLACED YOUR SKIN, *PETRIFYING* YOU. I'M SO SORRY, BILL.

I REMEMBER... FRAGMENTS.

CHARLIE UTTER... HE LIVES?

HE OWNS A SALOON IN *NEW MEXICO* NOW.

CAN YOU REMEMBER ANYTHING FROM *AFTER* YOUR DEATH? WHEN YOU WERE... *BROUGHT BACK?*

YES, I DO. I REMEMBER THAT WEASEL... *REYNARD.* I REMEMBER THE *ALIEN.*

BUT I ALSO REMEMBER... THE *OTHER* BODIES. *STONE,* LIKE ME... IS DEADWOOD... ATTACKING... THE HILLS YET?

THE *7TH CALVARY* WAS SETTING UP TO DO JUST THAT AS WE LEFT. WHY?

BECAUSE... THEY'RE WALKING... INTO A *TRAP.*

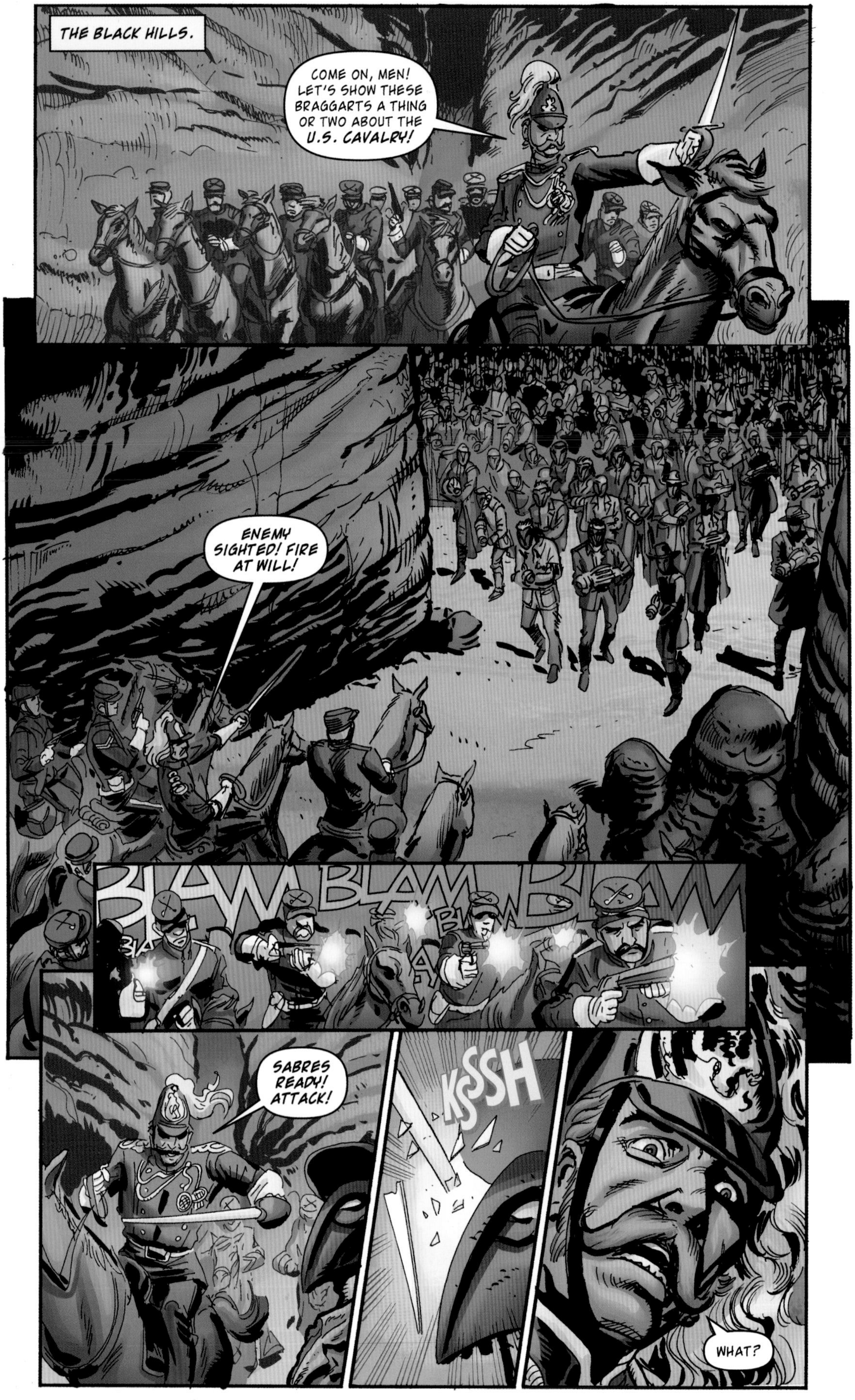
THE BLACK HILLS.
COME ON, MEN! LET'S SHOW THESE BRAGGARTS A THING OR TWO ABOUT THE U.S. CAVALRY!
ENEMY SIGHTED! FIRE AT WILL!
BLAM BLAM BLAM
SABRES READY! ATTACK!
KSSSH
WHAT?

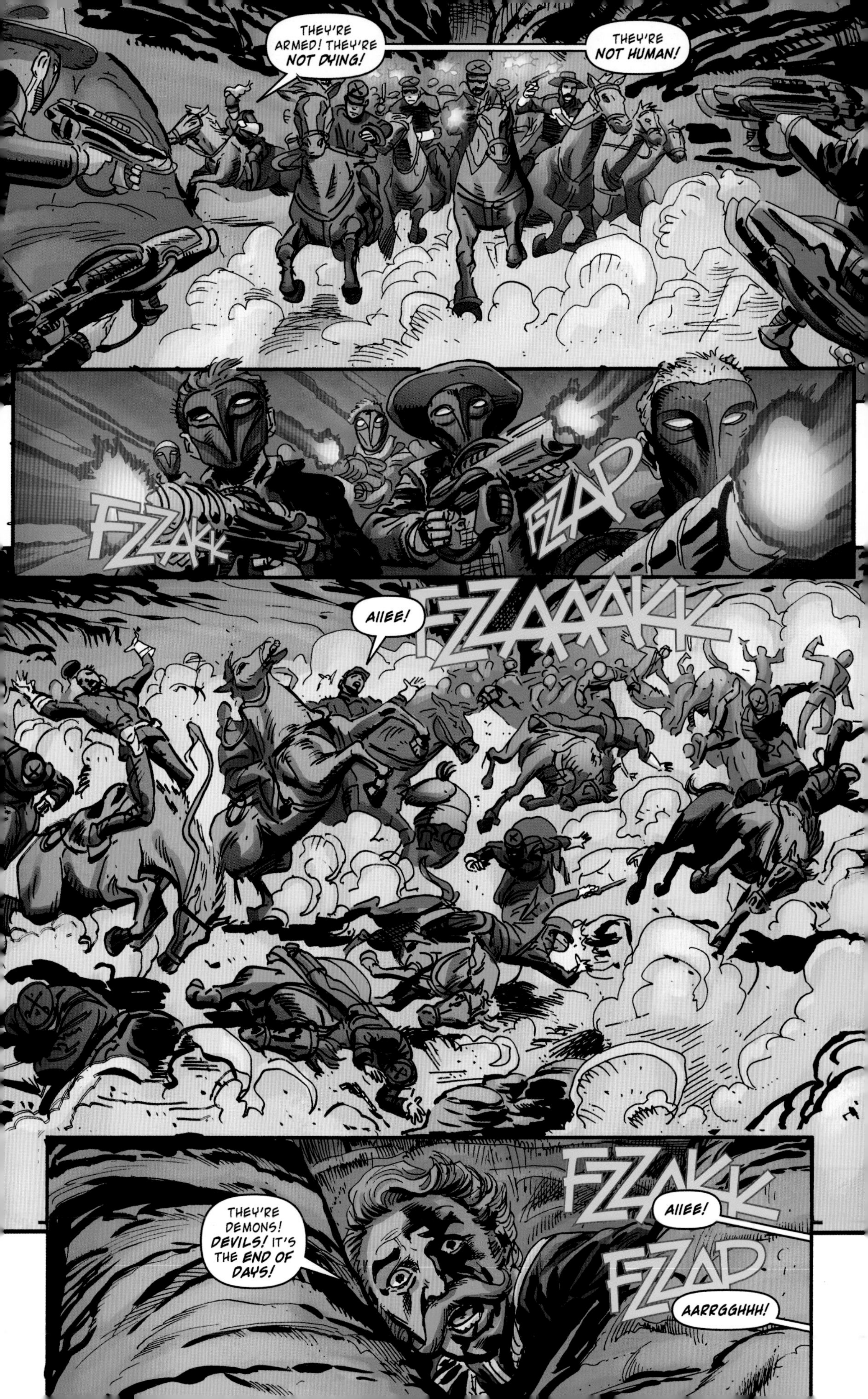

THEY'RE ARMED! THEY'RE NOT DYING!
THEY'RE NOT HUMAN!
FZZAKK
FZZAP
AIIEE!
FZZAAAKK
FZZAKK
THEY'RE DEMONS! DEVILS! IT'S THE END OF DAYS!
AIIEE!
FZZAP
AARRGGHHH!

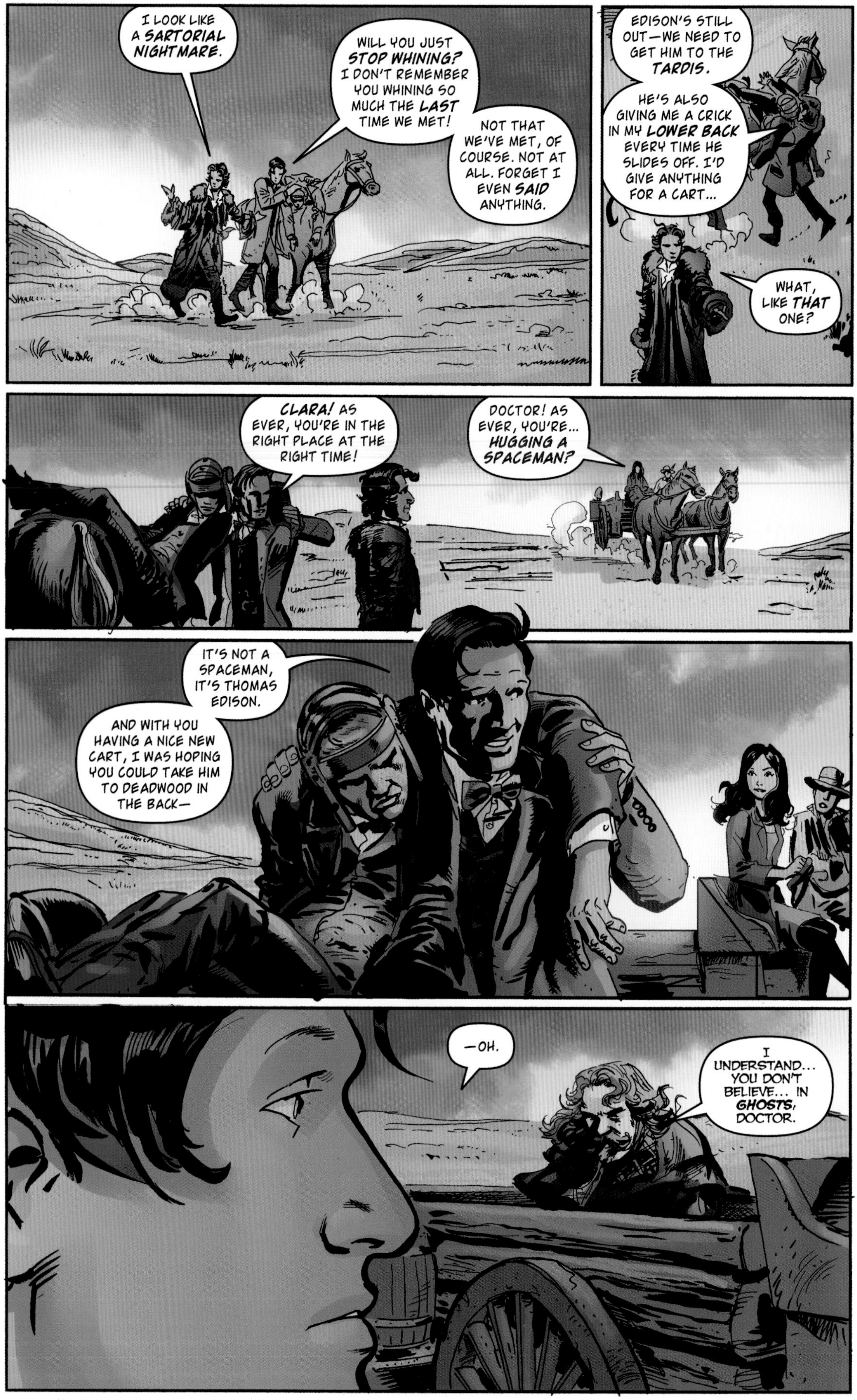

I LOOK LIKE A SARTORIAL NIGHTMARE.
WILL YOU JUST STOP WHINING? I DON'T REMEMBER YOU WHINING SO MUCH THE LAST TIME WE MET!
NOT THAT WE'VE MET, OF COURSE. NOT AT ALL. FORGET I EVEN SAID ANYTHING.
EDISON'S STILL OUT—WE NEED TO GET HIM TO THE TARDIS.
HE'S ALSO GIVING ME A CRICK IN MY LOWER BACK EVERY TIME HE SLIDES OFF. I'D GIVE ANYTHING FOR A CART...
WHAT, LIKE THAT ONE?
CLARA! AS EVER, YOU'RE IN THE RIGHT PLACE AT THE RIGHT TIME!
DOCTOR! AS EVER, YOU'RE... HUGGING A SPACEMAN?
IT'S NOT A SPACEMAN, IT'S THOMAS EDISON.
AND WITH YOU HAVING A NICE NEW CART, I WAS HOPING YOU COULD TAKE HIM TO DEADWOOD IN THE BACK—
—OH.
I UNDERSTAND... YOU DON'T BELIEVE... IN GHOSTS, DOCTOR.

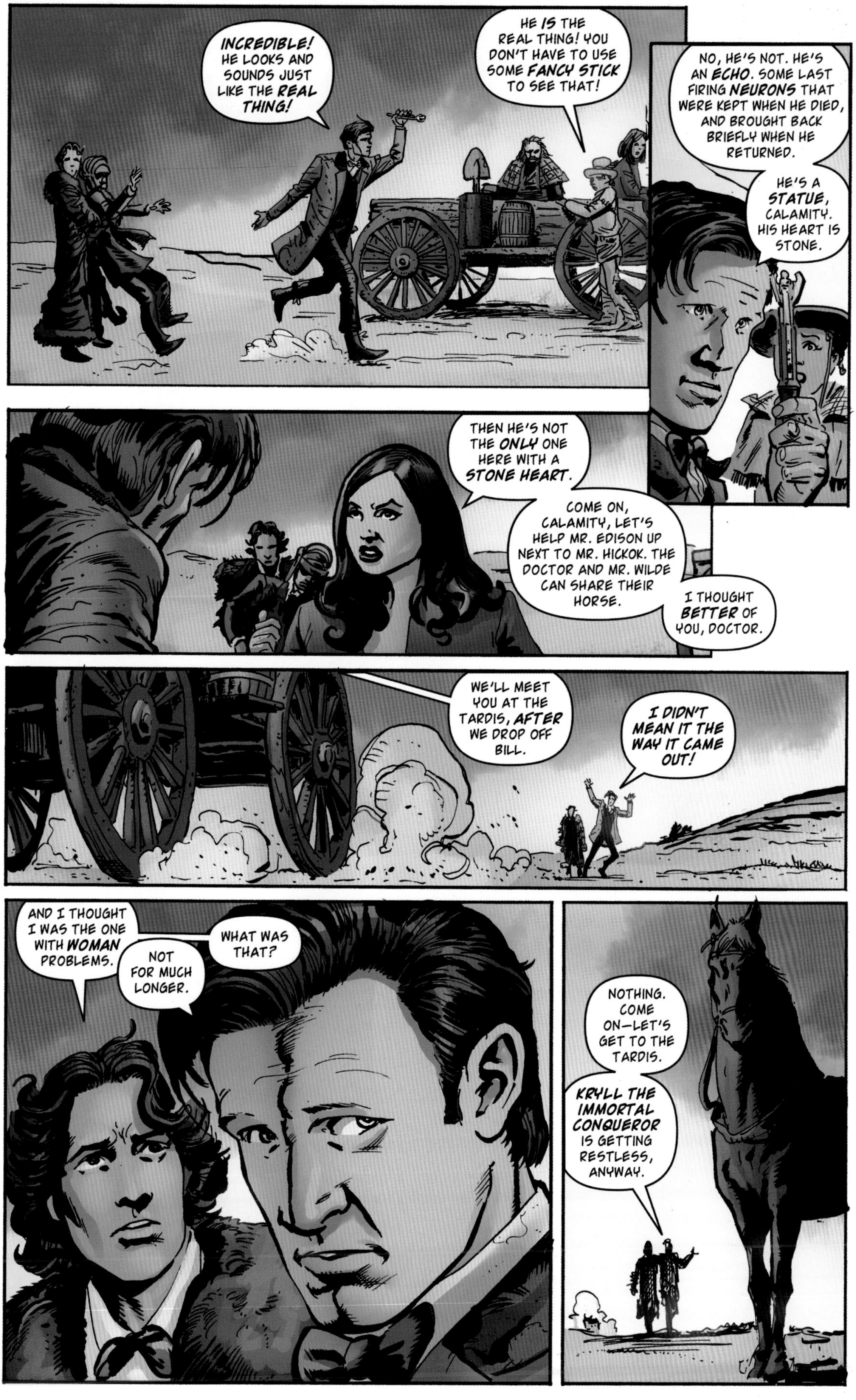
INCREDIBLE! HE LOOKS AND SOUNDS JUST LIKE THE REAL THING!
HE IS THE REAL THING! YOU DON'T HAVE TO USE SOME FANCY STICK TO SEE THAT!
NO, HE'S NOT. HE'S AN ECHO. SOME LAST FIRING NEURONS THAT WERE KEPT WHEN HE DIED, AND BROUGHT BACK BRIEFLY WHEN HE RETURNED.
HE'S A STATUE, CALAMITY. HIS HEART IS STONE.
THEN HE'S NOT THE ONLY ONE HERE WITH A STONE HEART.
COME ON, CALAMITY, LET'S HELP MR. EDISON UP NEXT TO MR. HICKOK. THE DOCTOR AND MR. WILDE CAN SHARE THEIR HORSE.
I THOUGHT BETTER OF YOU, DOCTOR.
WE'LL MEET YOU AT THE TARDIS, AFTER WE DROP OFF BILL.
I DIDN'T MEAN IT THE WAY IT CAME OUT!
AND I THOUGHT I WAS THE ONE WITH WOMAN PROBLEMS.
NOT FOR MUCH LONGER.
WHAT WAS THAT?
NOTHING. COME ON—LET'S GET TO THE TARDIS.
KRYLL THE IMMORTAL CONQUEROR IS GETTING RESTLESS, ANYWAY.

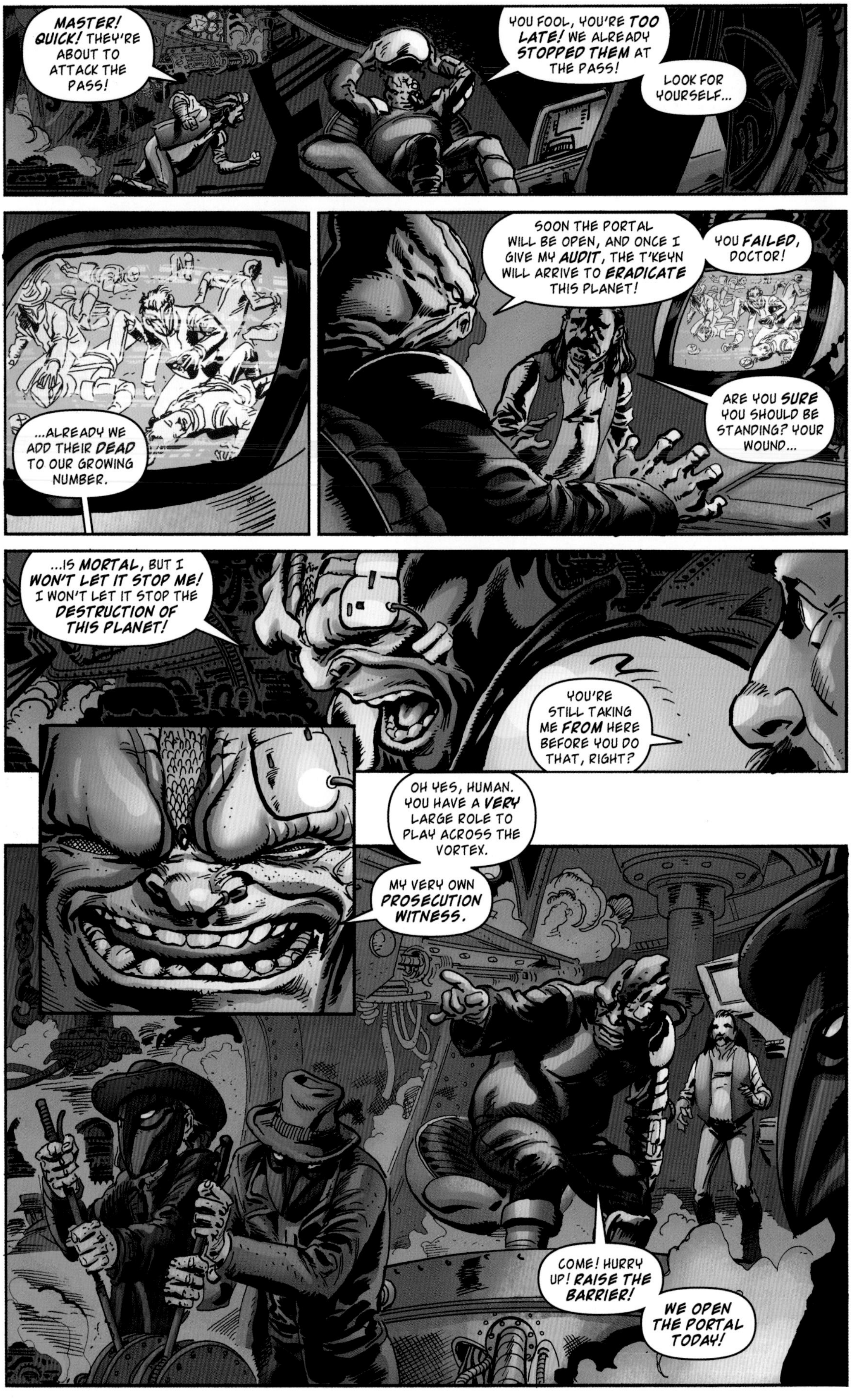
MASTER! QUICK! THEY'RE ABOUT TO ATTACK THE PASS!
YOU FOOL, YOU'RE TOO LATE! WE ALREADY STOPPED THEM AT THE PASS!
LOOK FOR YOURSELF...
...ALREADY WE ADD THEIR DEAD TO OUR GROWING NUMBER.
SOON THE PORTAL WILL BE OPEN, AND ONCE I GIVE MY AUDIT, THE T'KEYN WILL ARRIVE TO ERADICATE THIS PLANET!
YOU FAILED, DOCTOR!
ARE YOU SURE YOU SHOULD BE STANDING? YOUR WOUND...
...IS MORTAL, BUT I WON'T LET IT STOP ME! I WON'T LET IT STOP THE DESTRUCTION OF THIS PLANET!
YOU'RE STILL TAKING ME FROM HERE BEFORE YOU DO THAT, RIGHT?
OH YES, HUMAN. YOU HAVE A VERY LARGE ROLE TO PLAY ACROSS THE VORTEX.
MY VERY OWN PROSECUTION WITNESS.
COME! HURRY UP! RAISE THE BARRIER!
WE OPEN THE PORTAL TODAY!

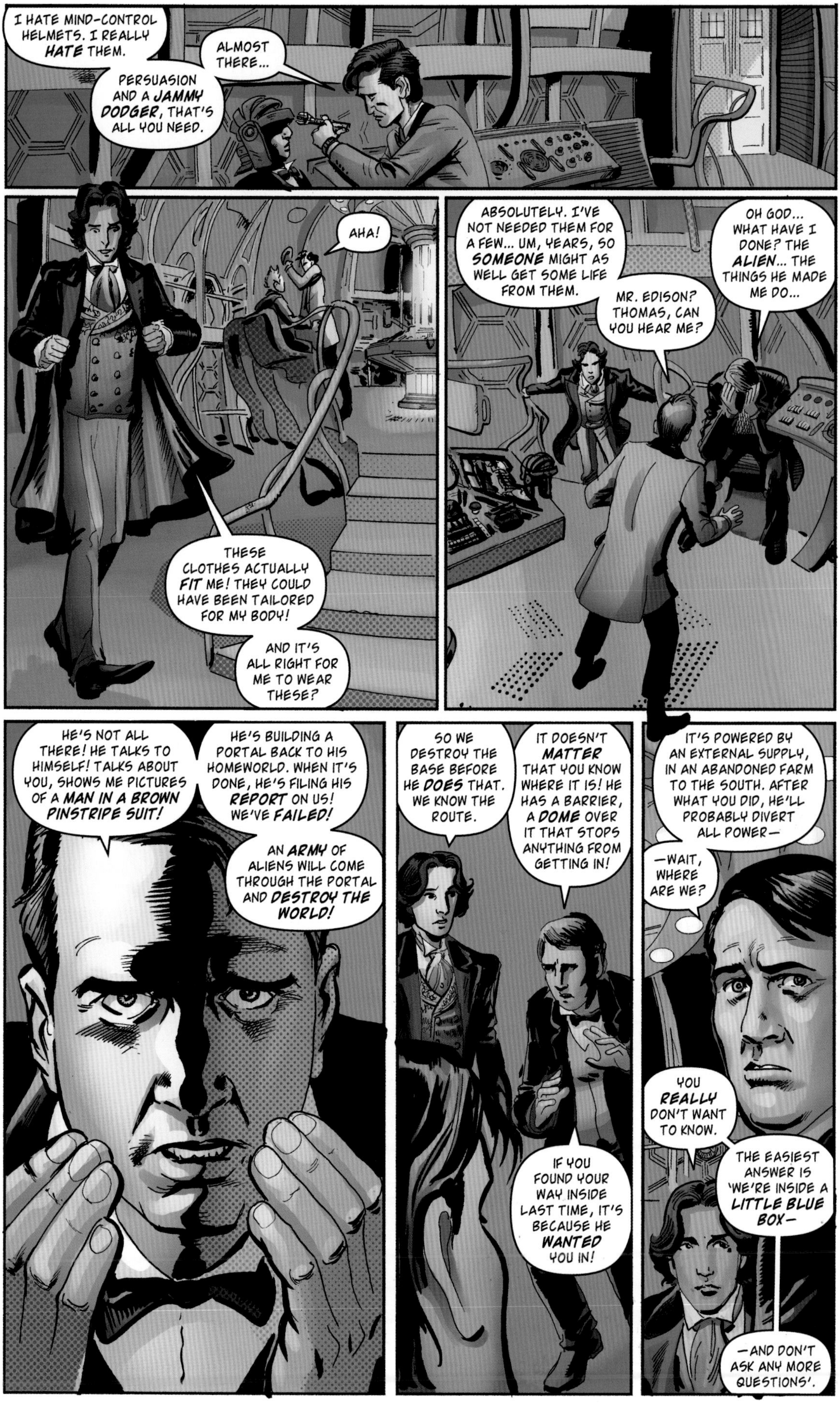
I HATE MIND-CONTROL HELMETS. I REALLY *HATE* THEM.
PERSUASION AND A *JAMMY DODGER*, THAT'S ALL YOU NEED.
ALMOST THERE...
AHA!
THESE CLOTHES ACTUALLY *FIT* ME! THEY COULD HAVE BEEN TAILORED FOR MY BODY!
AND IT'S ALL RIGHT FOR ME TO WEAR THESE?
ABSOLUTELY. I'VE NOT NEEDED THEM FOR A FEW... UM, YEARS, SO *SOMEONE* MIGHT AS WELL GET SOME LIFE FROM THEM.
MR. EDISON? THOMAS, CAN YOU HEAR ME?
OH GOD... WHAT HAVE I DONE? THE *ALIEN*... THE THINGS HE MADE ME DO...
HE'S NOT ALL THERE! HE TALKS TO HIMSELF! TALKS ABOUT YOU, SHOWS ME PICTURES OF A *MAN IN A BROWN PINSTRIPE SUIT!*
HE'S BUILDING A PORTAL BACK TO HIS HOMEWORLD. WHEN IT'S DONE, HE'S FILING HIS *REPORT* ON US! WE'VE *FAILED!*
AN *ARMY* OF ALIENS WILL COME THROUGH THE PORTAL AND *DESTROY THE WORLD!*
SO WE DESTROY THE BASE BEFORE HE *DOES* THAT. WE KNOW THE ROUTE.
IT DOESN'T *MATTER* THAT YOU KNOW WHERE IT IS! HE HAS A BARRIER, A *DOME* OVER IT THAT STOPS ANYTHING FROM GETTING IN!
IF YOU FOUND YOUR WAY INSIDE LAST TIME, IT'S BECAUSE HE *WANTED* YOU IN!
IT'S POWERED BY AN EXTERNAL SUPPLY, IN AN ABANDONED FARM TO THE SOUTH. AFTER WHAT YOU DID, HE'LL PROBABLY DIVERT ALL POWER—
—WAIT, WHERE ARE WE?
YOU *REALLY* DON'T WANT TO KNOW.
THE EASIEST ANSWER IS 'WE'RE INSIDE A *LITTLE BLUE BOX*—
—AND DON'T ASK ANY MORE QUESTIONS'.

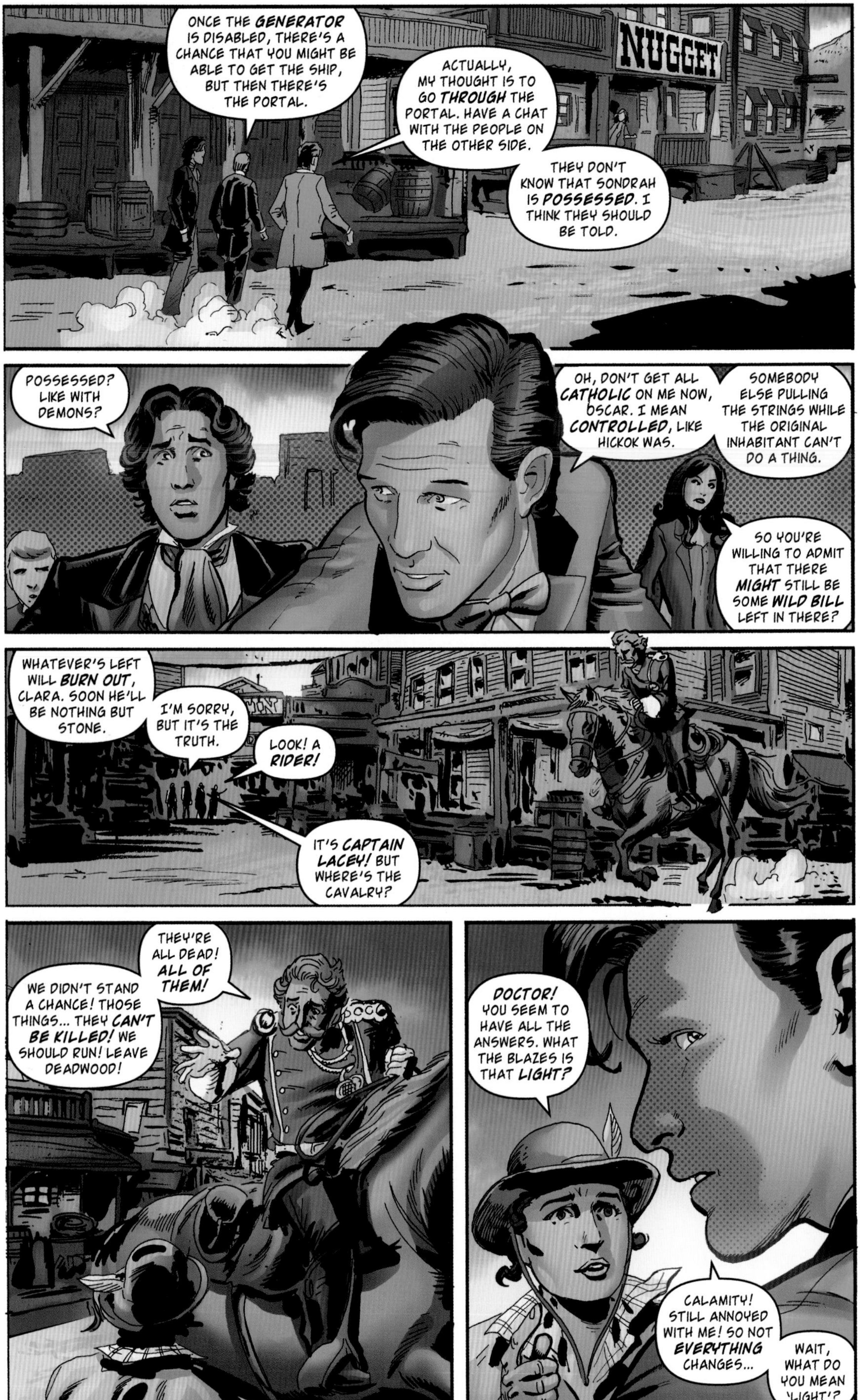
ONCE THE GENERATOR IS DISABLED, THERE'S A CHANCE THAT YOU MIGHT BE ABLE TO GET THE SHIP, BUT THEN THERE'S THE PORTAL.
ACTUALLY, MY THOUGHT IS TO GO THROUGH THE PORTAL. HAVE A CHAT WITH THE PEOPLE ON THE OTHER SIDE.
THEY DON'T KNOW THAT SONDRAH IS POSSESSED. I THINK THEY SHOULD BE TOLD.
NUGGET
POSSESSED? LIKE WITH DEMONS?
OH, DON'T GET ALL CATHOLIC ON ME NOW, OSCAR. I MEAN CONTROLLED, LIKE HICKOK WAS.
SOMEBODY ELSE PULLING THE STRINGS WHILE THE ORIGINAL INHABITANT CAN'T DO A THING.
SO YOU'RE WILLING TO ADMIT THAT THERE MIGHT STILL BE SOME WILD BILL LEFT IN THERE?
WHATEVER'S LEFT WILL BURN OUT, CLARA. SOON HE'LL BE NOTHING BUT STONE.
I'M SORRY, BUT IT'S THE TRUTH.
LOOK! A RIDER!
IT'S CAPTAIN LACEY! BUT WHERE'S THE CAVALRY?
THEY'RE ALL DEAD! ALL OF THEM!
WE DIDN'T STAND A CHANCE! THOSE THINGS... THEY CAN'T BE KILLED! WE SHOULD RUN! LEAVE DEADWOOD!
DOCTOR! YOU SEEM TO HAVE ALL THE ANSWERS. WHAT THE BLAZES IS THAT LIGHT?
CALAMITY! STILL ANNOYED WITH ME! SO NOT EVERYTHING CHANGES...
WAIT, WHAT DO YOU MEAN 'LIGHT'?

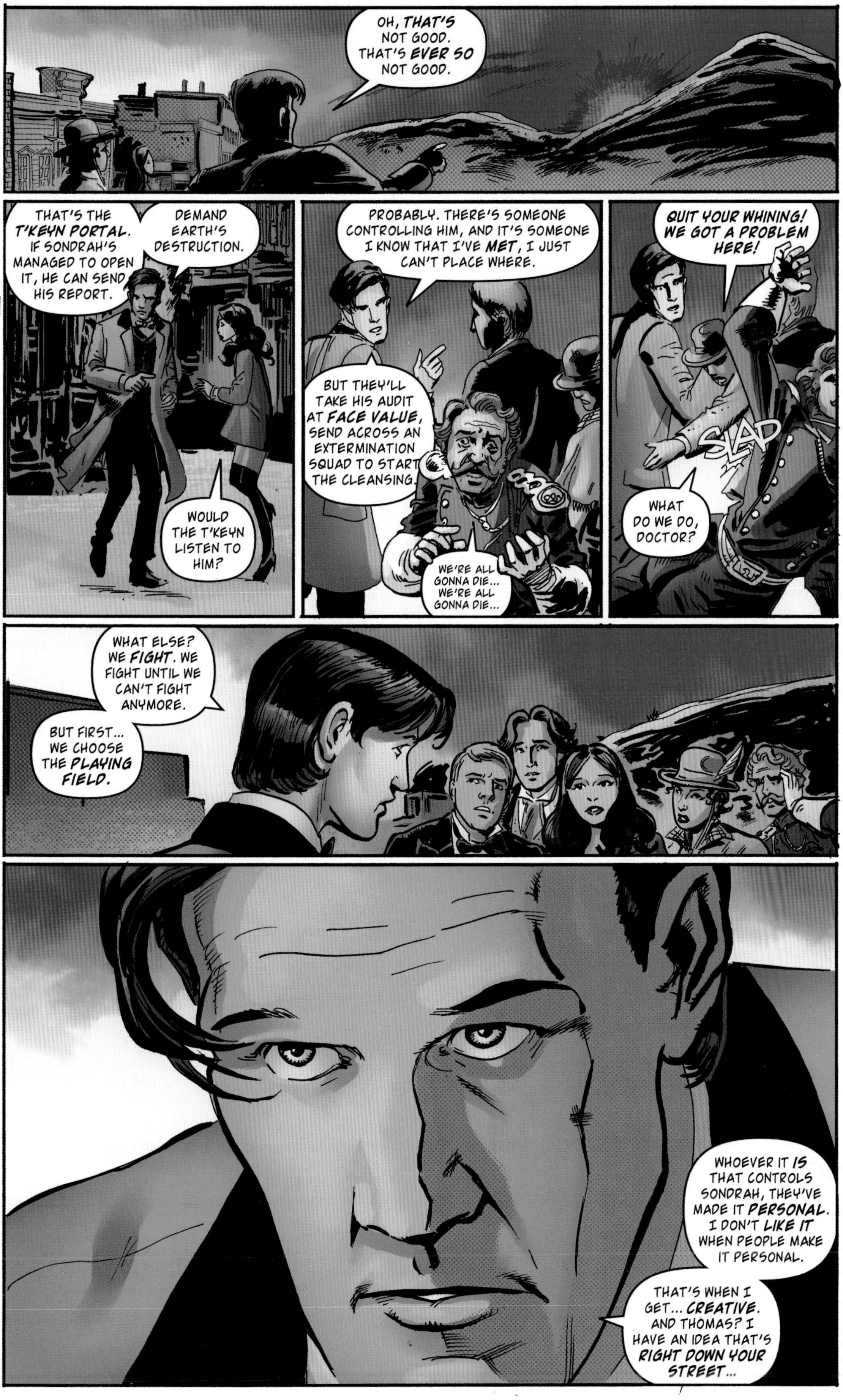
OH, THAT'S NOT GOOD. THAT'S EVER SO NOT GOOD.
THAT'S THE T'KEYN PORTAL. IF SONDRAH'S MANAGED TO OPEN IT, HE CAN SEND HIS REPORT.
DEMAND EARTH'S DESTRUCTION.
WOULD THE T'KEYN LISTEN TO HIM?
PROBABLY. THERE'S SOMEONE CONTROLLING HIM, AND IT'S SOMEONE I KNOW THAT I'VE MET, I JUST CAN'T PLACE WHERE.
BUT THEY'LL TAKE HIS AUDIT AT FACE VALUE, SEND ACROSS AN EXTERMINATION SQUAD TO START THE CLEANSING.
WE'RE ALL GONNA DIE... WE'RE ALL GONNA DIE...
QUIT YOUR WHINING! WE GOT A PROBLEM HERE!
SLAP
WHAT DO WE DO, DOCTOR?
WHAT ELSE? WE FIGHT. WE FIGHT UNTIL WE CAN'T FIGHT ANYMORE.
BUT FIRST... WE CHOOSE THE PLAYING FIELD.
WHOEVER IT IS THAT CONTROLS SONDRAH, THEY'VE MADE IT PERSONAL. I DON'T LIKE IT WHEN PEOPLE MAKE IT PERSONAL.
THAT'S WHEN I GET... CREATIVE. AND THOMAS? I HAVE AN IDEA THAT'S RIGHT DOWN YOUR STREET...

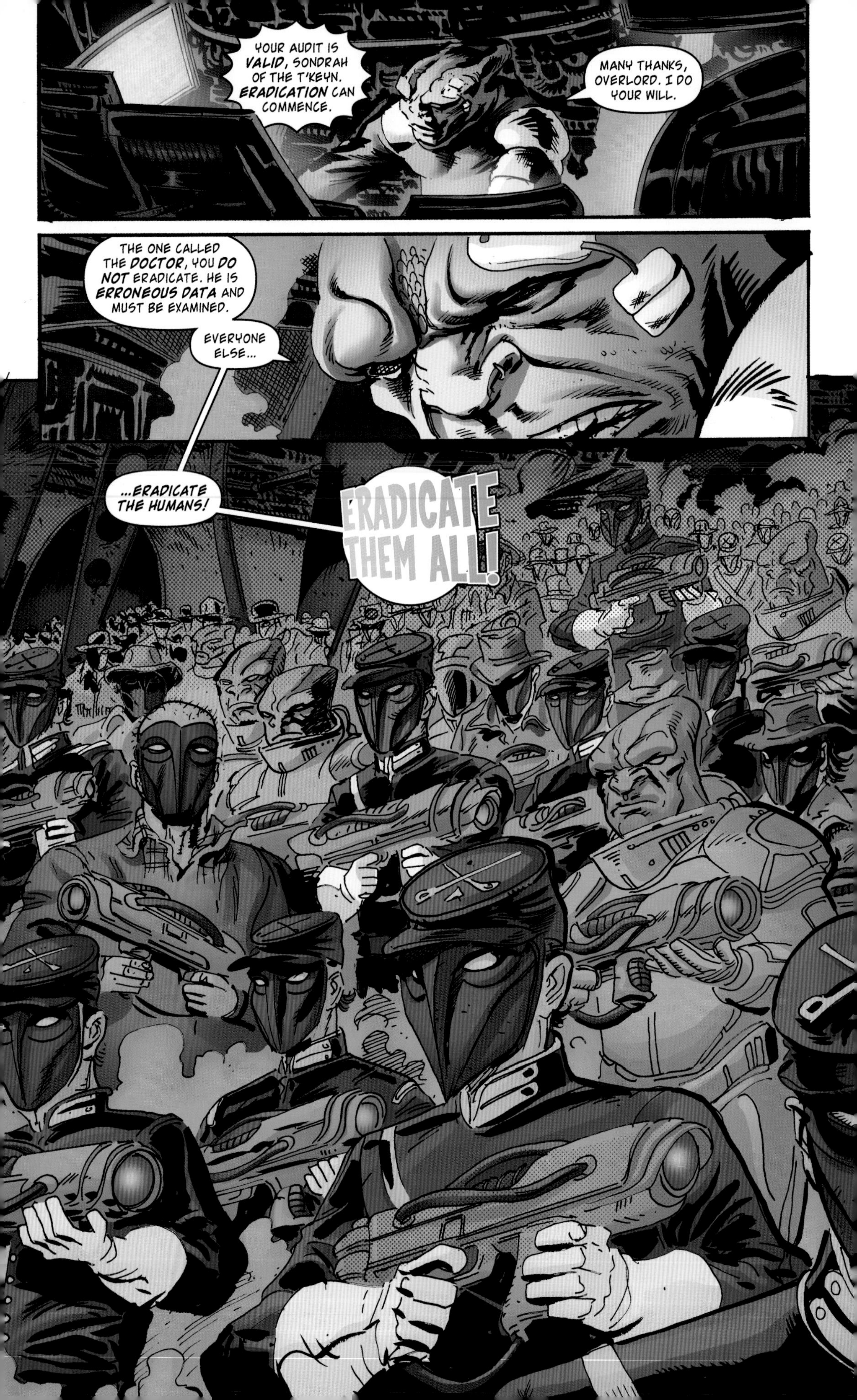
YOUR AUDIT IS VALID, SONDRAH OF THE T'KEYN. ERADICATION CAN COMMENCE.
MANY THANKS, OVERLORD. I DO YOUR WILL.
THE ONE CALLED THE DOCTOR, YOU DO NOT ERADICATE. HE IS ERRONEOUS DATA AND MUST BE EXAMINED.
EVERYONE ELSE...
...ERADICATE THE HUMANS!
ERADICATE THEM ALL!

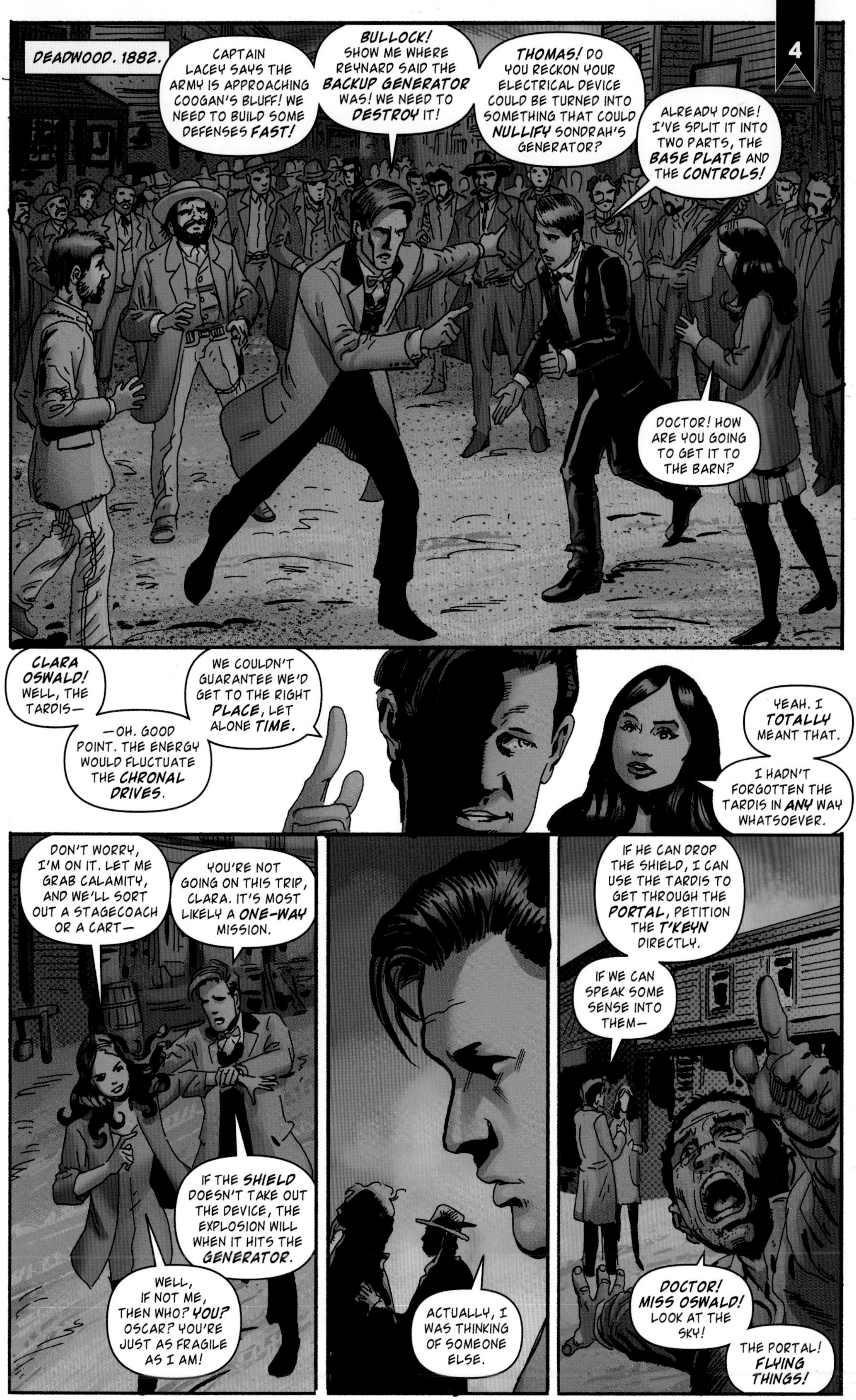
DEADWOOD. 1882.
CAPTAIN LACEY SAYS THE ARMY IS APPROACHING COOGAN'S BLUFF! WE NEED TO BUILD SOME DEFENSES FAST!
BULLOCK! SHOW ME WHERE REYNARD SAID THE BACKUP GENERATOR WAS! WE NEED TO DESTROY IT!
THOMAS! DO YOU RECKON YOUR ELECTRICAL DEVICE COULD BE TURNED INTO SOMETHING THAT COULD NULLIFY SONDRAH'S GENERATOR?
ALREADY DONE! I'VE SPLIT IT INTO TWO PARTS, THE BASE PLATE AND THE CONTROLS!
DOCTOR! HOW ARE YOU GOING TO GET IT TO THE BARN?
CLARA OSWALD! WELL, THE TARDIS—
—OH. GOOD POINT. THE ENERGY WOULD FLUCTUATE THE CHRONAL DRIVES.
WE COULDN'T GUARANTEE WE'D GET TO THE RIGHT PLACE, LET ALONE TIME.
YEAH. I TOTALLY MEANT THAT.
I HADN'T FORGOTTEN THE TARDIS IN ANY WAY WHATSOEVER.
DON'T WORRY, I'M ON IT. LET ME GRAB CALAMITY, AND WE'LL SORT OUT A STAGECOACH OR A CART—
YOU'RE NOT GOING ON THIS TRIP, CLARA. IT'S MOST LIKELY A ONE-WAY MISSION.
IF THE SHIELD DOESN'T TAKE OUT THE DEVICE, THE EXPLOSION WILL WHEN IT HITS THE GENERATOR.
WELL, IF NOT ME, THEN WHO? YOU? OSCAR? YOU'RE JUST AS FRAGILE AS I AM!
ACTUALLY, I WAS THINKING OF SOMEONE ELSE.
IF HE CAN DROP THE SHIELD, I CAN USE THE TARDIS TO GET THROUGH THE PORTAL, PETITION THE T'KEYN DIRECTLY.
IF WE CAN SPEAK SOME SENSE INTO THEM—
DOCTOR! MISS OSWALD! LOOK AT THE SKY!
THE PORTAL! FLYING THINGS!

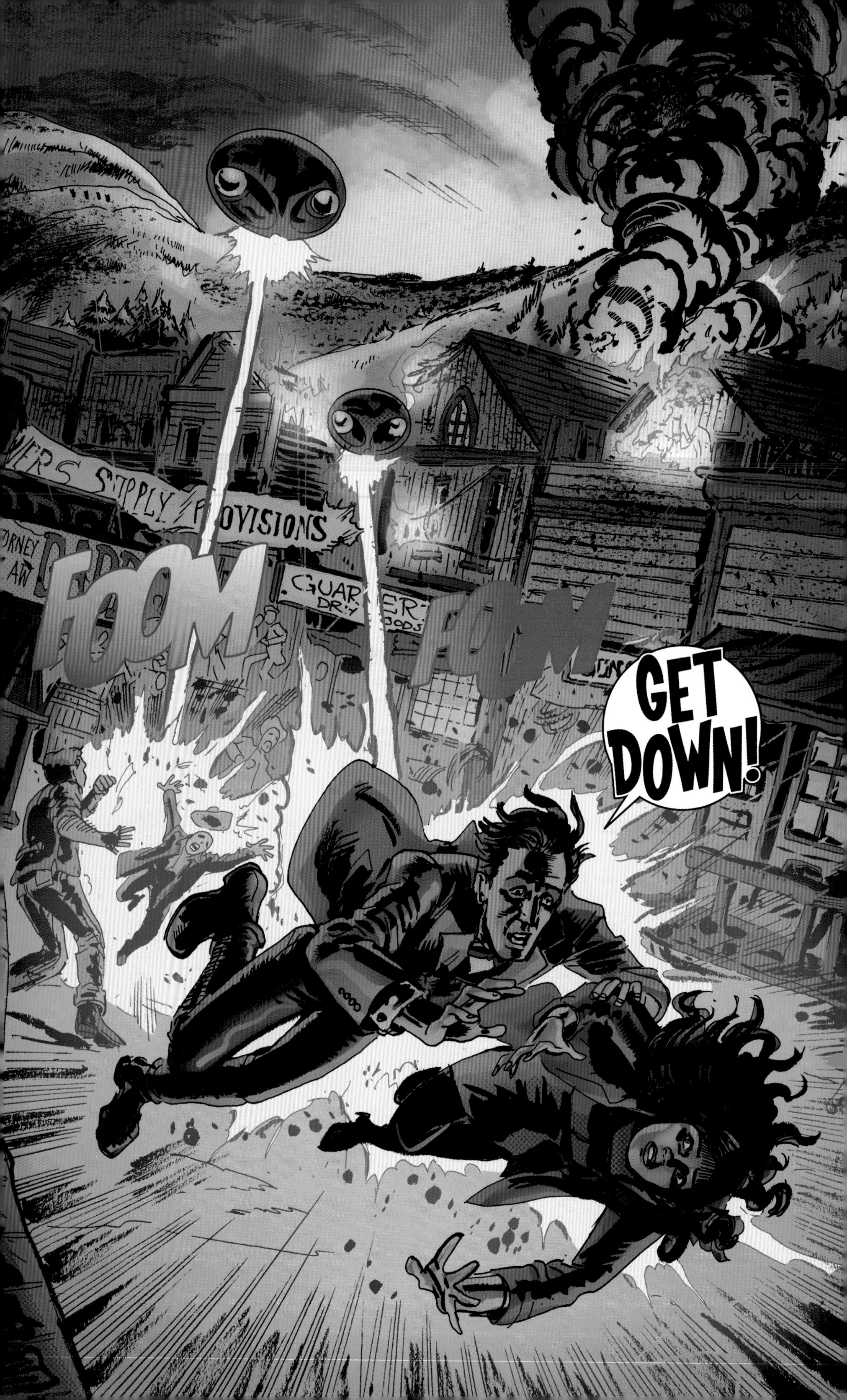
FOOM
FOOM
GET DOWN!

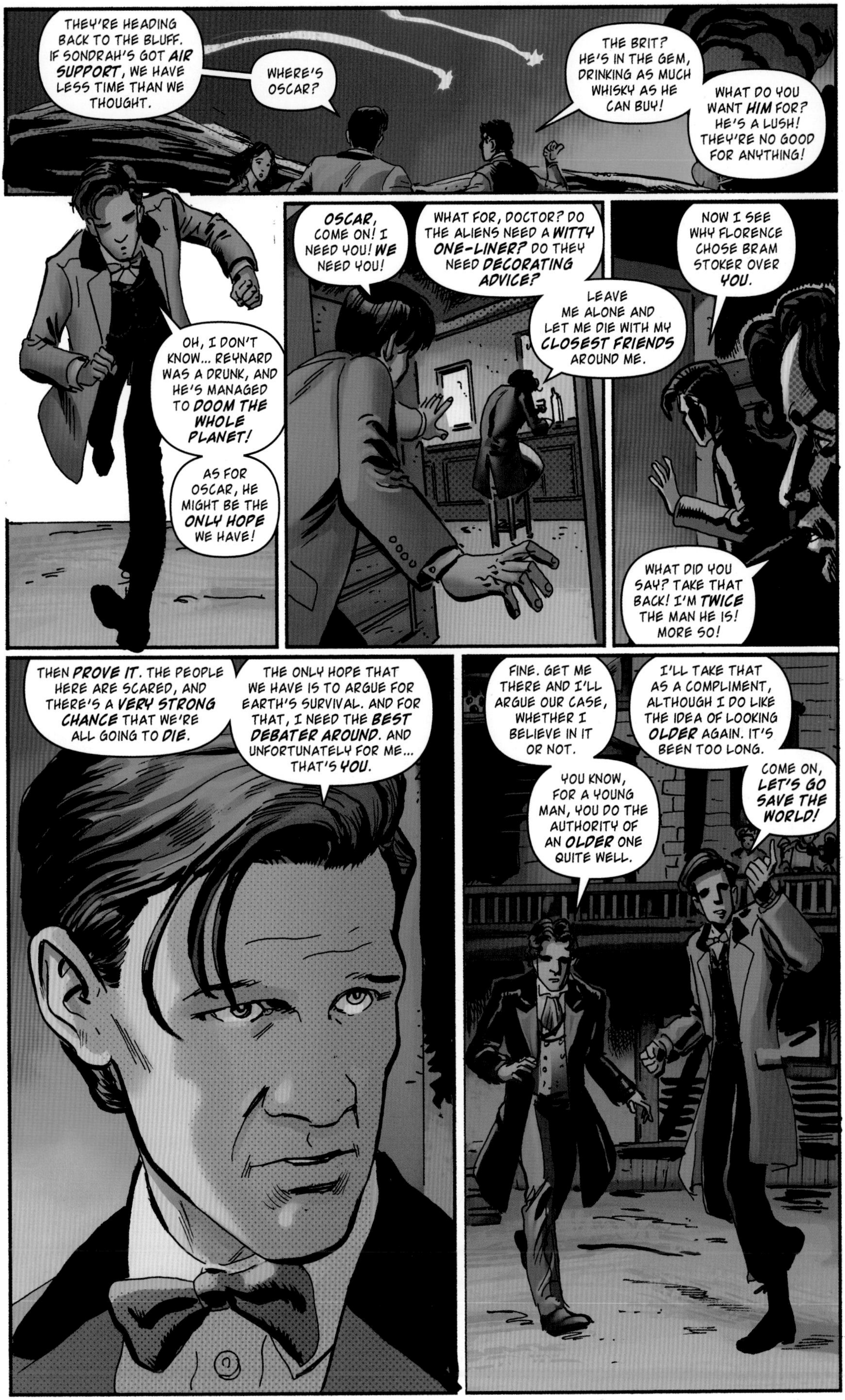
THEY'RE HEADING BACK TO THE BLUFF. IF SONDRAH'S GOT AIR SUPPORT, WE HAVE LESS TIME THAN WE THOUGHT.
WHERE'S OSCAR?
THE BRIT? HE'S IN THE GEM, DRINKING AS MUCH WHISKY AS HE CAN BUY!
WHAT DO YOU WANT HIM FOR? HE'S A LUSH! THEY'RE NO GOOD FOR ANYTHING!
OH, I DON'T KNOW... REYNARD WAS A DRUNK, AND HE'S MANAGED TO DOOM THE WHOLE PLANET!
AS FOR OSCAR, HE MIGHT BE THE ONLY HOPE WE HAVE!
OSCAR, COME ON! I NEED YOU! WE NEED YOU!
WHAT FOR, DOCTOR? DO THE ALIENS NEED A WITTY ONE-LINER? DO THEY NEED DECORATING ADVICE?
LEAVE ME ALONE AND LET ME DIE WITH MY CLOSEST FRIENDS AROUND ME.
NOW I SEE WHY FLORENCE CHOSE BRAM STOKER OVER YOU.
WHAT DID YOU SAY? TAKE THAT BACK! I'M TWICE THE MAN HE IS! MORE SO!
THEN PROVE IT. THE PEOPLE HERE ARE SCARED, AND THERE'S A VERY STRONG CHANCE THAT WE'RE ALL GOING TO DIE.
THE ONLY HOPE THAT WE HAVE IS TO ARGUE FOR EARTH'S SURVIVAL. AND FOR THAT, I NEED THE BEST DEBATER AROUND. AND UNFORTUNATELY FOR ME... THAT'S YOU.
FINE. GET ME THERE AND I'LL ARGUE OUR CASE, WHETHER I BELIEVE IN IT OR NOT.
YOU KNOW, FOR A YOUNG MAN, YOU DO THE AUTHORITY OF AN OLDER ONE QUITE WELL.
I'LL TAKE THAT AS A COMPLIMENT, ALTHOUGH I DO LIKE THE IDEA OF LOOKING OLDER AGAIN. IT'S BEEN TOO LONG.
COME ON, LET'S GO SAVE THE WORLD!

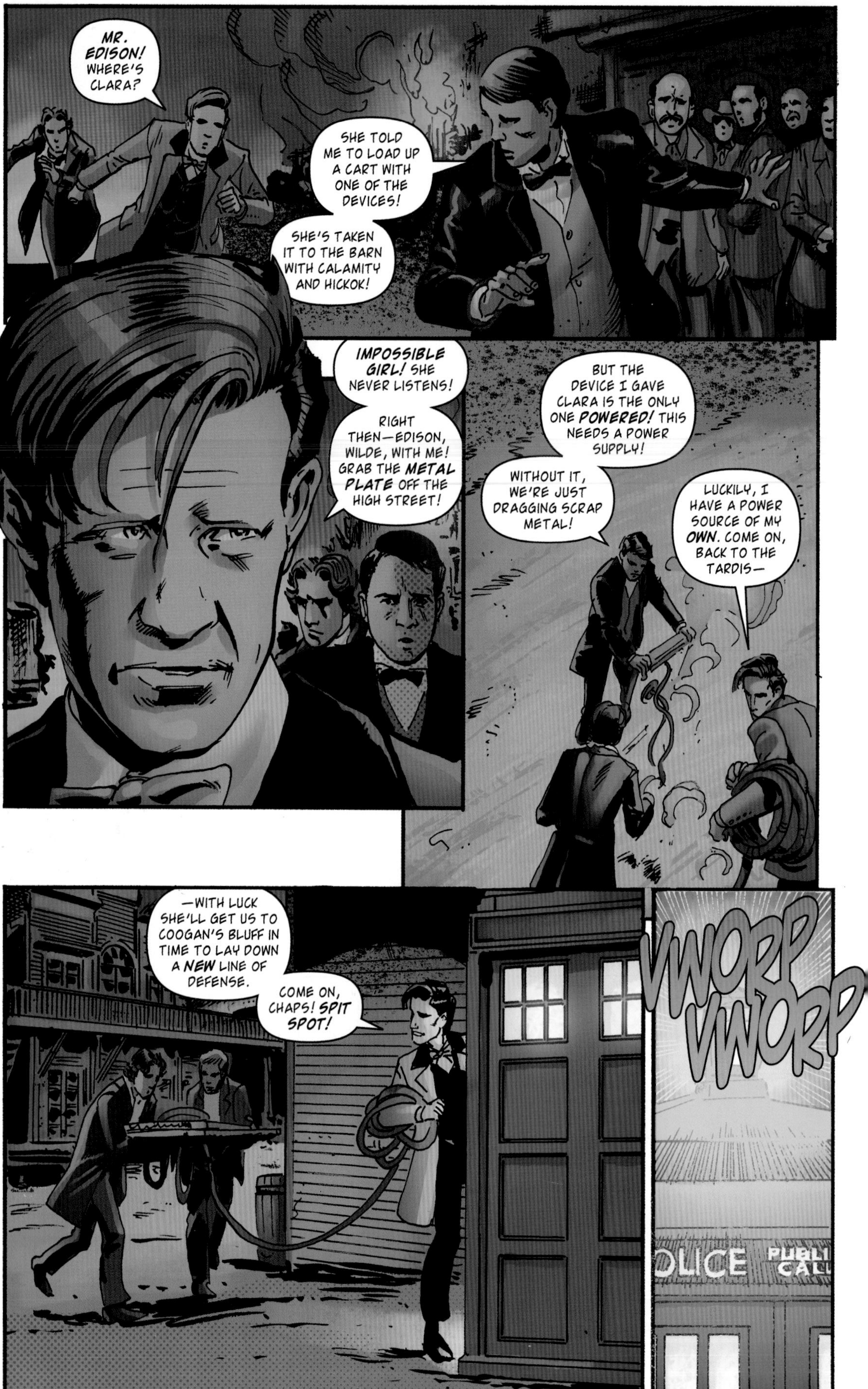
MR. EDISON! WHERE'S CLARA?
SHE TOLD ME TO LOAD UP A CART WITH ONE OF THE DEVICES!
SHE'S TAKEN IT TO THE BARN WITH CALAMITY AND HICKOK!
IMPOSSIBLE GIRL! SHE NEVER LISTENS!
RIGHT THEN—EDISON, WILDE, WITH ME! GRAB THE METAL PLATE OFF THE HIGH STREET!
BUT THE DEVICE I GAVE CLARA IS THE ONLY ONE POWERED! THIS NEEDS A POWER SUPPLY!
WITHOUT IT, WE'RE JUST DRAGGING SCRAP METAL!
LUCKILY, I HAVE A POWER SOURCE OF MY OWN. COME ON, BACK TO THE TARDIS—
—WITH LUCK SHE'LL GET US TO COOGAN'S BLUFF IN TIME TO LAY DOWN A NEW LINE OF DEFENSE.
COME ON, CHAPS! SPIT SPOT!
VWORP VWORP
OLICE PUBLI CALL

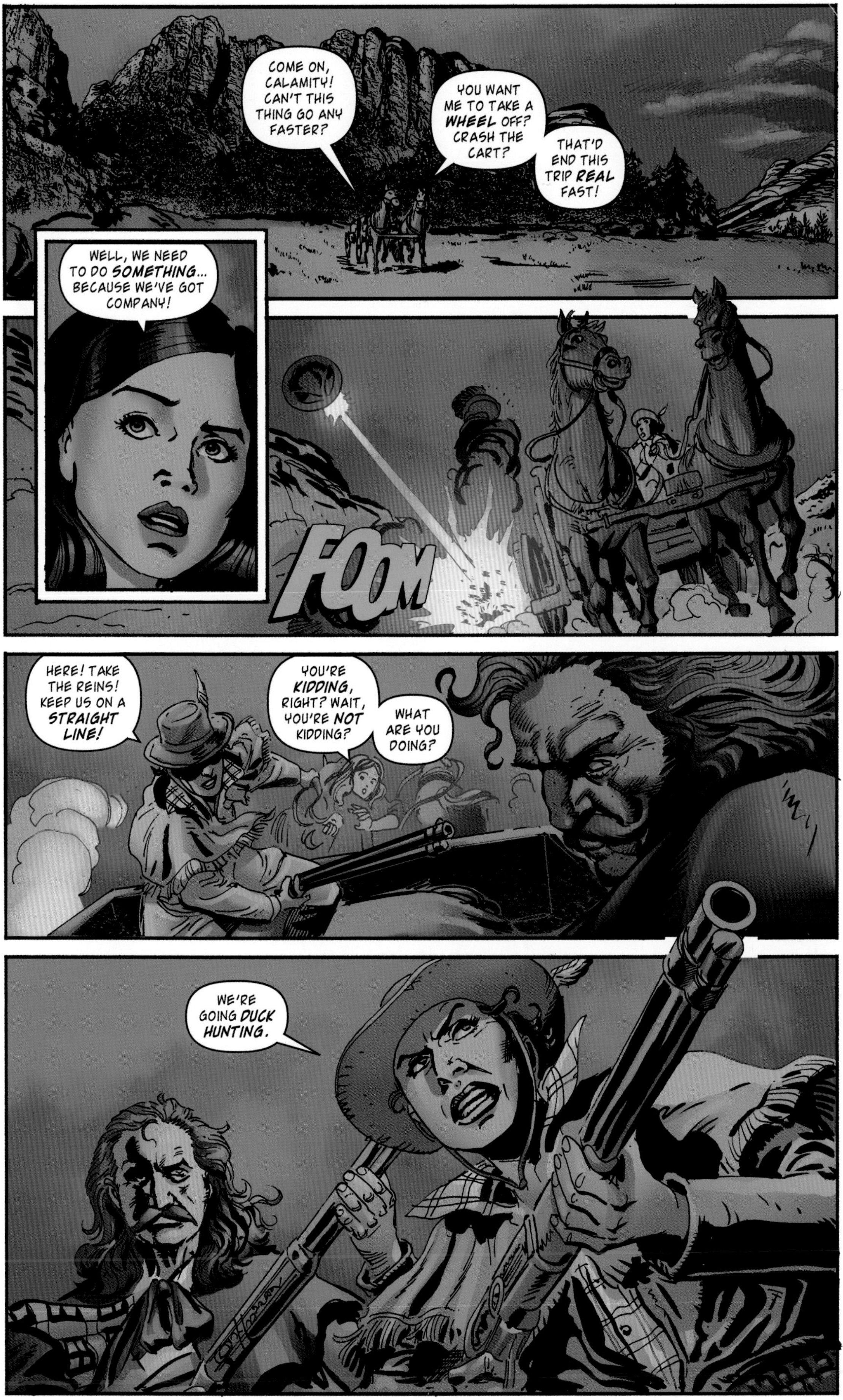
COME ON, CALAMITY! CAN'T THIS THING GO ANY FASTER?
YOU WANT ME TO TAKE A WHEEL OFF? CRASH THE CART?
THAT'D END THIS TRIP REAL FAST!
WELL, WE NEED TO DO SOMETHING... BECAUSE WE'VE GOT COMPANY!
FOOM
HERE! TAKE THE REINS! KEEP US ON A STRAIGHT LINE!
YOU'RE KIDDING, RIGHT? WAIT, YOU'RE NOT KIDDING?
WHAT ARE YOU DOING?
WE'RE GOING DUCK HUNTING.

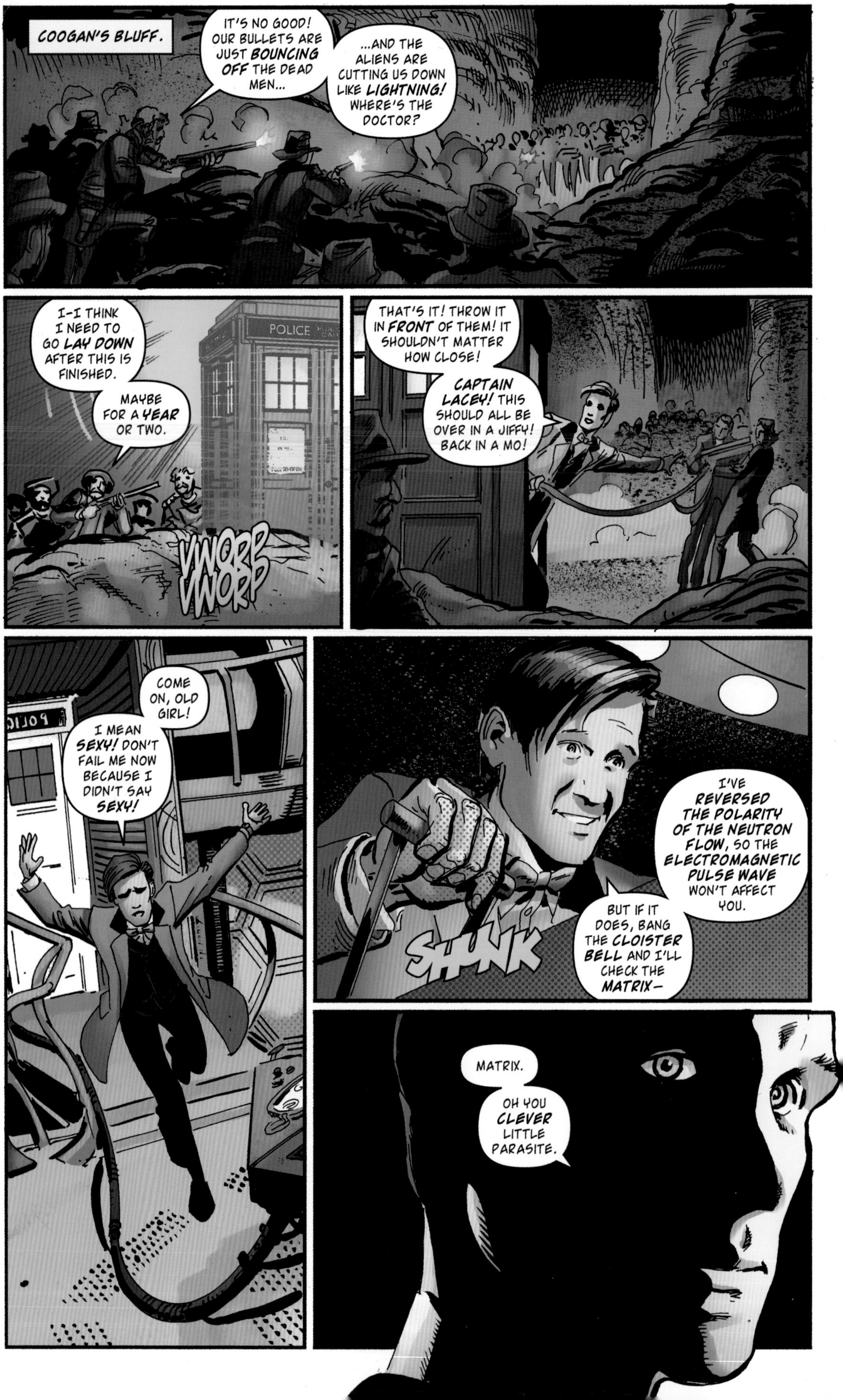
COOGAN'S BLUFF.
IT'S NO GOOD! OUR BULLETS ARE JUST BOUNCING OFF THE DEAD MEN...
...AND THE ALIENS ARE CUTTING US DOWN LIKE LIGHTNING! WHERE'S THE DOCTOR?
I-I THINK I NEED TO GO LAY DOWN AFTER THIS IS FINISHED.
MAYBE FOR A YEAR OR TWO.
POLICE
VWORP VWORP
THAT'S IT! THROW IT IN FRONT OF THEM! IT SHOULDN'T MATTER HOW CLOSE!
CAPTAIN LACEY! THIS SHOULD ALL BE OVER IN A JIFFY! BACK IN A MO!
COME ON, OLD GIRL!
I MEAN SEXY! DON'T FAIL ME NOW BECAUSE I DIDN'T SAY SEXY!
I'VE REVERSED THE POLARITY OF THE NEUTRON FLOW, SO THE ELECTROMAGNETIC PULSE WAVE WON'T AFFECT YOU.
SHUNK
BUT IF IT DOES, BANG THE CLOISTER BELL AND I'LL CHECK THE MATRIX—
MATRIX.
OH YOU CLEVER LITTLE PARASITE.

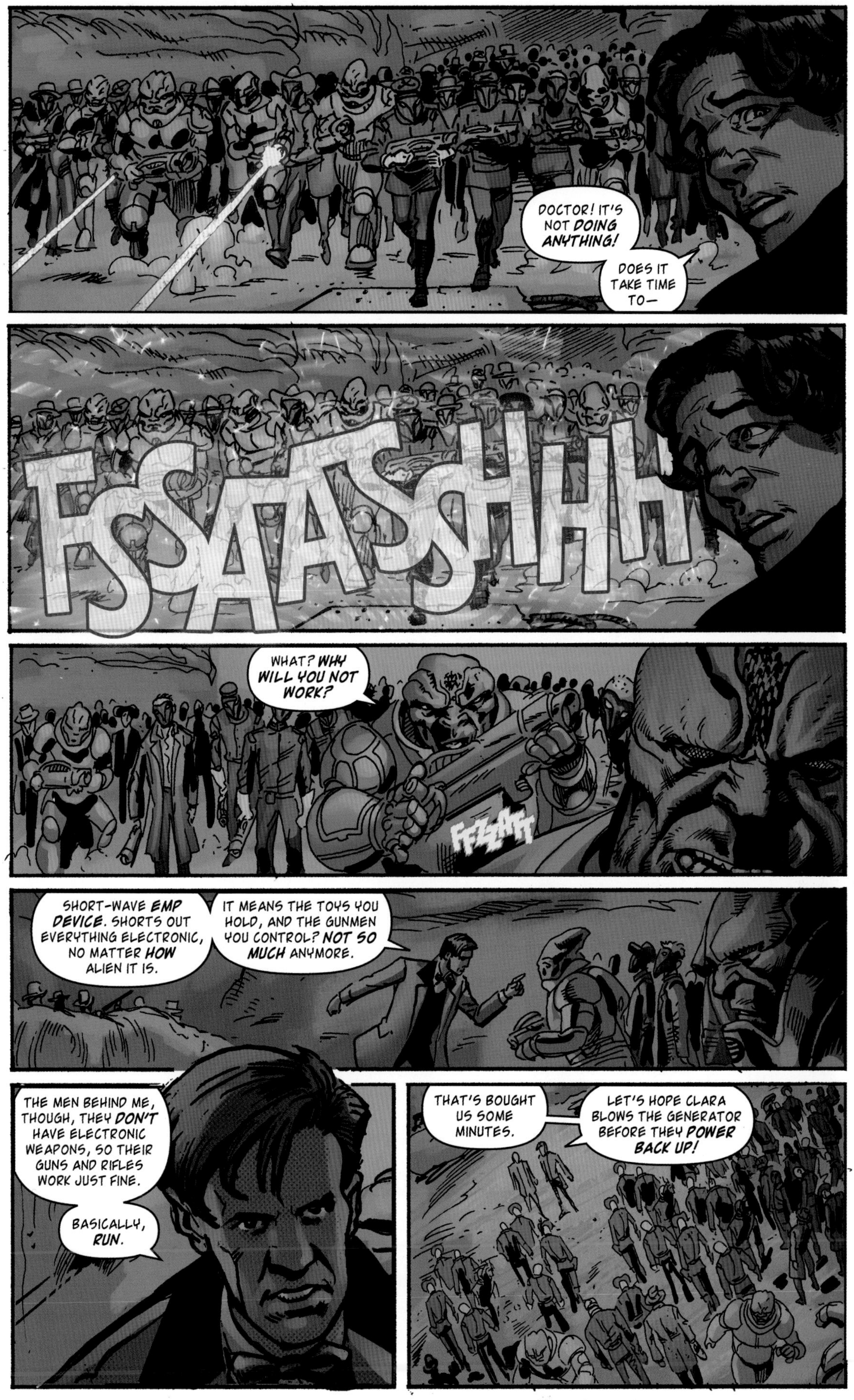
DOCTOR! IT'S NOT DOING ANYTHING!
DOES IT TAKE TIME TO—
FSSSSHHH
WHAT? WHY WILL YOU NOT WORK?
FFZZAPP
SHORT-WAVE EMP DEVICE. SHORTS OUT EVERYTHING ELECTRONIC, NO MATTER HOW ALIEN IT IS.
IT MEANS THE TOYS YOU HOLD, AND THE GUNMEN YOU CONTROL? NOT SO MUCH ANYMORE.
THE MEN BEHIND ME, THOUGH, THEY DON'T HAVE ELECTRONIC WEAPONS, SO THEIR GUNS AND RIFLES WORK JUST FINE.
BASICALLY, RUN.
THAT'S BOUGHT US SOME MINUTES.
LET'S HOPE CLARA BLOWS THE GENERATOR BEFORE THEY POWER BACK UP!

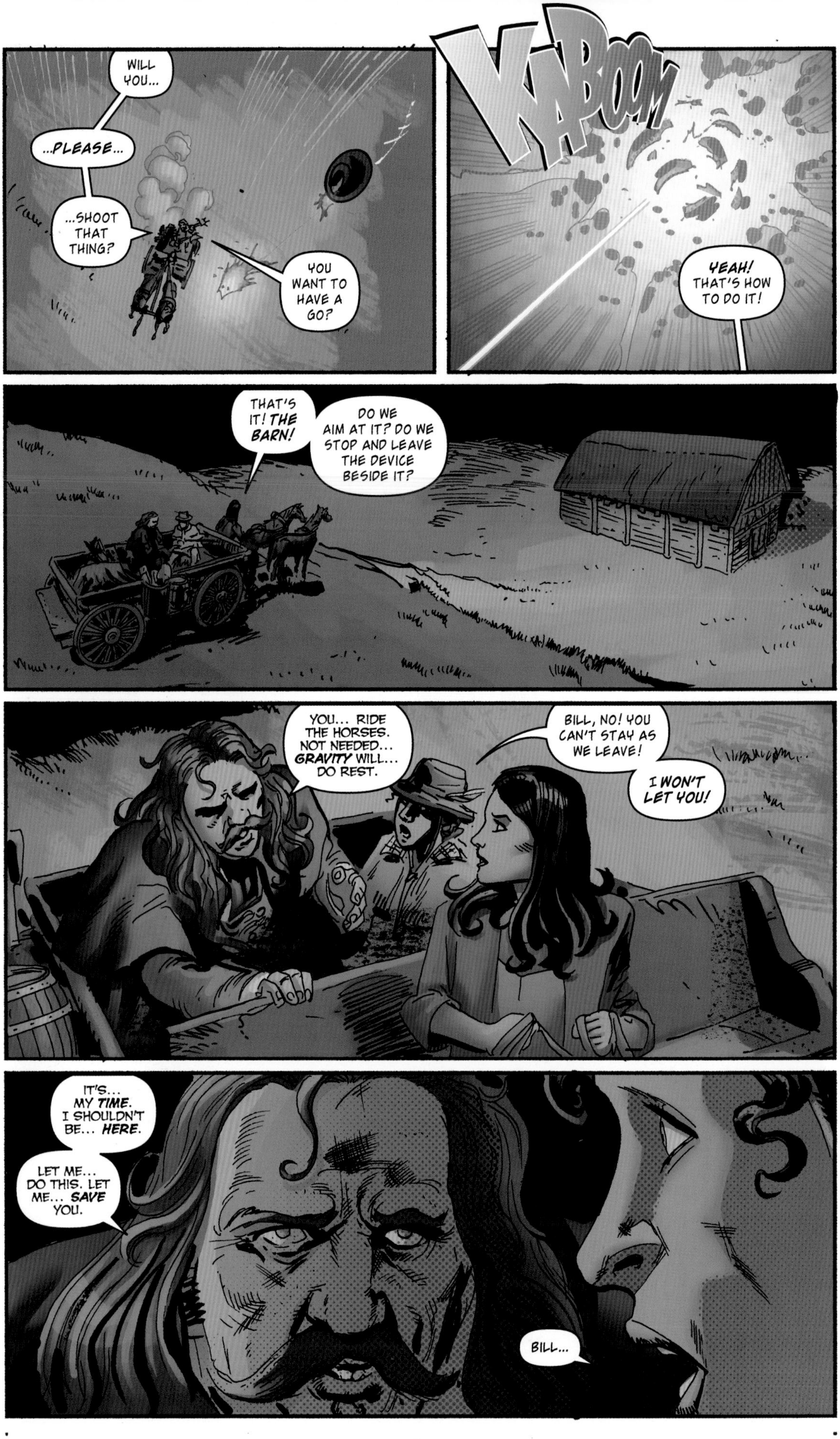
WILL YOU...
...PLEASE...
...SHOOT THAT THING?
YOU WANT TO HAVE A GO?
KABOOM
YEAH! THAT'S HOW TO DO IT!
THAT'S IT! THE BARN!
DO WE AIM AT IT? DO WE STOP AND LEAVE THE DEVICE BESIDE IT?
YOU... RIDE THE HORSES. NOT NEEDED... GRAVITY WILL... DO REST.
BILL, NO! YOU CAN'T STAY AS WE LEAVE!
I WON'T LET YOU!
IT'S... MY TIME. I SHOULDN'T BE... HERE.
LET ME... DO THIS. LET ME... SAVE YOU.
BILL...

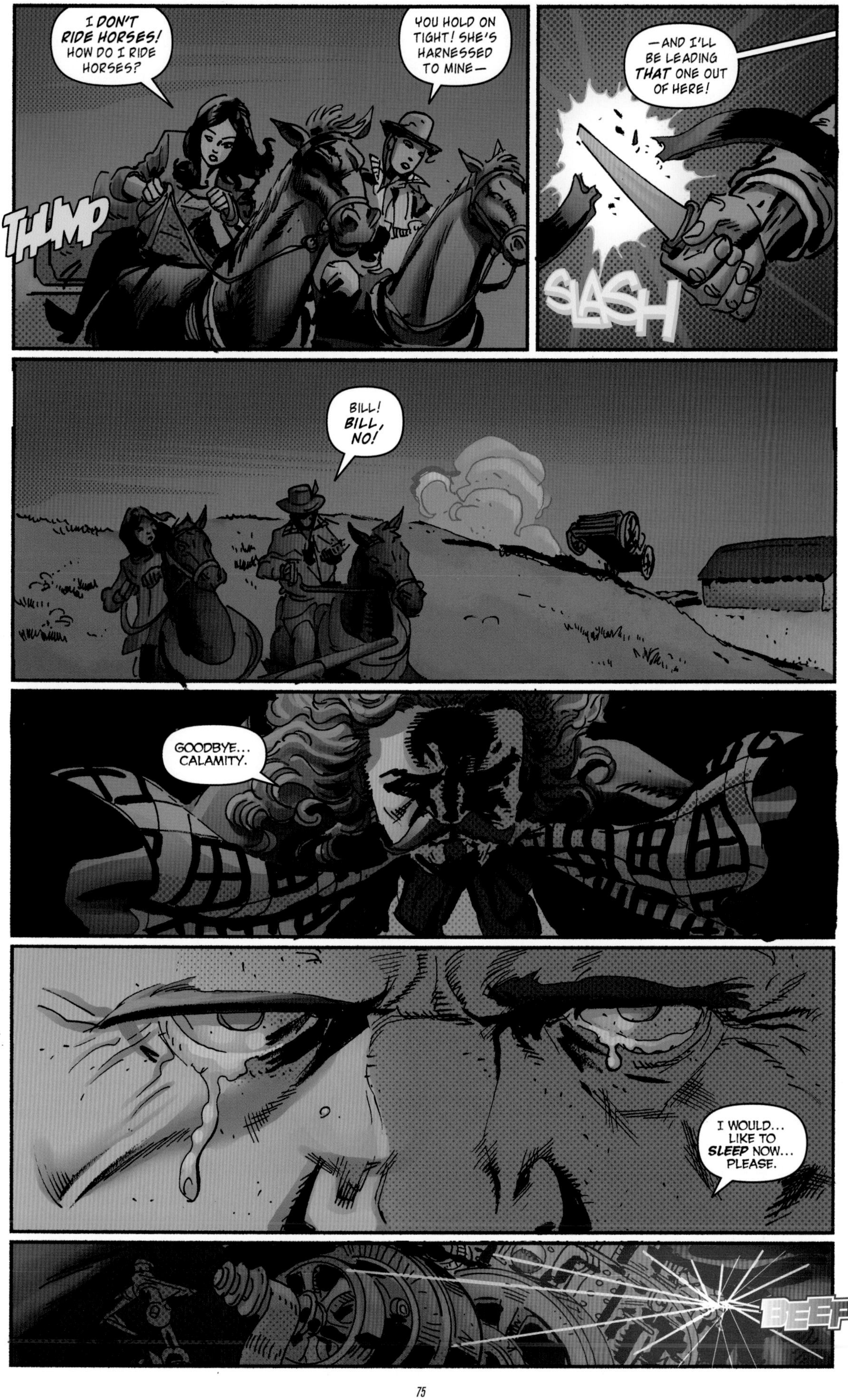
I DON'T RIDE HORSES! HOW DO I RIDE HORSES?
YOU HOLD ON TIGHT! SHE'S HARNESSED TO MINE—
THUMP
—AND I'LL BE LEADING THAT ONE OUT OF HERE!
SLASH
BILL! BILL, NO!
GOODBYE... CALAMITY.
I WOULD... LIKE TO SLEEP NOW... PLEASE.
BEEP

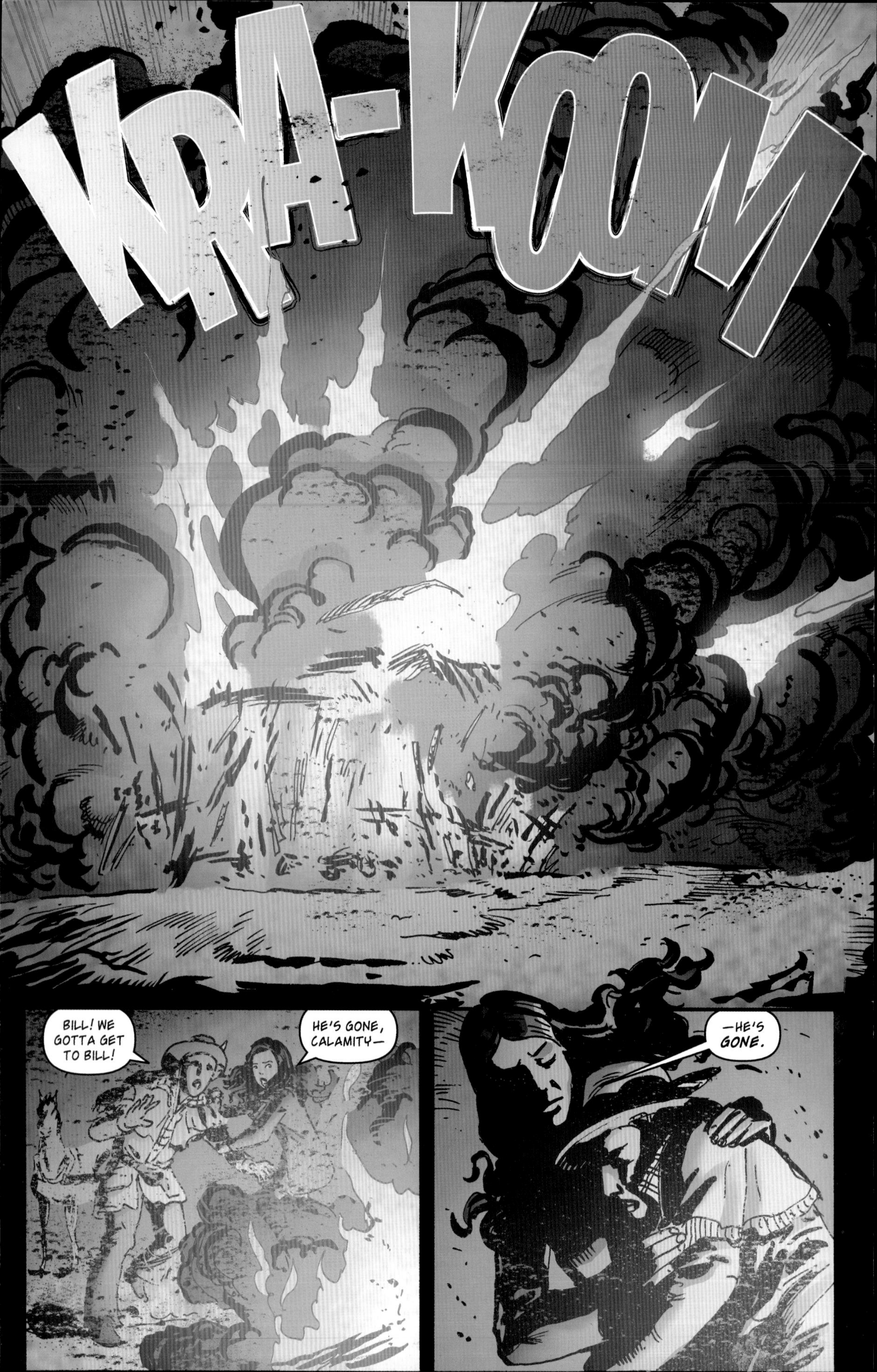
KRA-KOOM
BILL! WE GOTTA GET TO BILL!
HE'S GONE, CALAMITY—
—HE'S **GONE.**

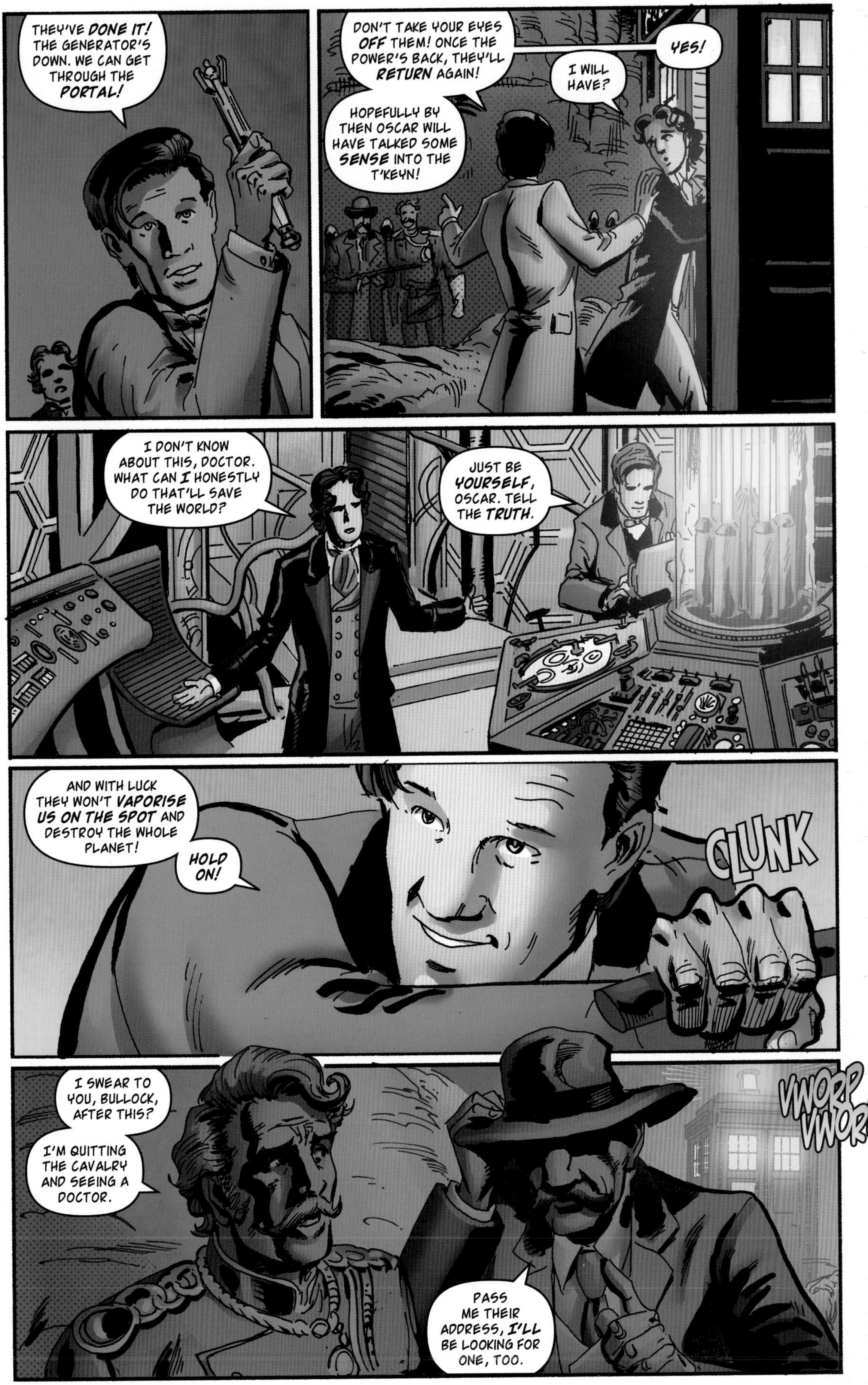
THEY'VE DONE IT! THE GENERATOR'S DOWN. WE CAN GET THROUGH THE PORTAL!
DON'T TAKE YOUR EYES OFF THEM! ONCE THE POWER'S BACK, THEY'LL RETURN AGAIN!
YES!
HOPEFULLY BY THEN OSCAR WILL HAVE TALKED SOME SENSE INTO THE T'KEYN!
I WILL HAVE?
I DON'T KNOW ABOUT THIS, DOCTOR. WHAT CAN I HONESTLY DO THAT'LL SAVE THE WORLD?
JUST BE YOURSELF, OSCAR. TELL THE TRUTH.
AND WITH LUCK THEY WON'T VAPORISE US ON THE SPOT AND DESTROY THE WHOLE PLANET!
HOLD ON!
CLUNK
I SWEAR TO YOU, BULLOCK, AFTER THIS?
I'M QUITTING THE CAVALRY AND SEEING A DOCTOR.
VWORP VWOR
PASS ME THEIR ADDRESS, I'LL BE LOOKING FOR ONE, TOO.

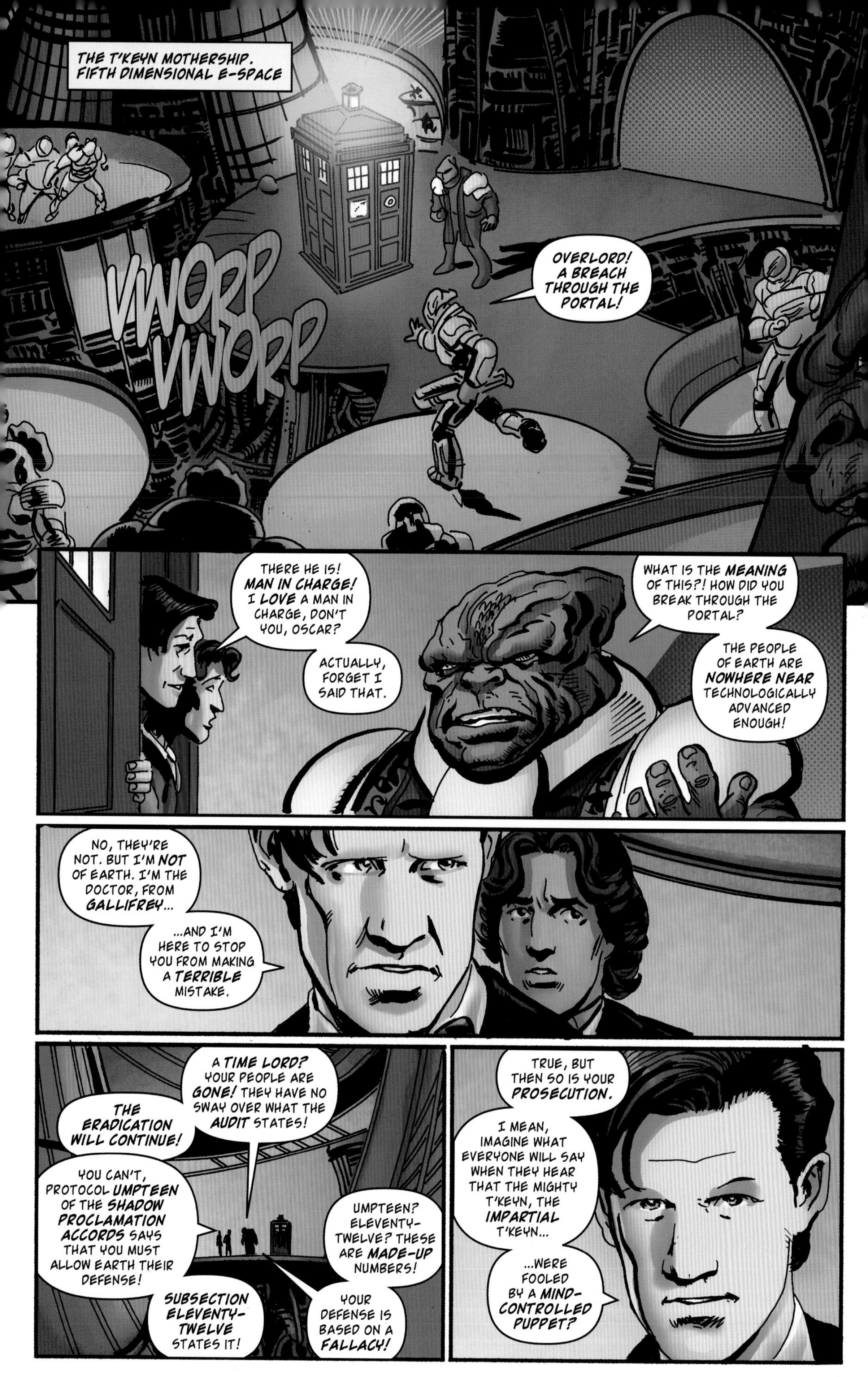
THE T'KEYN MOTHERSHIP. FIFTH DIMENSIONAL E-SPACE
VWORP VWORP
OVERLORD! A BREACH THROUGH THE PORTAL!
THERE HE IS! MAN IN CHARGE! I LOVE A MAN IN CHARGE, DON'T YOU, OSCAR?
ACTUALLY, FORGET I SAID THAT.
WHAT IS THE MEANING OF THIS?! HOW DID YOU BREAK THROUGH THE PORTAL?
THE PEOPLE OF EARTH ARE NOWHERE NEAR TECHNOLOGICALLY ADVANCED ENOUGH!
NO, THEY'RE NOT. BUT I'M NOT OF EARTH. I'M THE DOCTOR, FROM GALLIFREY...
...AND I'M HERE TO STOP YOU FROM MAKING A TERRIBLE MISTAKE.
A TIME LORD? YOUR PEOPLE ARE GONE! THEY HAVE NO SWAY OVER WHAT THE AUDIT STATES!
THE ERADICATION WILL CONTINUE!
YOU CAN'T, PROTOCOL UMPTEEN OF THE SHADOW PROCLAMATION ACCORDS SAYS THAT YOU MUST ALLOW EARTH THEIR DEFENSE!
UMPTEEN? ELEVENTY-TWELVE? THESE ARE MADE-UP NUMBERS!
SUBSECTION ELEVENTY-TWELVE STATES IT!
YOUR DEFENSE IS BASED ON A FALLACY!
TRUE, BUT THEN SO IS YOUR PROSECUTION.
I MEAN, IMAGINE WHAT EVERYONE WILL SAY WHEN THEY HEAR THAT THE MIGHTY T'KEYN, THE IMPARTIAL T'KEYN...
...WERE FOOLED BY A MIND-CONTROLLED PUPPET?

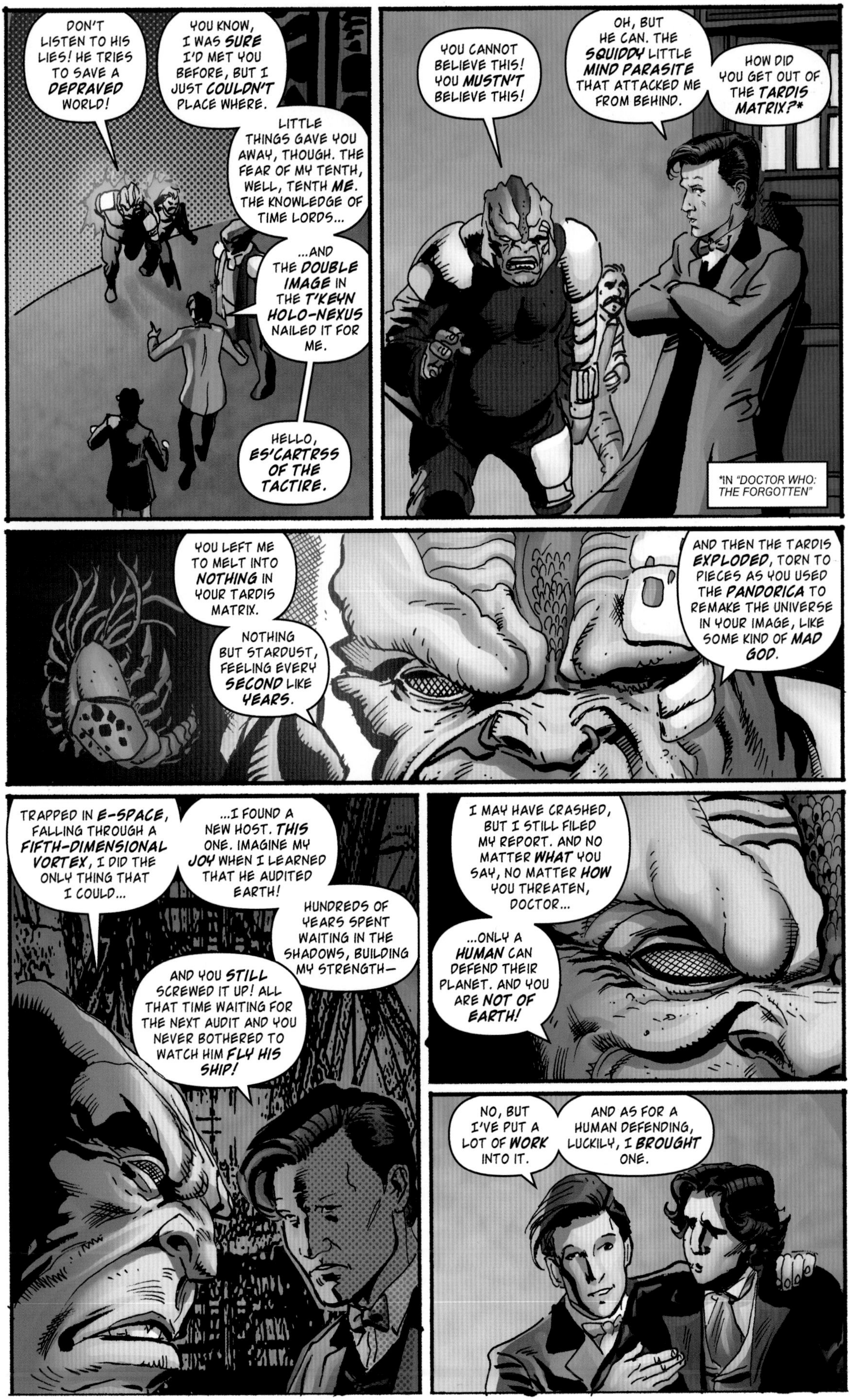
DON'T LISTEN TO HIS LIES! HE TRIES TO SAVE A DEPRAVED WORLD!
YOU KNOW, I WAS SURE I'D MET YOU BEFORE, BUT I JUST COULDN'T PLACE WHERE.
LITTLE THINGS GAVE YOU AWAY, THOUGH. THE FEAR OF MY TENTH, WELL, TENTH ME. THE KNOWLEDGE OF TIME LORDS...
...AND THE DOUBLE IMAGE IN THE T'KEYN HOLO-NEXUS NAILED IT FOR ME.
HELLO, ES'CARTRSS OF THE TACTIRE.
YOU CANNOT BELIEVE THIS! YOU MUSTN'T BELIEVE THIS!
OH, BUT HE CAN. THE SQUIDDY LITTLE MIND PARASITE THAT ATTACKED ME FROM BEHIND.
HOW DID YOU GET OUT OF THE TARDIS MATRIX?*
*IN "DOCTOR WHO: THE FORGOTTEN"
YOU LEFT ME TO MELT INTO NOTHING IN YOUR TARDIS MATRIX.
NOTHING BUT STARDUST, FEELING EVERY SECOND LIKE YEARS.
AND THEN THE TARDIS EXPLODED, TORN TO PIECES AS YOU USED THE PANDORICA TO REMAKE THE UNIVERSE IN YOUR IMAGE, LIKE SOME KIND OF MAD GOD.
TRAPPED IN E-SPACE, FALLING THROUGH A FIFTH-DIMENSIONAL VORTEX, I DID THE ONLY THING THAT I COULD...
...I FOUND A NEW HOST. THIS ONE. IMAGINE MY JOY WHEN I LEARNED THAT HE AUDITED EARTH!
HUNDREDS OF YEARS SPENT WAITING IN THE SHADOWS, BUILDING MY STRENGTH—
AND YOU STILL SCREWED IT UP! ALL THAT TIME WAITING FOR THE NEXT AUDIT AND YOU NEVER BOTHERED TO WATCH HIM FLY HIS SHIP!
I MAY HAVE CRASHED, BUT I STILL FILED MY REPORT. AND NO MATTER WHAT YOU SAY, NO MATTER HOW YOU THREATEN, DOCTOR...
...ONLY A HUMAN CAN DEFEND THEIR PLANET. AND YOU ARE NOT OF EARTH!
NO, BUT I'VE PUT A LOT OF WORK INTO IT.
AND AS FOR A HUMAN DEFENDING, LUCKILY, I BROUGHT ONE.

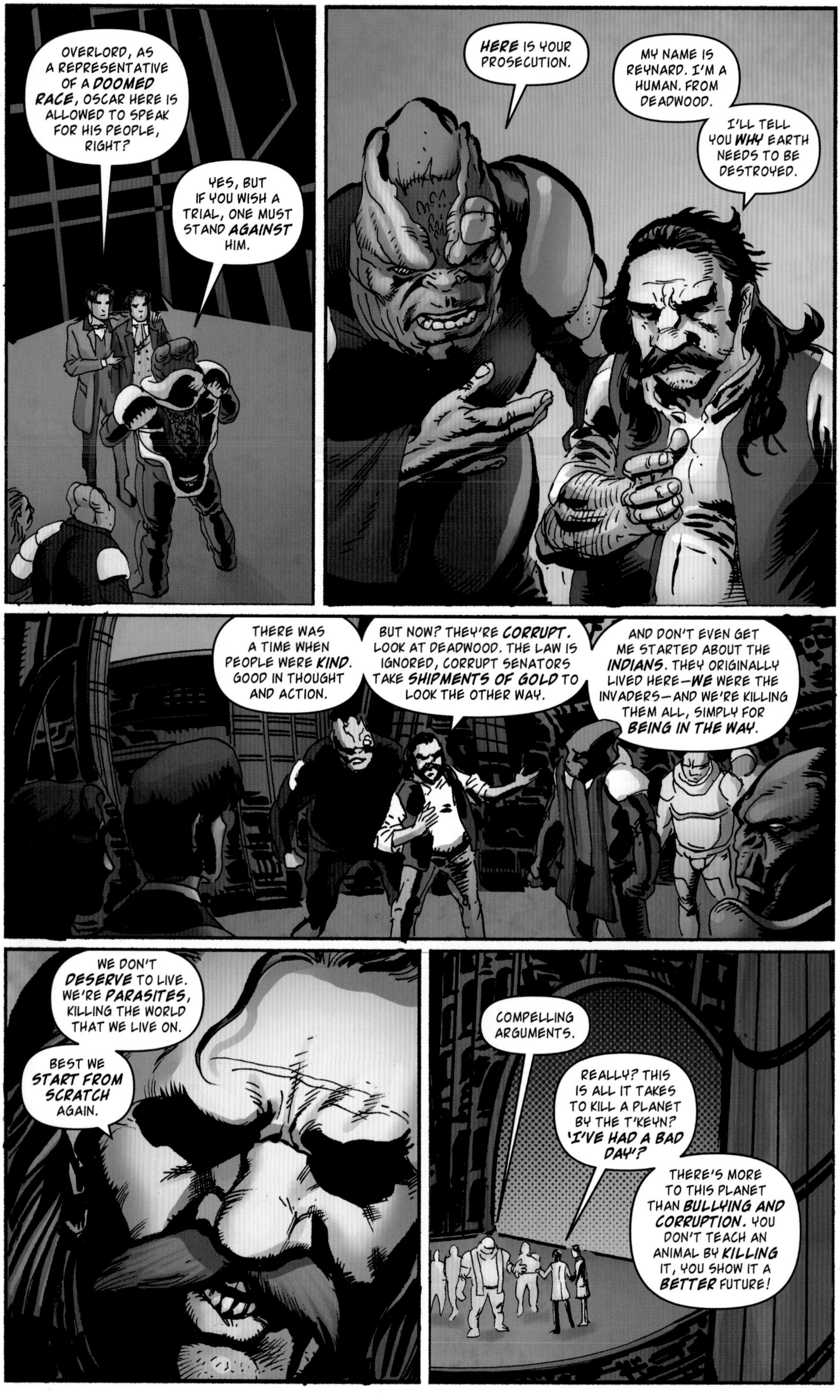
OVERLORD, AS A REPRESENTATIVE OF A DOOMED RACE, OSCAR HERE IS ALLOWED TO SPEAK FOR HIS PEOPLE, RIGHT?
YES, BUT IF YOU WISH A TRIAL, ONE MUST STAND AGAINST HIM.
HERE IS YOUR PROSECUTION.
MY NAME IS REYNARD. I'M A HUMAN. FROM DEADWOOD.
I'LL TELL YOU WHY EARTH NEEDS TO BE DESTROYED.
THERE WAS A TIME WHEN PEOPLE WERE KIND. GOOD IN THOUGHT AND ACTION.
BUT NOW? THEY'RE CORRUPT. LOOK AT DEADWOOD. THE LAW IS IGNORED, CORRUPT SENATORS TAKE SHIPMENTS OF GOLD TO LOOK THE OTHER WAY.
AND DON'T EVEN GET ME STARTED ABOUT THE INDIANS. THEY ORIGINALLY LIVED HERE—WE WERE THE INVADERS—AND WE'RE KILLING THEM ALL, SIMPLY FOR BEING IN THE WAY.
WE DON'T DESERVE TO LIVE. WE'RE PARASITES, KILLING THE WORLD THAT WE LIVE ON.
BEST WE START FROM SCRATCH AGAIN.
COMPELLING ARGUMENTS.
REALLY? THIS IS ALL IT TAKES TO KILL A PLANET BY THE T'KEYN? 'I'VE HAD A BAD DAY'?
THERE'S MORE TO THIS PLANET THAN BULLYING AND CORRUPTION. YOU DON'T TEACH AN ANIMAL BY KILLING IT, YOU SHOW IT A BETTER FUTURE!

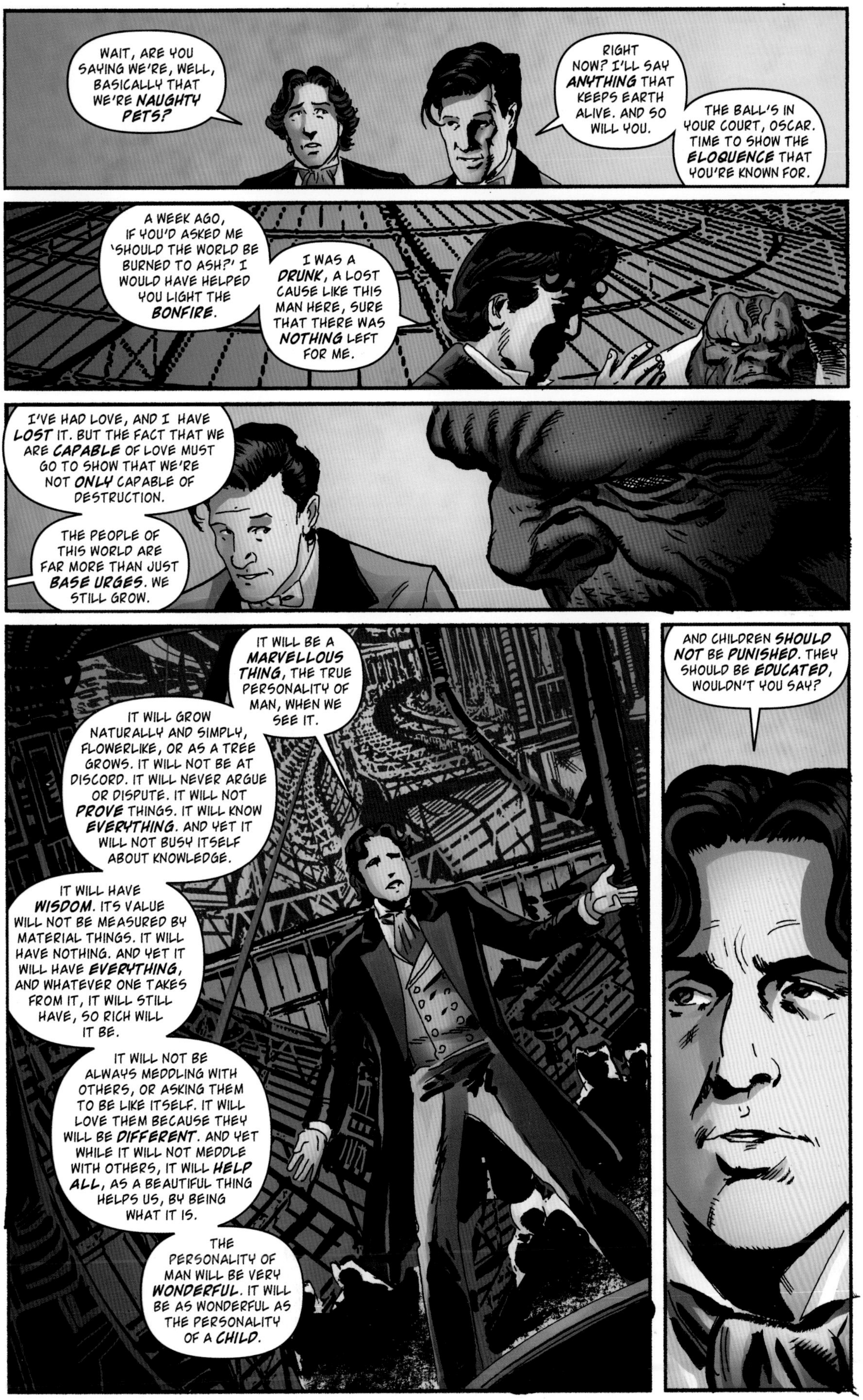
WAIT, ARE YOU SAYING WE'RE, WELL, BASICALLY THAT WE'RE NAUGHTY PETS?
RIGHT NOW? I'LL SAY ANYTHING THAT KEEPS EARTH ALIVE. AND SO WILL YOU.
THE BALL'S IN YOUR COURT, OSCAR. TIME TO SHOW THE ELOQUENCE THAT YOU'RE KNOWN FOR.
A WEEK AGO, IF YOU'D ASKED ME 'SHOULD THE WORLD BE BURNED TO ASH?' I WOULD HAVE HELPED YOU LIGHT THE BONFIRE.
I WAS A DRUNK, A LOST CAUSE LIKE THIS MAN HERE, SURE THAT THERE WAS NOTHING LEFT FOR ME.
I'VE HAD LOVE, AND I HAVE LOST IT. BUT THE FACT THAT WE ARE CAPABLE OF LOVE MUST GO TO SHOW THAT WE'RE NOT ONLY CAPABLE OF DESTRUCTION.
THE PEOPLE OF THIS WORLD ARE FAR MORE THAN JUST BASE URGES. WE STILL GROW.
IT WILL BE A MARVELLOUS THING, THE TRUE PERSONALITY OF MAN, WHEN WE SEE IT.
IT WILL GROW NATURALLY AND SIMPLY, FLOWERLIKE, OR AS A TREE GROWS. IT WILL NOT BE AT DISCORD. IT WILL NEVER ARGUE OR DISPUTE. IT WILL NOT PROVE THINGS. IT WILL KNOW EVERYTHING. AND YET IT WILL NOT BUSY ITSELF ABOUT KNOWLEDGE.
IT WILL HAVE WISDOM. ITS VALUE WILL NOT BE MEASURED BY MATERIAL THINGS. IT WILL HAVE NOTHING. AND YET IT WILL HAVE EVERYTHING, AND WHATEVER ONE TAKES FROM IT, IT WILL STILL HAVE, SO RICH WILL IT BE.
IT WILL NOT BE ALWAYS MEDDLING WITH OTHERS, OR ASKING THEM TO BE LIKE ITSELF. IT WILL LOVE THEM BECAUSE THEY WILL BE DIFFERENT. AND YET WHILE IT WILL NOT MEDDLE WITH OTHERS, IT WILL HELP ALL, AS A BEAUTIFUL THING HELPS US, BY BEING WHAT IT IS.
THE PERSONALITY OF MAN WILL BE VERY WONDERFUL. IT WILL BE AS WONDERFUL AS THE PERSONALITY OF A CHILD.
AND CHILDREN SHOULD NOT BE PUNISHED. THEY SHOULD BE EDUCATED, WOULDN'T YOU SAY?

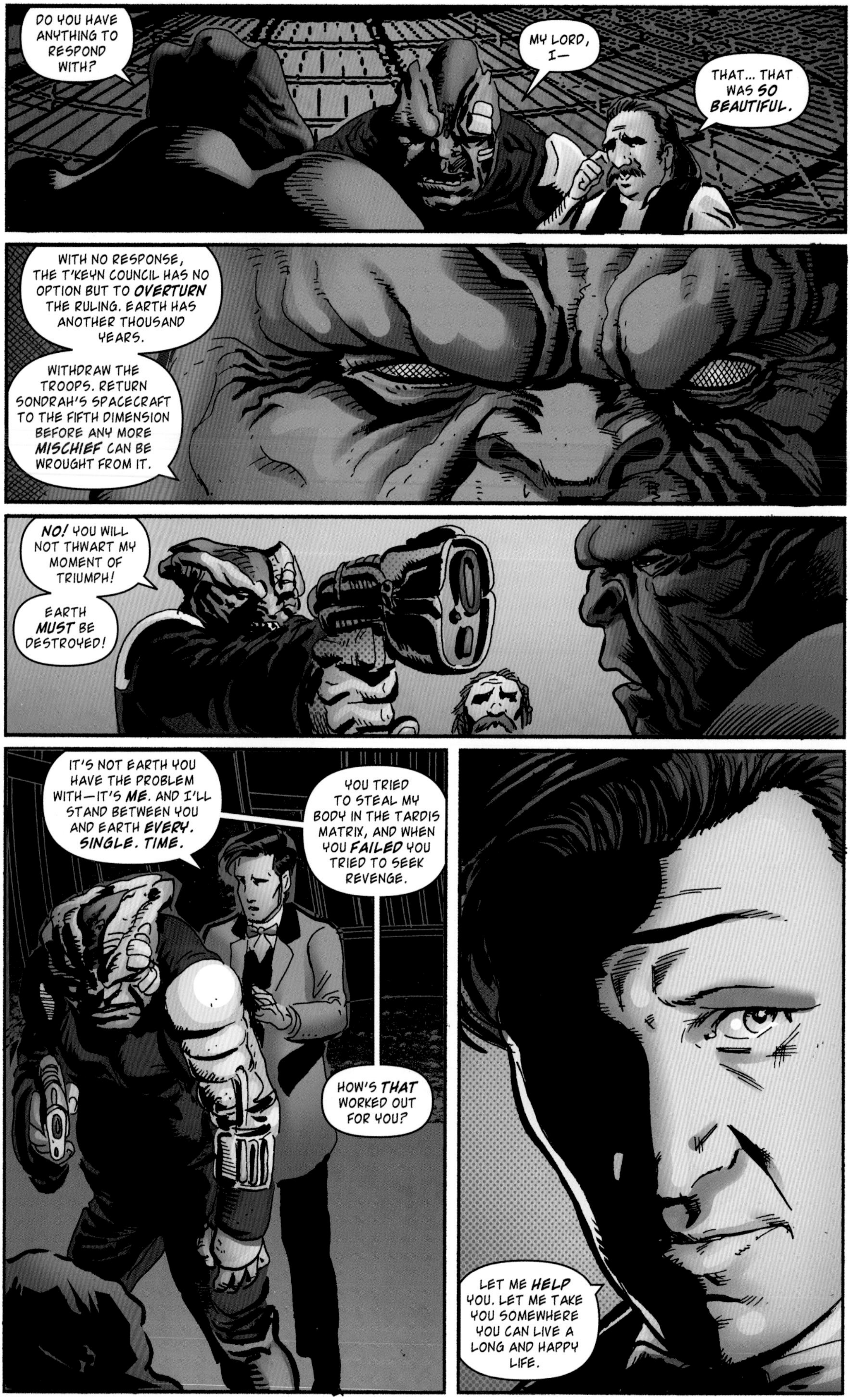

DO YOU HAVE ANYTHING TO RESPOND WITH?
MY LORD, I—
THAT... THAT WAS SO BEAUTIFUL.
WITH NO RESPONSE, THE T'KEYN COUNCIL HAS NO OPTION BUT TO OVERTURN THE RULING. EARTH HAS ANOTHER THOUSAND YEARS.
WITHDRAW THE TROOPS. RETURN SONDRAH'S SPACECRAFT TO THE FIFTH DIMENSION BEFORE ANY MORE MISCHIEF CAN BE WROUGHT FROM IT.
NO! YOU WILL NOT THWART MY MOMENT OF TRIUMPH!
EARTH MUST BE DESTROYED!
IT'S NOT EARTH YOU HAVE THE PROBLEM WITH—IT'S ME. AND I'LL STAND BETWEEN YOU AND EARTH EVERY. SINGLE. TIME.
YOU TRIED TO STEAL MY BODY IN THE TARDIS MATRIX, AND WHEN YOU FAILED YOU TRIED TO SEEK REVENGE.
HOW'S THAT WORKED OUT FOR YOU?
LET ME HELP YOU. LET ME TAKE YOU SOMEWHERE YOU CAN LIVE A LONG AND HAPPY LIFE.

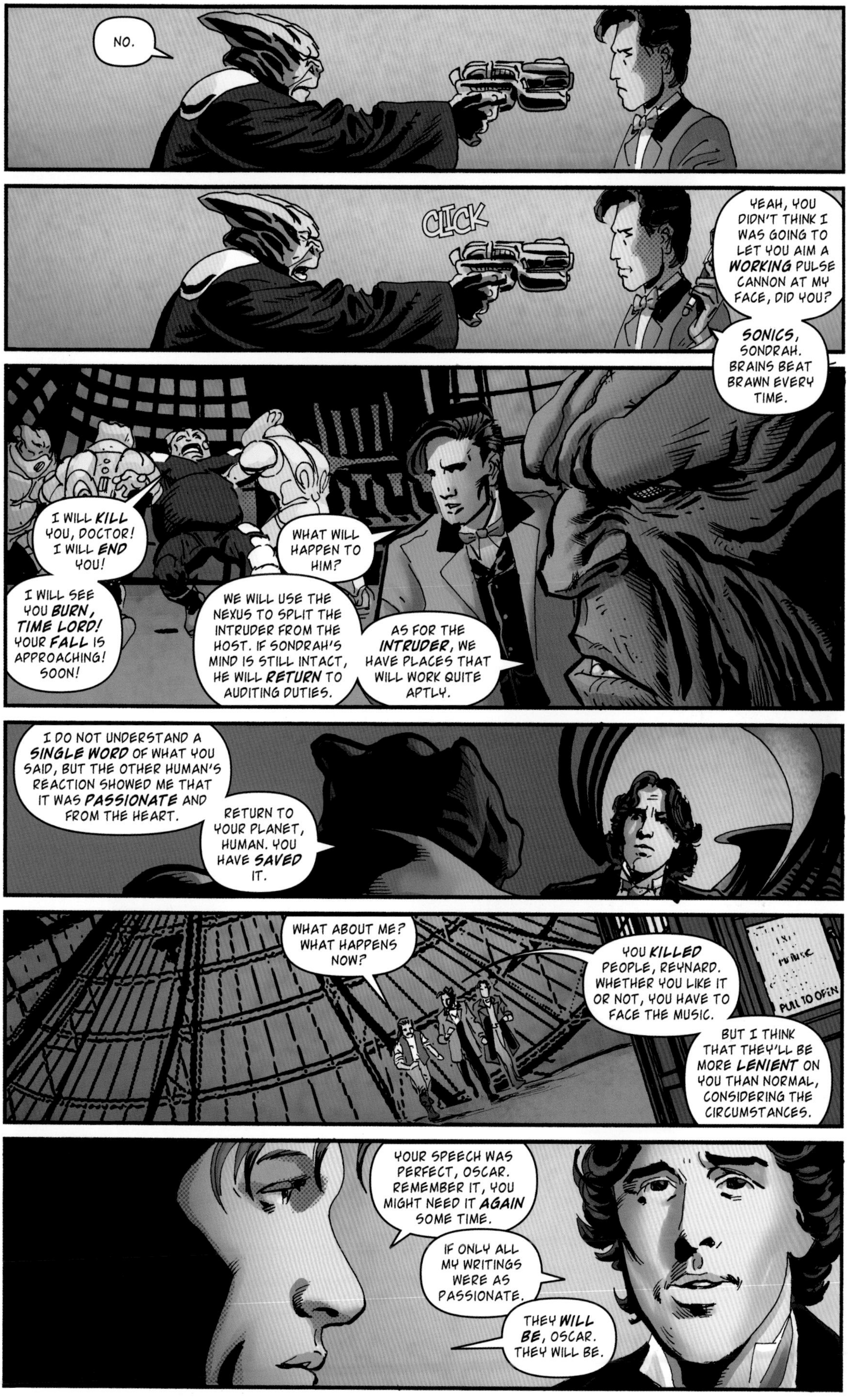
NO.
CLICK
YEAH, YOU DIDN'T THINK I WAS GOING TO LET YOU AIM A WORKING PULSE CANNON AT MY FACE, DID YOU?
SONICS, SONDRAH. BRAINS BEAT BRAWN EVERY TIME.
I WILL KILL YOU, DOCTOR! I WILL END YOU!
I WILL SEE YOU BURN, TIME LORD! YOUR FALL IS APPROACHING! SOON!
WHAT WILL HAPPEN TO HIM?
WE WILL USE THE NEXUS TO SPLIT THE INTRUDER FROM THE HOST. IF SONDRAH'S MIND IS STILL INTACT, HE WILL RETURN TO AUDITING DUTIES.
AS FOR THE INTRUDER, WE HAVE PLACES THAT WILL WORK QUITE APTLY.
I DO NOT UNDERSTAND A SINGLE WORD OF WHAT YOU SAID, BUT THE OTHER HUMAN'S REACTION SHOWED ME THAT IT WAS PASSIONATE AND FROM THE HEART.
RETURN TO YOUR PLANET, HUMAN. YOU HAVE SAVED IT.
WHAT ABOUT ME? WHAT HAPPENS NOW?
YOU KILLED PEOPLE, REYNARD. WHETHER YOU LIKE IT OR NOT, YOU HAVE TO FACE THE MUSIC.
BUT I THINK THAT THEY'LL BE MORE LENIENT ON YOU THAN NORMAL, CONSIDERING THE CIRCUMSTANCES.
PULL TO OPEN
YOUR SPEECH WAS PERFECT, OSCAR. REMEMBER IT, YOU MIGHT NEED IT AGAIN SOME TIME.
IF ONLY ALL MY WRITINGS WERE AS PASSIONATE.
THEY WILL BE, OSCAR. THEY WILL BE.

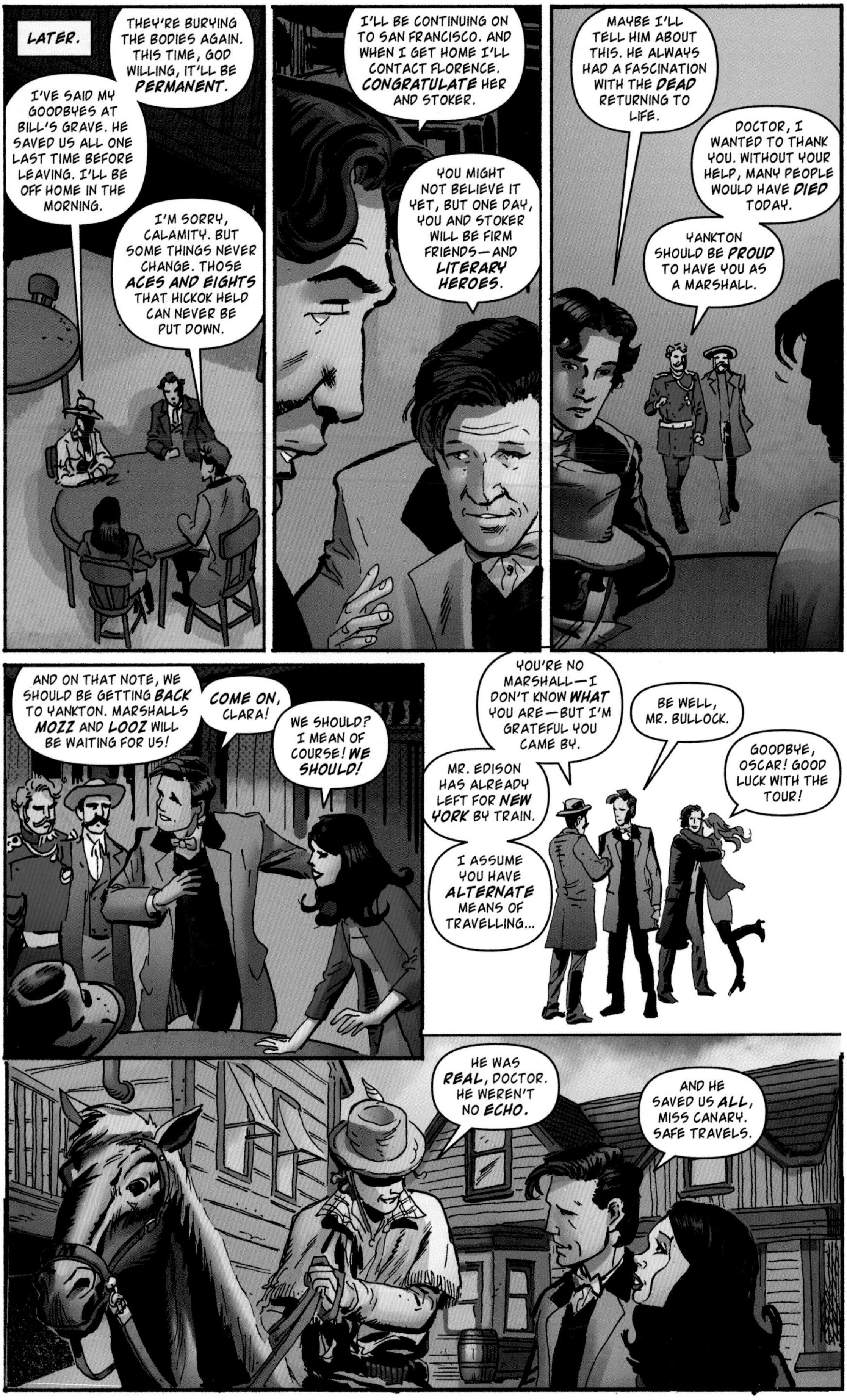
LATER.
THEY'RE BURYING THE BODIES AGAIN. THIS TIME, GOD WILLING, IT'LL BE PERMANENT.
I'VE SAID MY GOODBYES AT BILL'S GRAVE. HE SAVED US ALL ONE LAST TIME BEFORE LEAVING. I'LL BE OFF HOME IN THE MORNING.
I'M SORRY, CALAMITY. BUT SOME THINGS NEVER CHANGE. THOSE ACES AND EIGHTS THAT HICKOK HELD CAN NEVER BE PUT DOWN.
I'LL BE CONTINUING ON TO SAN FRANCISCO. AND WHEN I GET HOME I'LL CONTACT FLORENCE. CONGRATULATE HER AND STOKER.
YOU MIGHT NOT BELIEVE IT YET, BUT ONE DAY, YOU AND STOKER WILL BE FIRM FRIENDS—AND LITERARY HEROES.
MAYBE I'LL TELL HIM ABOUT THIS. HE ALWAYS HAD A FASCINATION WITH THE DEAD RETURNING TO LIFE.
DOCTOR, I WANTED TO THANK YOU. WITHOUT YOUR HELP, MANY PEOPLE WOULD HAVE DIED TODAY.
YANKTON SHOULD BE PROUD TO HAVE YOU AS A MARSHALL.
AND ON THAT NOTE, WE SHOULD BE GETTING BACK TO YANKTON. MARSHALLS MOZZ AND LOOZ WILL BE WAITING FOR US!
COME ON, CLARA!
WE SHOULD? I MEAN OF COURSE! WE SHOULD!
YOU'RE NO MARSHALL—I DON'T KNOW WHAT YOU ARE—BUT I'M GRATEFUL YOU CAME BY.
MR. EDISON HAS ALREADY LEFT FOR NEW YORK BY TRAIN.
I ASSUME YOU HAVE ALTERNATE MEANS OF TRAVELLING...
BE WELL, MR. BULLOCK.
GOODBYE, OSCAR! GOOD LUCK WITH THE TOUR!
HE WAS REAL, DOCTOR. HE WEREN'T NO ECHO.
AND HE SAVED US ALL, MISS CANARY. SAFE TRAVELS.

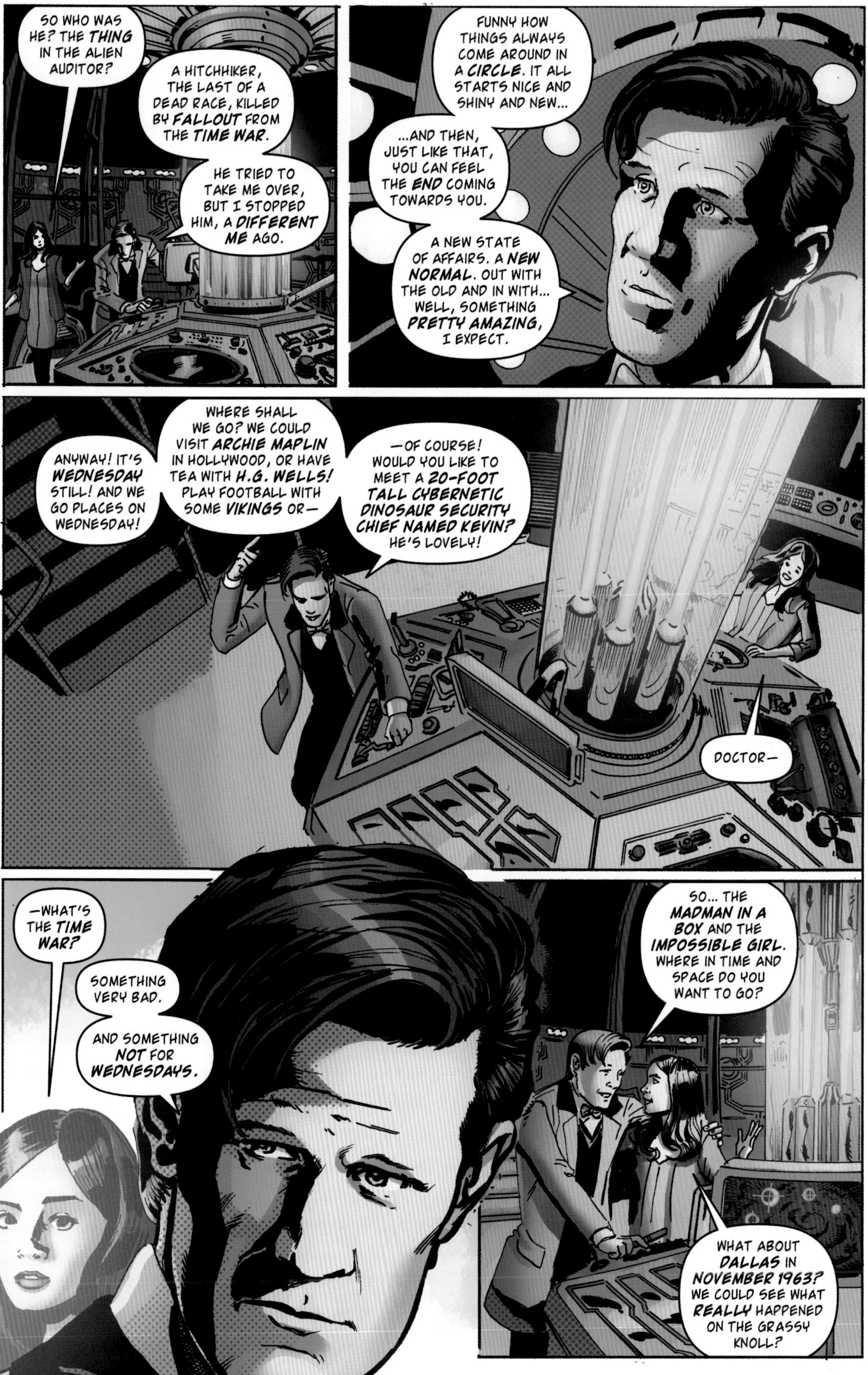

SO WHO WAS HE? THE THING IN THE ALIEN AUDITOR?
A HITCHHIKER, THE LAST OF A DEAD RACE, KILLED BY FALLOUT FROM THE TIME WAR.
HE TRIED TO TAKE ME OVER, BUT I STOPPED HIM, A DIFFERENT ME AGO.
FUNNY HOW THINGS ALWAYS COME AROUND IN A CIRCLE. IT ALL STARTS NICE AND SHINY AND NEW...
...AND THEN, JUST LIKE THAT, YOU CAN FEEL THE END COMING TOWARDS YOU.
A NEW STATE OF AFFAIRS. A NEW NORMAL. OUT WITH THE OLD AND IN WITH... WELL, SOMETHING PRETTY AMAZING, I EXPECT.
ANYWAY! IT'S WEDNESDAY STILL! AND WE GO PLACES ON WEDNESDAY!
WHERE SHALL WE GO? WE COULD VISIT ARCHIE MAPLIN IN HOLLYWOOD, OR HAVE TEA WITH H.G. WELLS! PLAY FOOTBALL WITH SOME VIKINGS OR—
—OF COURSE! WOULD YOU LIKE TO MEET A 20-FOOT TALL CYBERNETIC DINOSAUR SECURITY CHIEF NAMED KEVIN? HE'S LOVELY!
DOCTOR—
—WHAT'S THE TIME WAR?
SOMETHING VERY BAD.
AND SOMETHING NOT FOR WEDNESDAYS.
SO... THE MADMAN IN A BOX AND THE IMPOSSIBLE GIRL. WHERE IN TIME AND SPACE DO YOU WANT TO GO?
WHAT ABOUT DALLAS IN NOVEMBER 1963? WE COULD SEE WHAT REALLY HAPPENED ON THE GRASSY KNOLL?

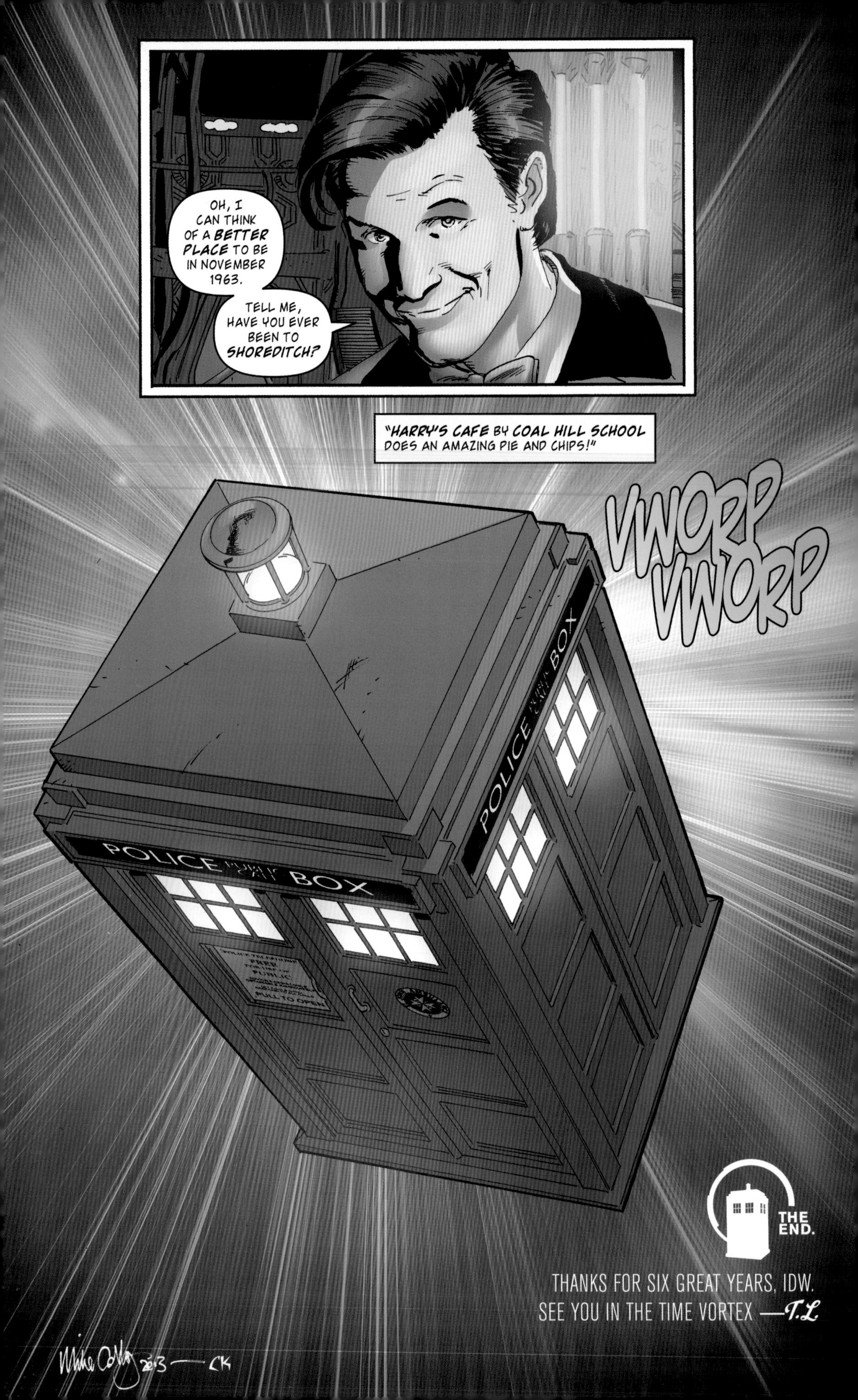

OH, I CAN THINK OF A BETTER PLACE TO BE IN NOVEMBER 1963.
TELL ME, HAVE YOU EVER BEEN TO SHOREDITCH?
"HARRY'S CAFE BY COAL HILL SCHOOL DOES AN AMAZING PIE AND CHIPS!"
VWORP VWORP
POLICE BOX
THE END.
THANKS FOR SIX GREAT YEARS, IDW.
SEE YOU IN THE TIME VORTEX —T.L.

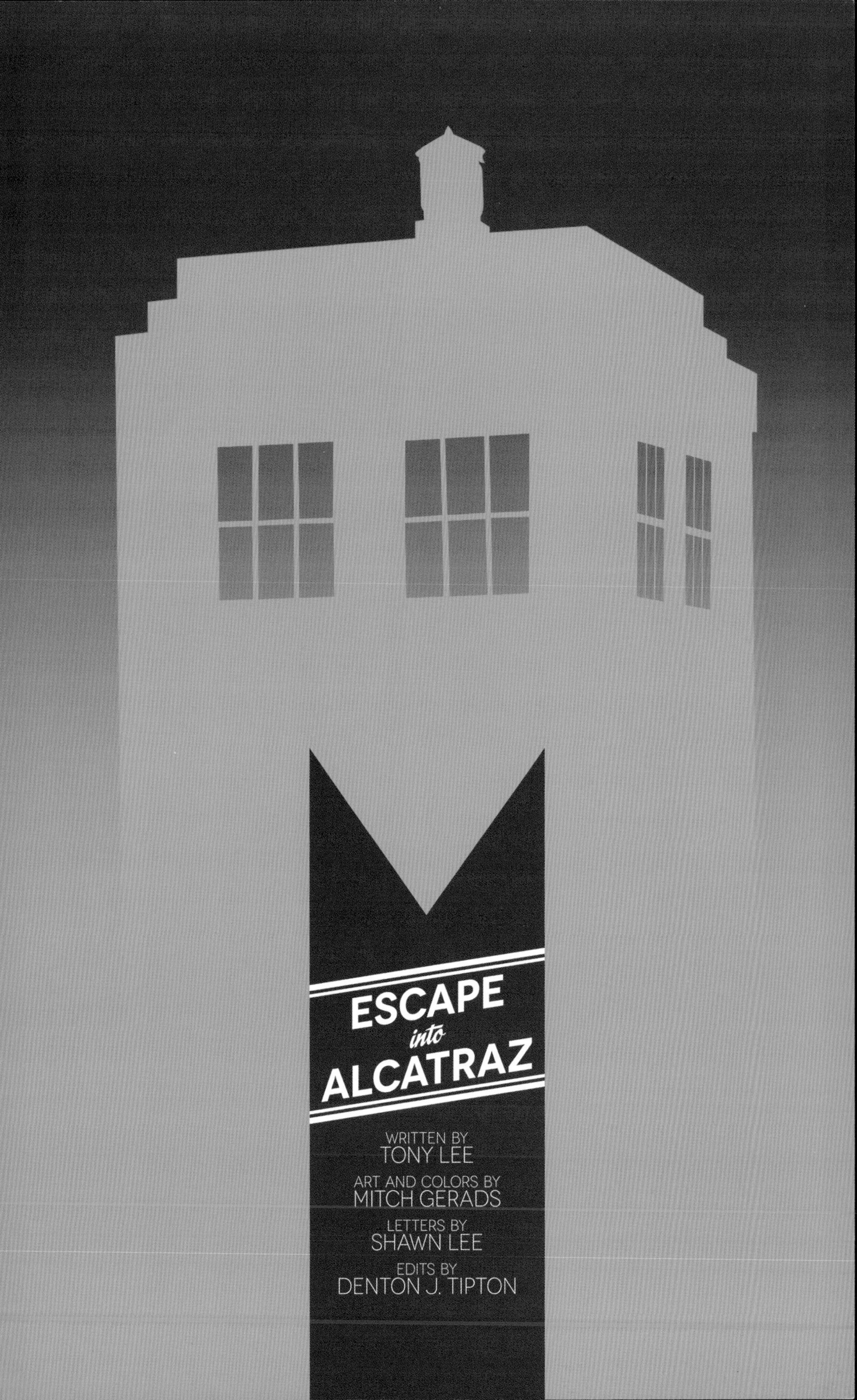
ESCAPE
into
ALCATRAZ
WRITTEN BY
TONY LEE
ART AND COLORS BY
MITCH GERADS
LETTERS BY
SHAWN LEE
EDITS BY
DENTON J. TIPTON

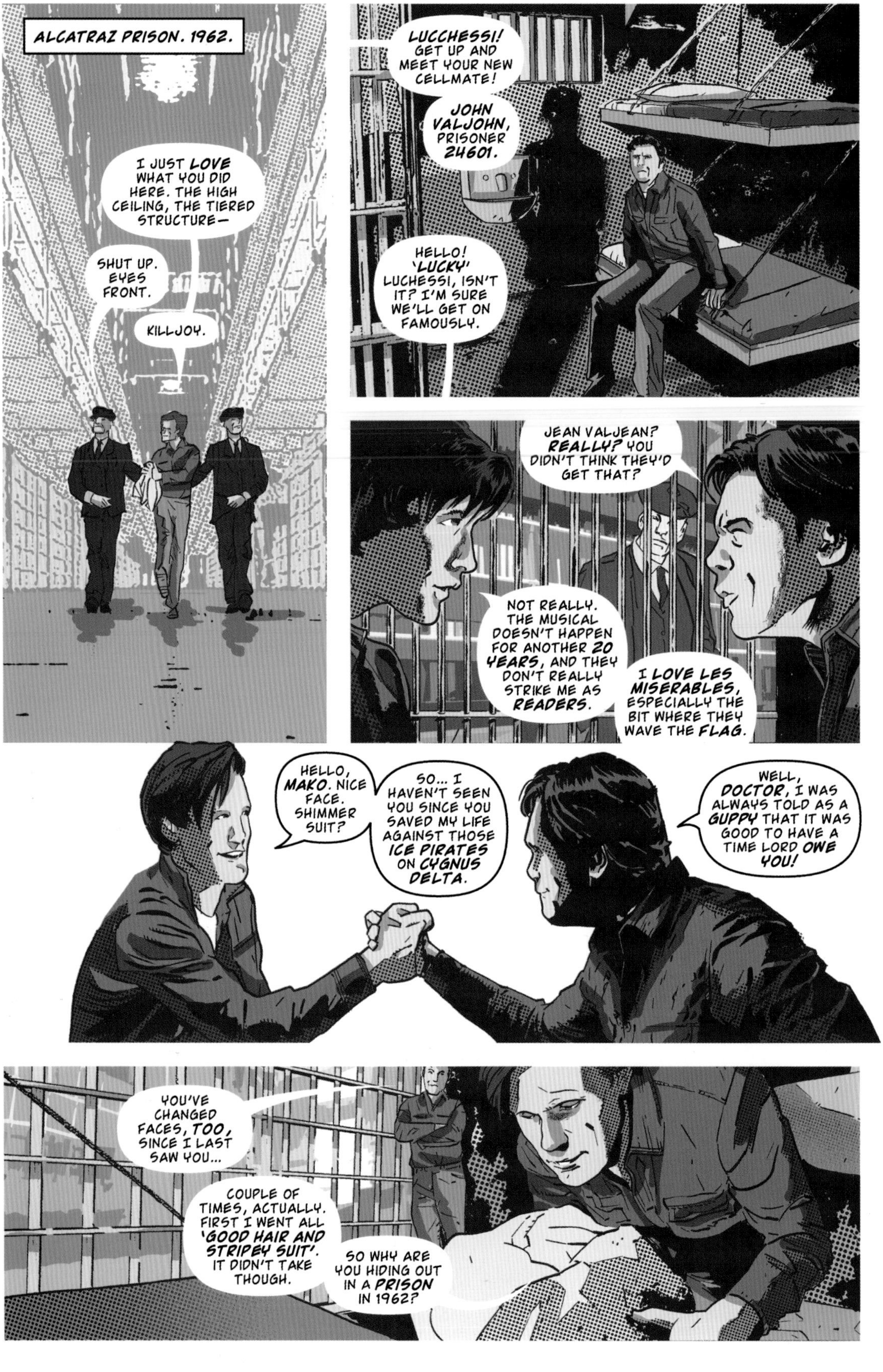
ALCATRAZ PRISON. 1962.
I JUST LOVE WHAT YOU DID HERE. THE HIGH CEILING, THE TIERED STRUCTURE—
SHUT UP. EYES FRONT.
KILLJOY.
LUCCHESSI! GET UP AND MEET YOUR NEW CELLMATE!
JOHN VALJOHN, PRISONER 24601.
HELLO! 'LUCKY' LUCHESSI, ISN'T IT? I'M SURE WE'LL GET ON FAMOUSLY.
JEAN VALJEAN? REALLY? YOU DIDN'T THINK THEY'D GET THAT?
NOT REALLY. THE MUSICAL DOESN'T HAPPEN FOR ANOTHER 20 YEARS, AND THEY DON'T REALLY STRIKE ME AS READERS.
I LOVE LES MISERABLES, ESPECIALLY THE BIT WHERE THEY WAVE THE FLAG.
HELLO, MAKO. NICE FACE. SHIMMER SUIT?
SO... I HAVEN'T SEEN YOU SINCE YOU SAVED MY LIFE AGAINST THOSE ICE PIRATES ON CYGNUS DELTA.
WELL, DOCTOR, I WAS ALWAYS TOLD AS A GUPPY THAT IT WAS GOOD TO HAVE A TIME LORD OWE YOU!
YOU'VE CHANGED FACES, TOO, SINCE I LAST SAW YOU...
COUPLE OF TIMES, ACTUALLY. FIRST I WENT ALL 'GOOD HAIR AND STRIPEY SUIT'. IT DIDN'T TAKE THOUGH.
SO WHY ARE YOU HIDING OUT IN A PRISON IN 1962?

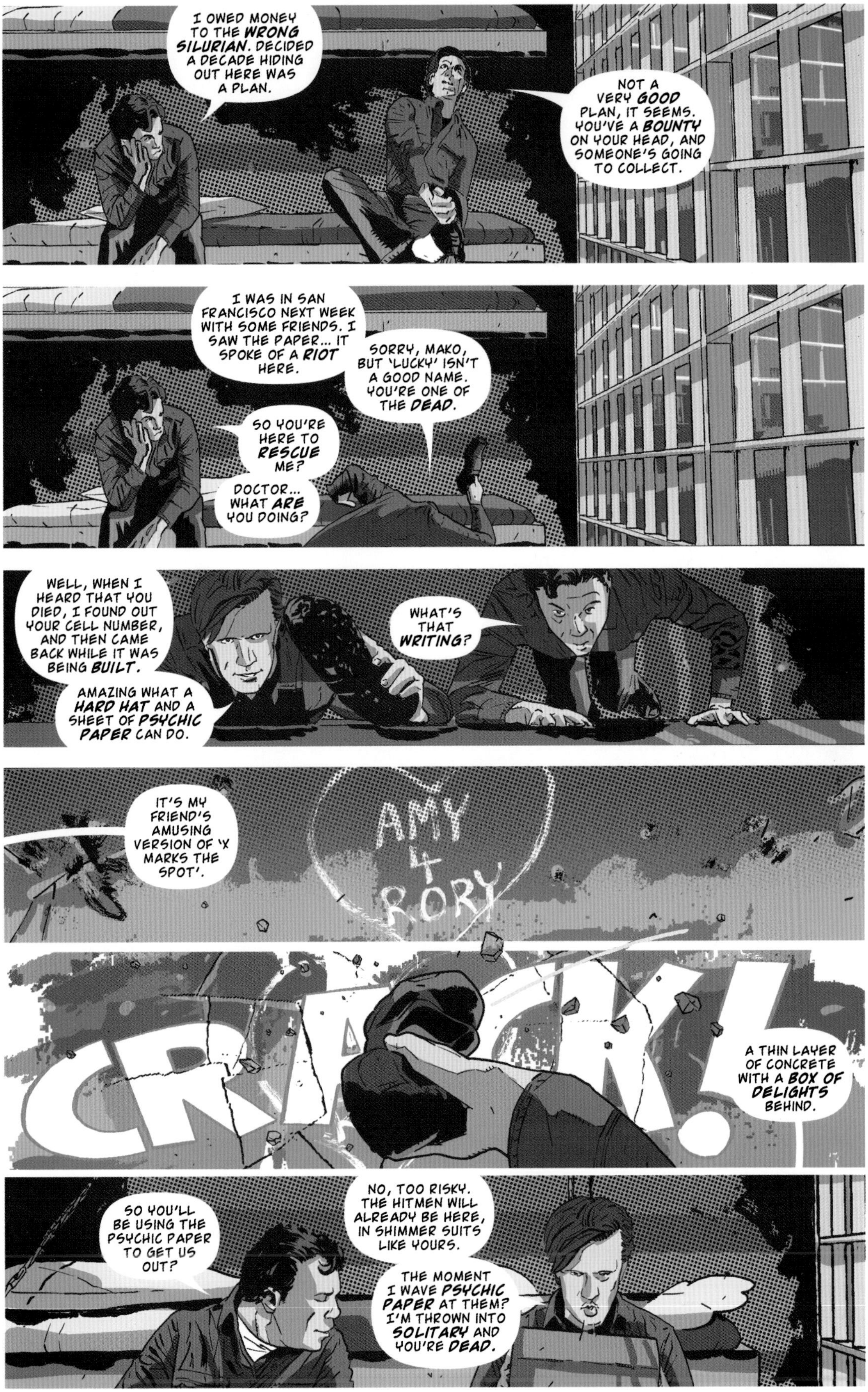
I OWED MONEY TO THE WRONG SILURIAN. DECIDED A DECADE HIDING OUT HERE WAS A PLAN.
NOT A VERY GOOD PLAN, IT SEEMS. YOU'VE A BOUNTY ON YOUR HEAD, AND SOMEONE'S GOING TO COLLECT.
I WAS IN SAN FRANCISCO NEXT WEEK WITH SOME FRIENDS. I SAW THE PAPER... IT SPOKE OF A RIOT HERE.
SORRY, MAKO, BUT 'LUCKY' ISN'T A GOOD NAME. YOU'RE ONE OF THE DEAD.
SO YOU'RE HERE TO RESCUE ME?
DOCTOR... WHAT ARE YOU DOING?
WELL, WHEN I HEARD THAT YOU DIED, I FOUND OUT YOUR CELL NUMBER, AND THEN CAME BACK WHILE IT WAS BEING BUILT.
AMAZING WHAT A HARD HAT AND A SHEET OF PSYCHIC PAPER CAN DO.
WHAT'S THAT WRITING?
IT'S MY FRIEND'S AMUSING VERSION OF 'X MARKS THE SPOT'.
AMY 4 RORY
CRACK!
A THIN LAYER OF CONCRETE WITH A BOX OF DELIGHTS BEHIND.
SO YOU'LL BE USING THE PSYCHIC PAPER TO GET US OUT?
NO, TOO RISKY. THE HITMEN WILL ALREADY BE HERE, IN SHIMMER SUITS LIKE YOURS.
THE MOMENT I WAVE PSYCHIC PAPER AT THEM? I'M THROWN INTO SOLITARY AND YOU'RE DEAD.

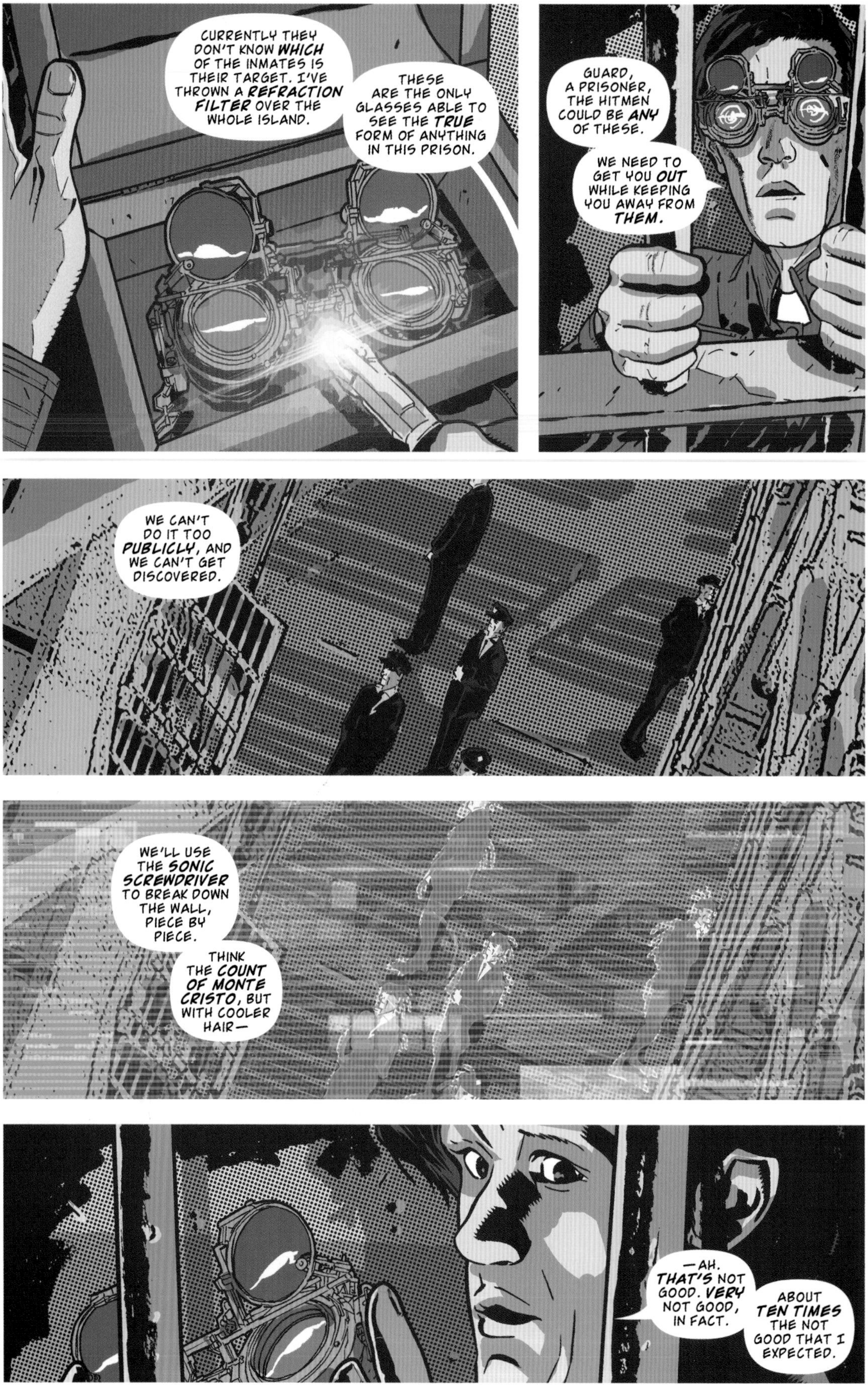
CURRENTLY THEY DON'T KNOW WHICH OF THE INMATES IS THEIR TARGET. I'VE THROWN A REFRACTION FILTER OVER THE WHOLE ISLAND.
THESE ARE THE ONLY GLASSES ABLE TO SEE THE TRUE FORM OF ANYTHING IN THIS PRISON.
GUARD, A PRISONER, THE HITMEN COULD BE ANY OF THESE.
WE NEED TO GET YOU OUT WHILE KEEPING YOU AWAY FROM THEM.
WE CAN'T DO IT TOO PUBLICLY, AND WE CAN'T GET DISCOVERED.
WE'LL USE THE SONIC SCREWDRIVER TO BREAK DOWN THE WALL, PIECE BY PIECE.
THINK THE COUNT OF MONTE CRISTO, BUT WITH COOLER HAIR—
—AH. THAT'S NOT GOOD. VERY NOT GOOD, IN FACT.
ABOUT TEN TIMES THE NOT GOOD THAT I EXPECTED.

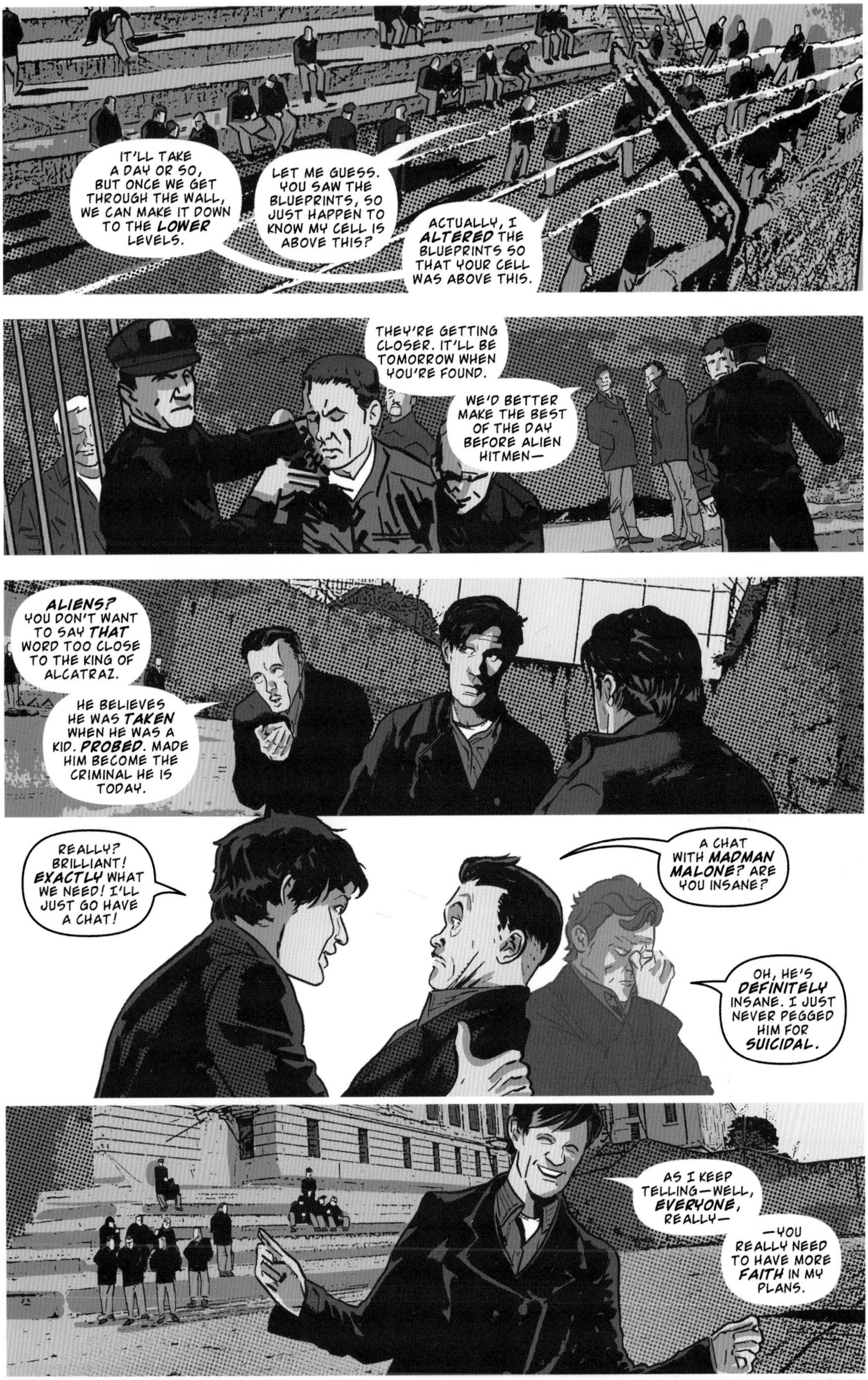
IT'LL TAKE A DAY OR SO, BUT ONCE WE GET THROUGH THE WALL, WE CAN MAKE IT DOWN TO THE LOWER LEVELS.
LET ME GUESS. YOU SAW THE BLUEPRINTS, SO JUST HAPPEN TO KNOW MY CELL IS ABOVE THIS?
ACTUALLY, I ALTERED THE BLUEPRINTS SO THAT YOUR CELL WAS ABOVE THIS.
THEY'RE GETTING CLOSER. IT'LL BE TOMORROW WHEN YOU'RE FOUND.
WE'D BETTER MAKE THE BEST OF THE DAY BEFORE ALIEN HITMEN—
ALIENS? YOU DON'T WANT TO SAY THAT WORD TOO CLOSE TO THE KING OF ALCATRAZ.
HE BELIEVES HE WAS TAKEN WHEN HE WAS A KID. PROBED. MADE HIM BECOME THE CRIMINAL HE IS TODAY.
REALLY? BRILLIANT! EXACTLY WHAT WE NEED! I'LL JUST GO HAVE A CHAT!
A CHAT WITH MADMAN MALONE? ARE YOU INSANE?
OH, HE'S DEFINITELY INSANE. I JUST NEVER PEGGED HIM FOR SUICIDAL.
AS I KEEP TELLING—WELL, EVERYONE, REALLY—
—YOU REALLY NEED TO HAVE MORE FAITH IN MY PLANS.

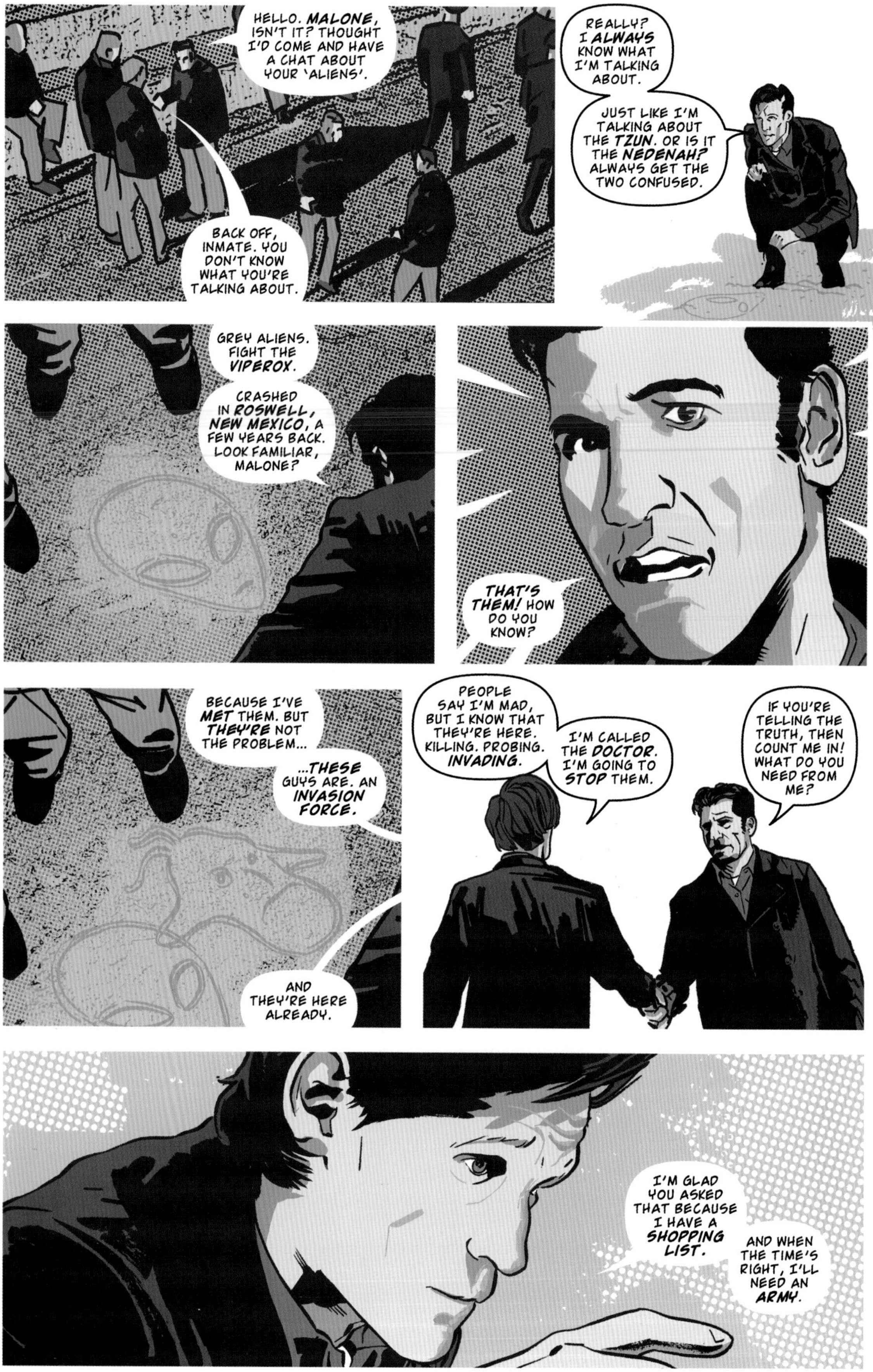
HELLO. MALONE, ISN'T IT? THOUGHT I'D COME AND HAVE A CHAT ABOUT YOUR 'ALIENS'.
BACK OFF, INMATE. YOU DON'T KNOW WHAT YOU'RE TALKING ABOUT.
REALLY? I ALWAYS KNOW WHAT I'M TALKING ABOUT.
JUST LIKE I'M TALKING ABOUT THE TZUN. OR IS IT THE NEDENAH? ALWAYS GET THE TWO CONFUSED.
GREY ALIENS. FIGHT THE VIPEROX.
CRASHED IN ROSWELL, NEW MEXICO, A FEW YEARS BACK. LOOK FAMILIAR, MALONE?
THAT'S THEM! HOW DO YOU KNOW?
BECAUSE I'VE MET THEM. BUT THEY'RE NOT THE PROBLEM...
...THESE GUYS ARE. AN INVASION FORCE.
AND THEY'RE HERE ALREADY.
PEOPLE SAY I'M MAD, BUT I KNOW THAT THEY'RE HERE. KILLING. PROBING. INVADING.
I'M CALLED THE DOCTOR. I'M GOING TO STOP THEM.
IF YOU'RE TELLING THE TRUTH, THEN COUNT ME IN! WHAT DO YOU NEED FROM ME?
I'M GLAD YOU ASKED THAT BECAUSE I HAVE A SHOPPING LIST.
AND WHEN THE TIME'S RIGHT, I'LL NEED AN ARMY.

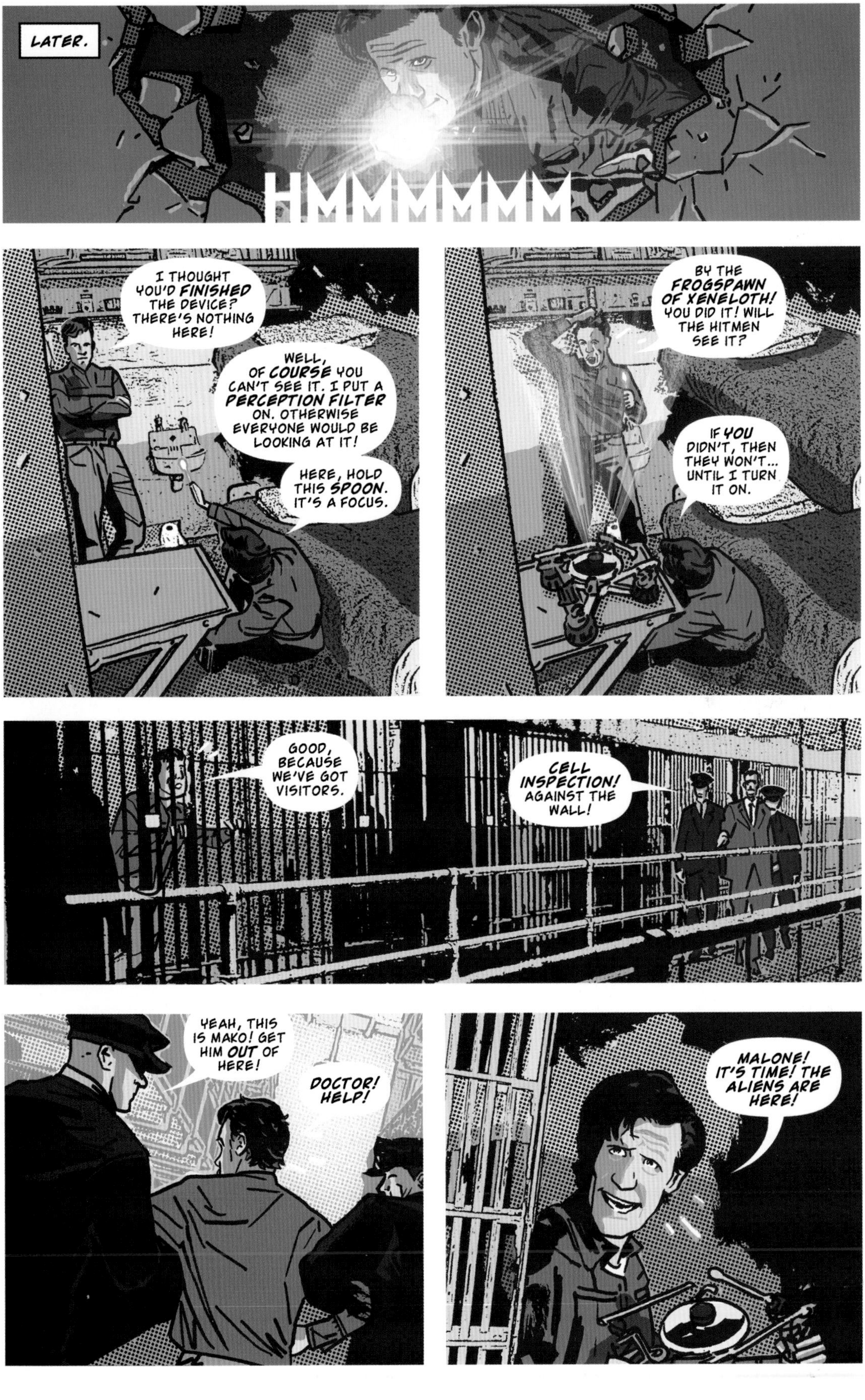
LATER.
HMMMMMM
I THOUGHT YOU'D FINISHED THE DEVICE? THERE'S NOTHING HERE!
WELL, OF COURSE YOU CAN'T SEE IT. I PUT A PERCEPTION FILTER ON. OTHERWISE EVERYONE WOULD BE LOOKING AT IT!
HERE, HOLD THIS SPOON. IT'S A FOCUS.
BY THE FROGSPAWN OF XENELOTH! YOU DID IT! WILL THE HITMEN SEE IT?
IF YOU DIDN'T, THEN THEY WON'T... UNTIL I TURN IT ON.
GOOD, BECAUSE WE'VE GOT VISITORS.
CELL INSPECTION! AGAINST THE WALL!
YEAH, THIS IS MAKO! GET HIM OUT OF HERE!
DOCTOR! HELP!
MALONE! IT'S TIME! THE ALIENS ARE HERE!

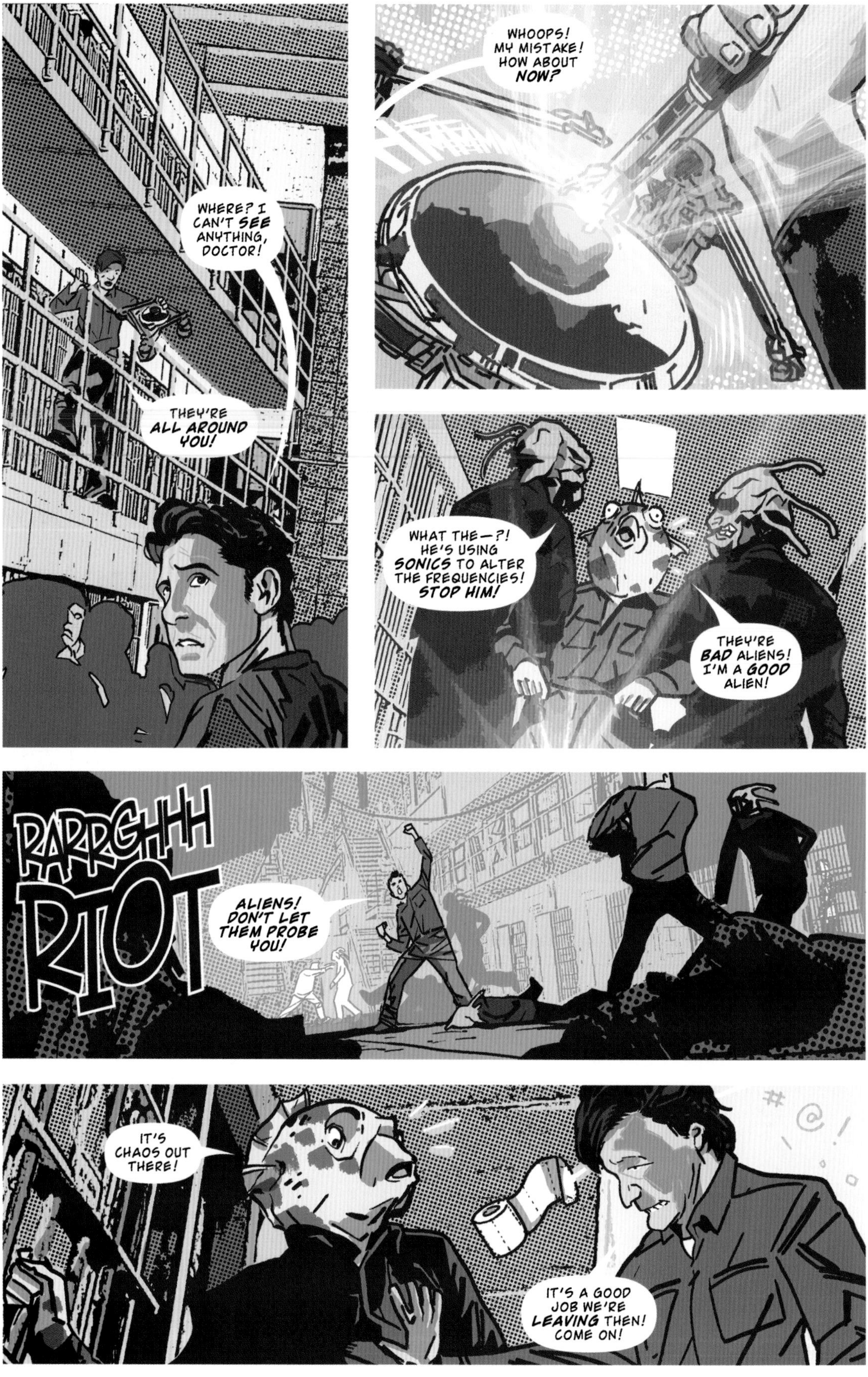
WHERE? I CAN'T SEE ANYTHING, DOCTOR!
THEY'RE ALL AROUND YOU!
WHOOPS! MY MISTAKE! HOW ABOUT NOW?
WHAT THE—?! HE'S USING SONICS TO ALTER THE FREQUENCIES! STOP HIM!
THEY'RE BAD ALIENS! I'M A GOOD ALIEN!
RARRGHHH
RIOT
ALIENS! DON'T LET THEM PROBE YOU!
IT'S CHAOS OUT THERE!
@ !
IT'S A GOOD JOB WE'RE LEAVING THEN! COME ON!

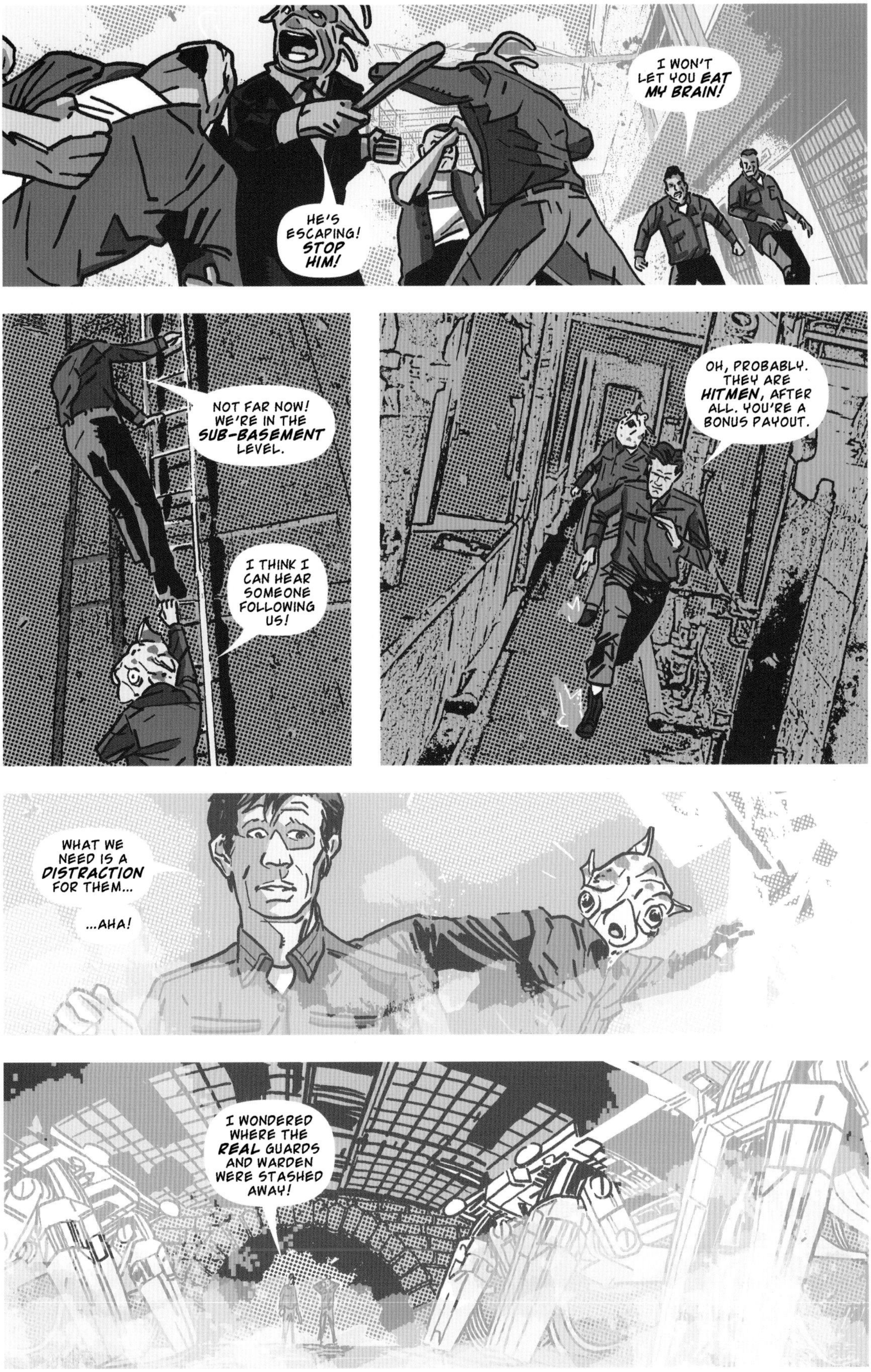
HE'S ESCAPING! STOP HIM!
I WON'T LET YOU EAT MY BRAIN!
NOT FAR NOW! WE'RE IN THE SUB-BASEMENT LEVEL.
I THINK I CAN HEAR SOMEONE FOLLOWING US!
OH, PROBABLY. THEY ARE HITMEN, AFTER ALL. YOU'RE A BONUS PAYOUT.
WHAT WE NEED IS A DISTRACTION FOR THEM...
...AHA!
I WONDERED WHERE THE REAL GUARDS AND WARDEN WERE STASHED AWAY!

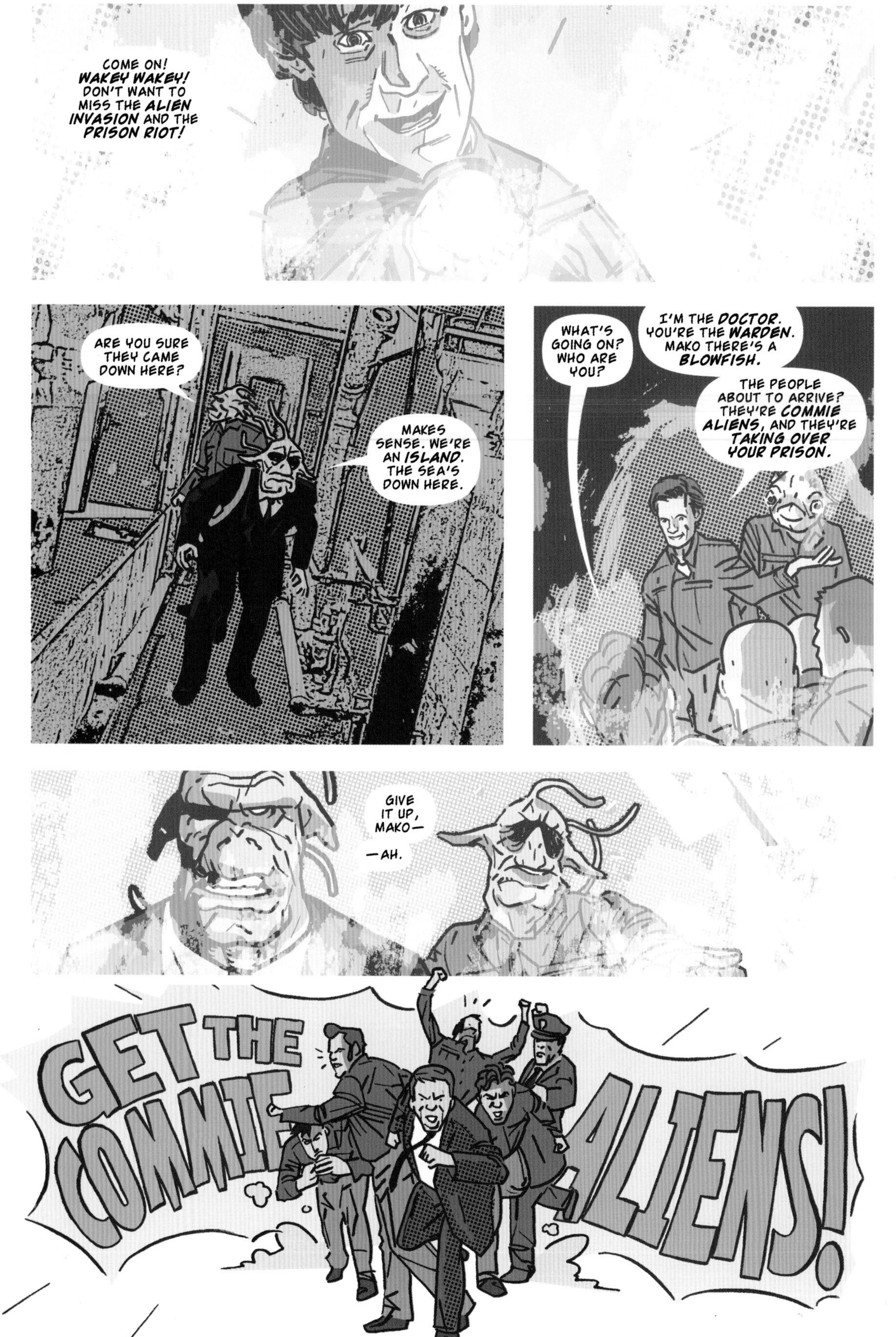
COME ON! WAKEY WAKEY! DON'T WANT TO MISS THE ALIEN INVASION AND THE PRISON RIOT!
ARE YOU SURE THEY CAME DOWN HERE?
MAKES SENSE. WE'RE AN ISLAND. THE SEA'S DOWN HERE.
WHAT'S GOING ON? WHO ARE YOU?
I'M THE DOCTOR. YOU'RE THE WARDEN. MAKO THERE'S A BLOWFISH.
THE PEOPLE ABOUT TO ARRIVE? THEY'RE COMMIE ALIENS, AND THEY'RE TAKING OVER YOUR PRISON.
GIVE IT UP, MAKO—
—AH.
GET THE COMMIE ALIENS!

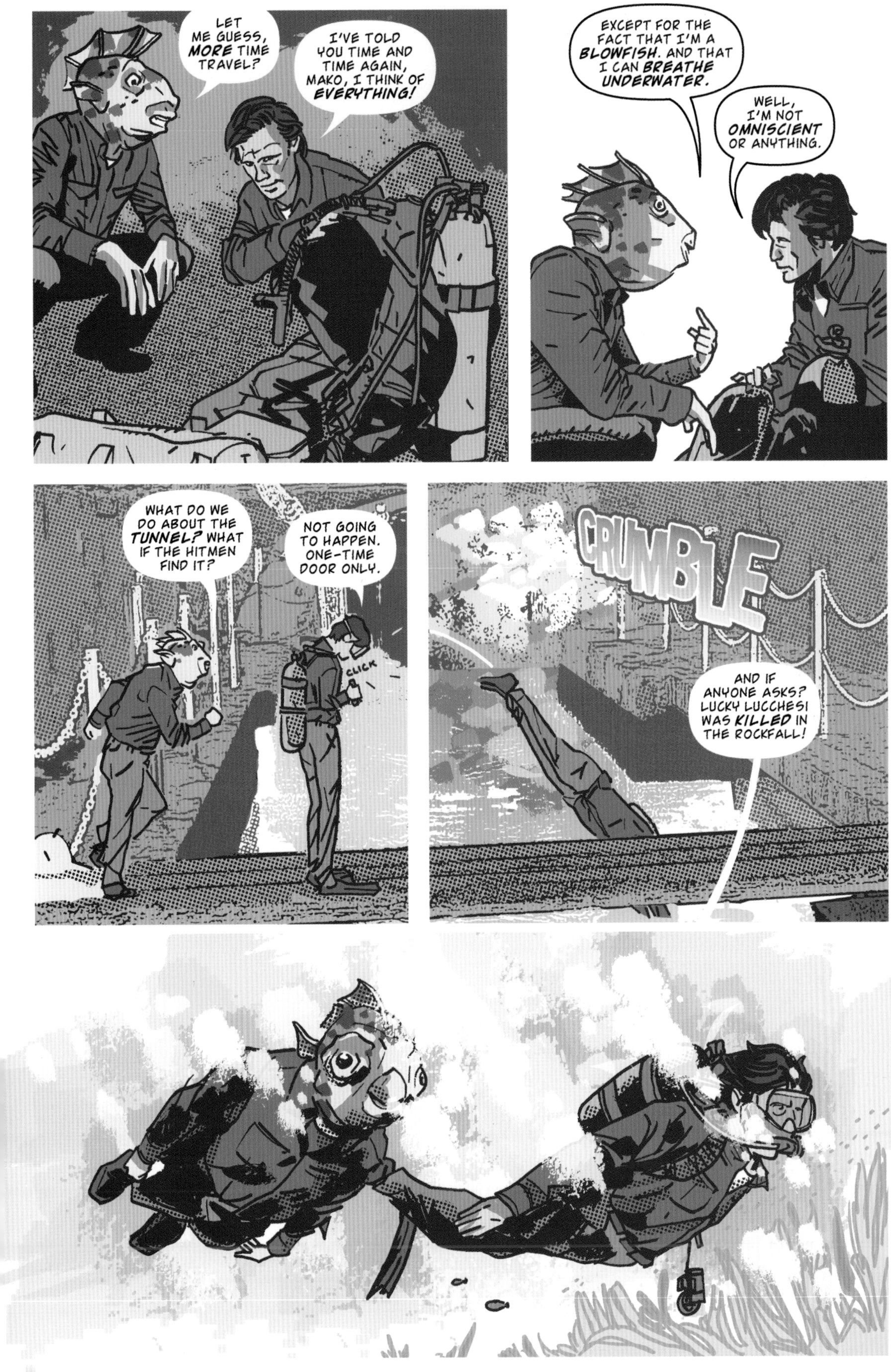
LET ME GUESS, MORE TIME TRAVEL?
I'VE TOLD YOU TIME AND TIME AGAIN, MAKO, I THINK OF EVERYTHING!
EXCEPT FOR THE FACT THAT I'M A BLOWFISH. AND THAT I CAN BREATHE UNDERWATER.
WELL, I'M NOT OMNISCIENT OR ANYTHING.
WHAT DO WE DO ABOUT THE TUNNEL? WHAT IF THE HITMEN FIND IT?
NOT GOING TO HAPPEN. ONE-TIME DOOR ONLY.
CLICK
CRUMBLE
AND IF ANYONE ASKS? LUCKY LUCCHESI WAS KILLED IN THE ROCKFALL!

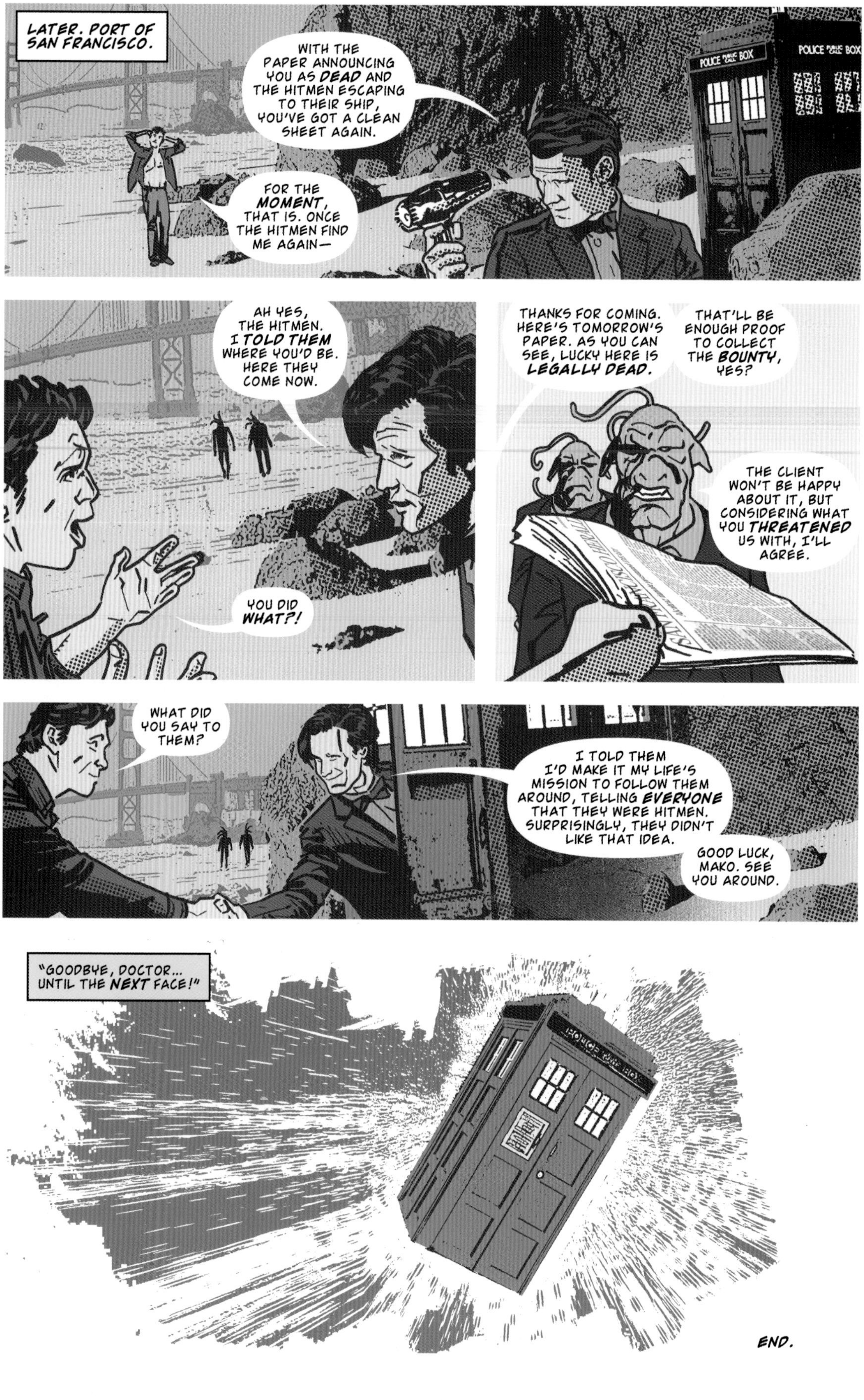
LATER. PORT OF SAN FRANCISCO.
WITH THE PAPER ANNOUNCING YOU AS DEAD AND THE HITMEN ESCAPING TO THEIR SHIP, YOU'VE GOT A CLEAN SHEET AGAIN.
FOR THE MOMENT, THAT IS. ONCE THE HITMEN FIND ME AGAIN—
AH YES, THE HITMEN. I TOLD THEM WHERE YOU'D BE. HERE THEY COME NOW.
YOU DID WHAT?!
THANKS FOR COMING. HERE'S TOMORROW'S PAPER. AS YOU CAN SEE, LUCKY HERE IS LEGALLY DEAD.
THAT'LL BE ENOUGH PROOF TO COLLECT THE BOUNTY, YES?
THE CLIENT WON'T BE HAPPY ABOUT IT, BUT CONSIDERING WHAT YOU THREATENED US WITH, I'LL AGREE.
WHAT DID YOU SAY TO THEM?
I TOLD THEM I'D MAKE IT MY LIFE'S MISSION TO FOLLOW THEM AROUND, TELLING EVERYONE THAT THEY WERE HITMEN. SURPRISINGLY, THEY DIDN'T LIKE THAT IDEA.
GOOD LUCK, MAKO. SEE YOU AROUND.
"GOODBYE, DOCTOR... UNTIL THE NEXT FACE!"
END.

Art by Mark Buckingham
Colors by Charlie Kirchoff

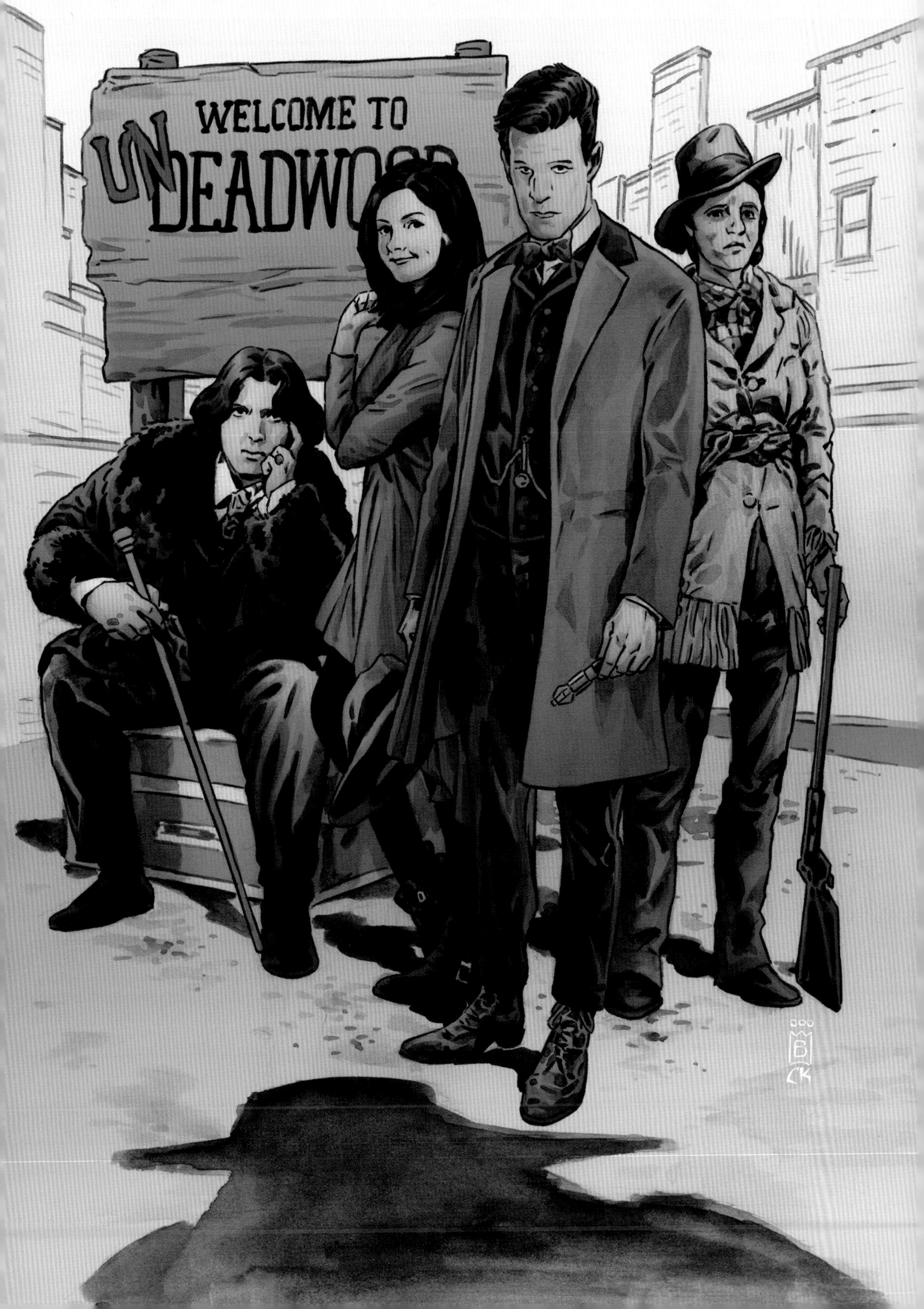
WELCOME TO
UNDEADWO

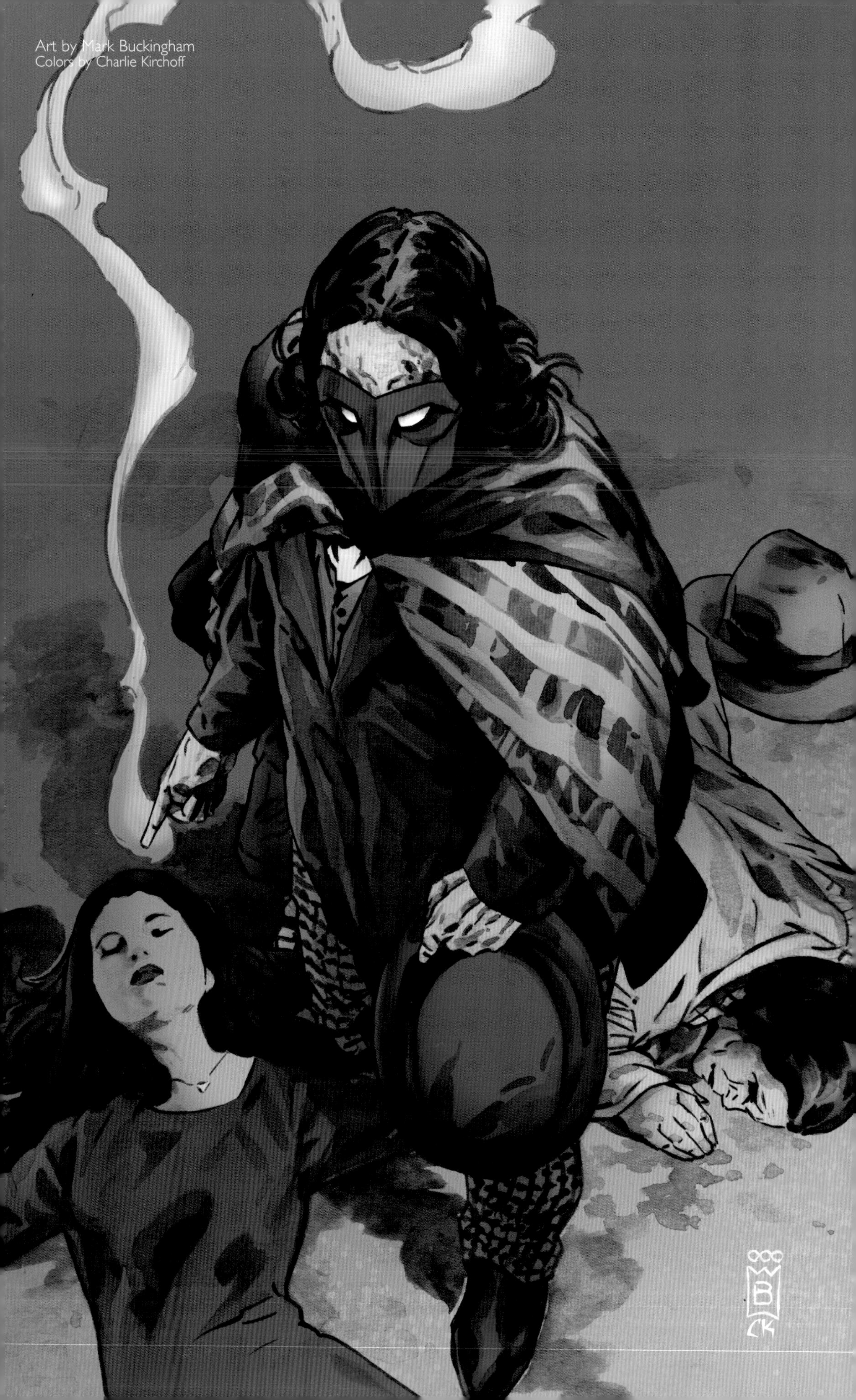

Art by Mark Buckingham
Colors by Charlie Kirchoff

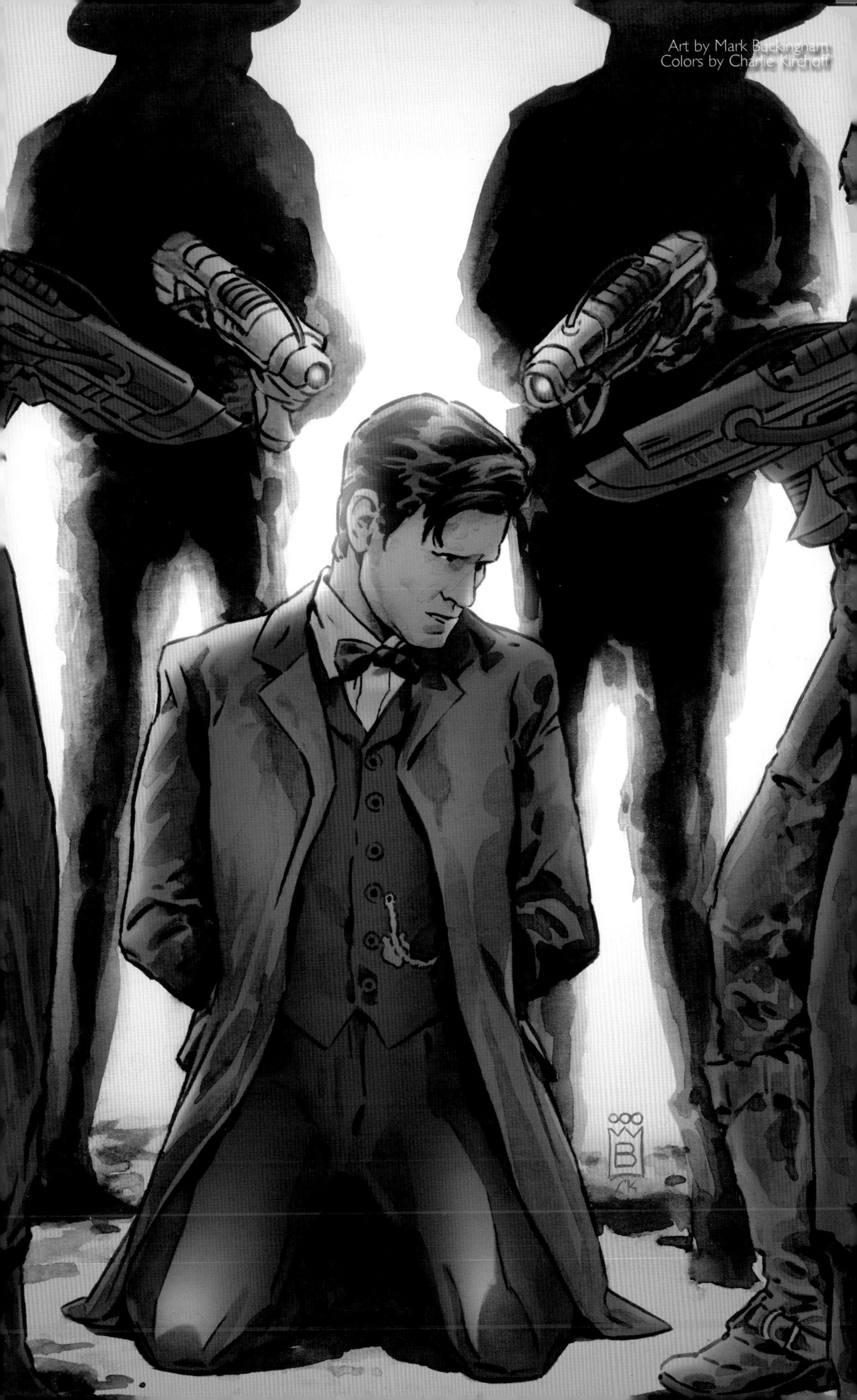
Art by Mark Buckingham
Colors by Charlie Kirchoff

Art by Mark Buckingham
Colors by Charlie Kirchoff

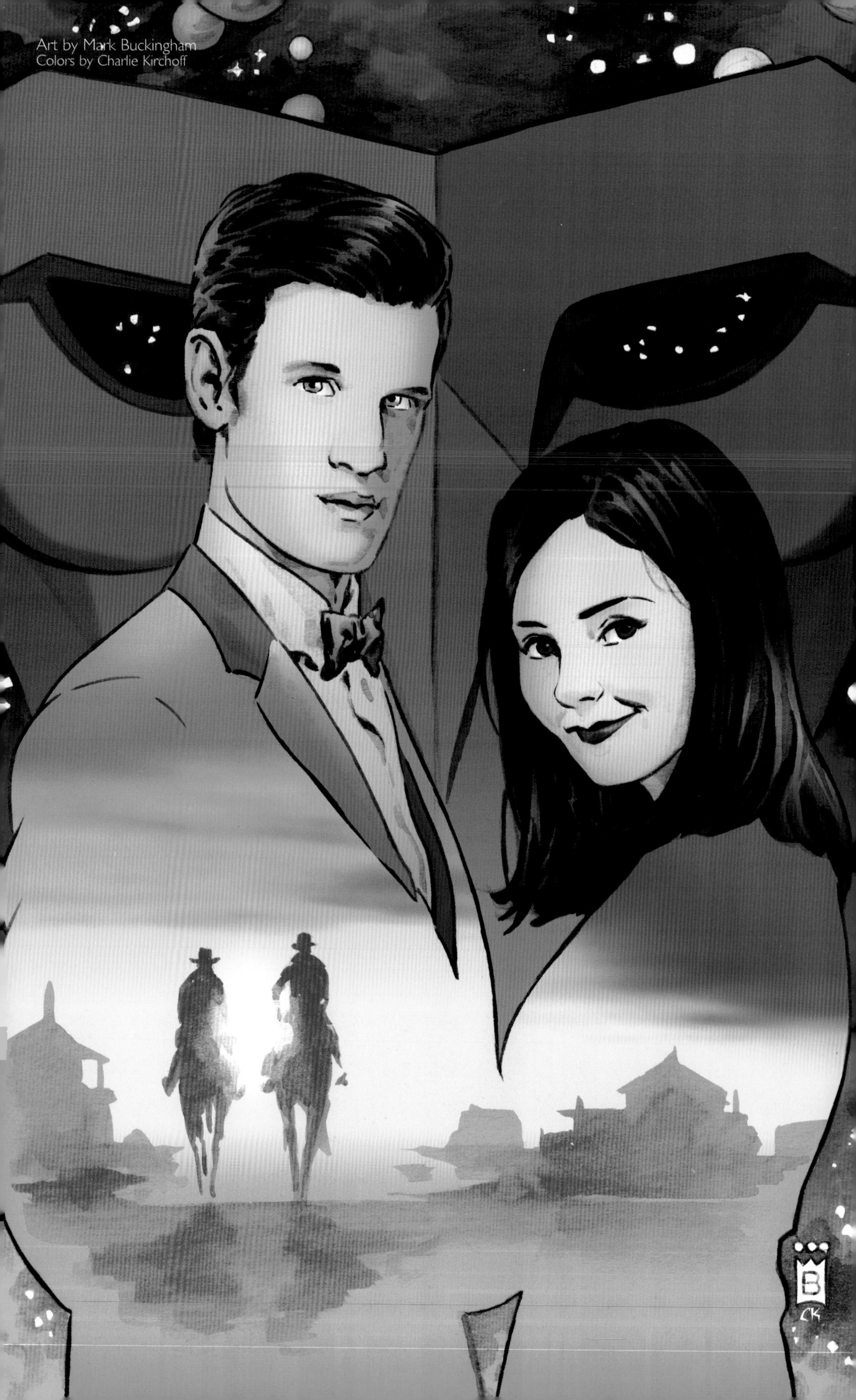

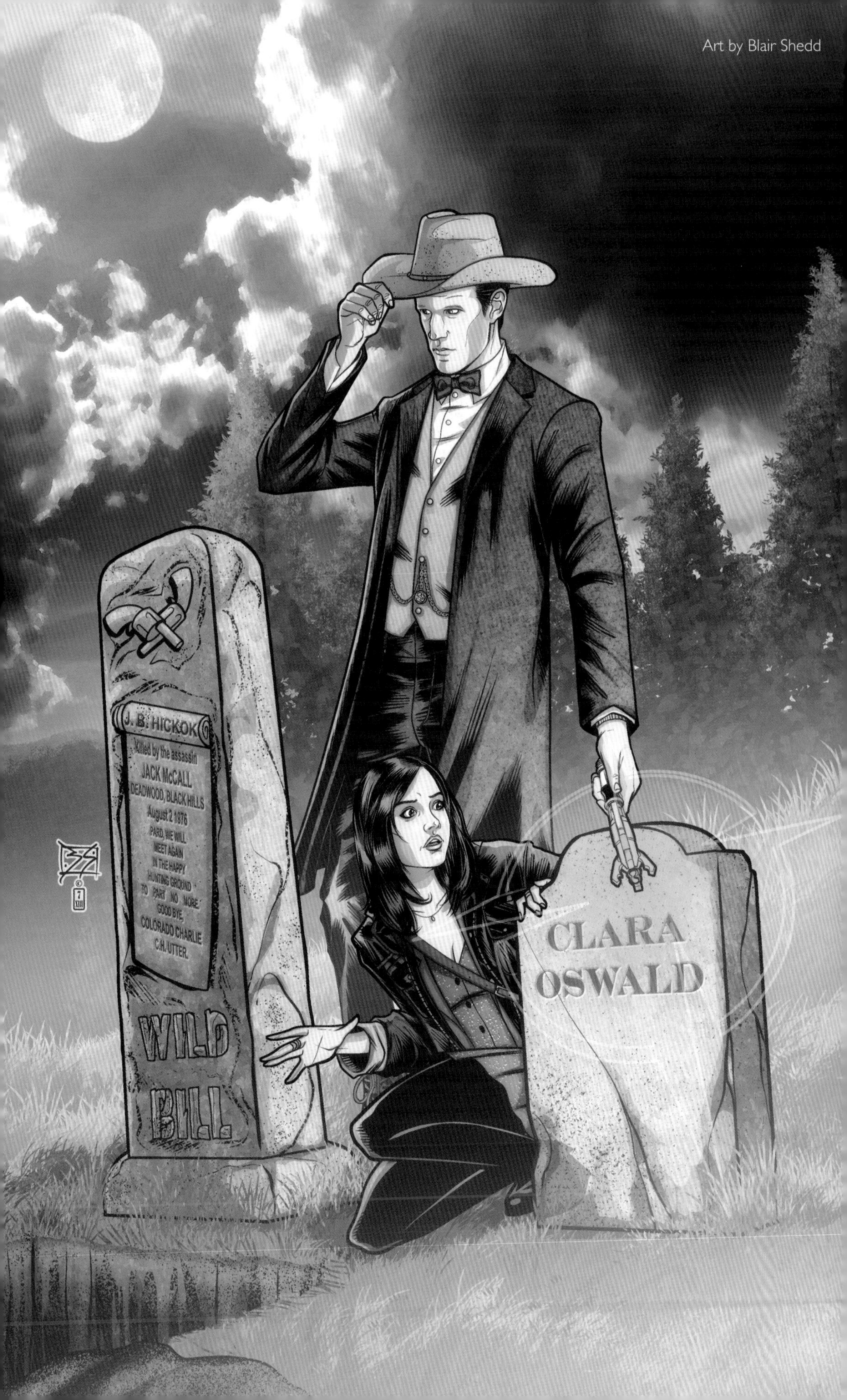
J. B. HICKOK
Killed by the assassin
JACK McCALL
DEADWOOD, BLACK HILLS
August 2 1876
PARD, WE WILL
MEET AGAIN
IN THE HAPPY
HUNTING GROUND
TO PART NO MORE.
GOOD BYE,
COLORADO CHARLIE
C.H. UTTER.
WILD
BILL
CLARA
OSWALD
Art by Blair Shedd

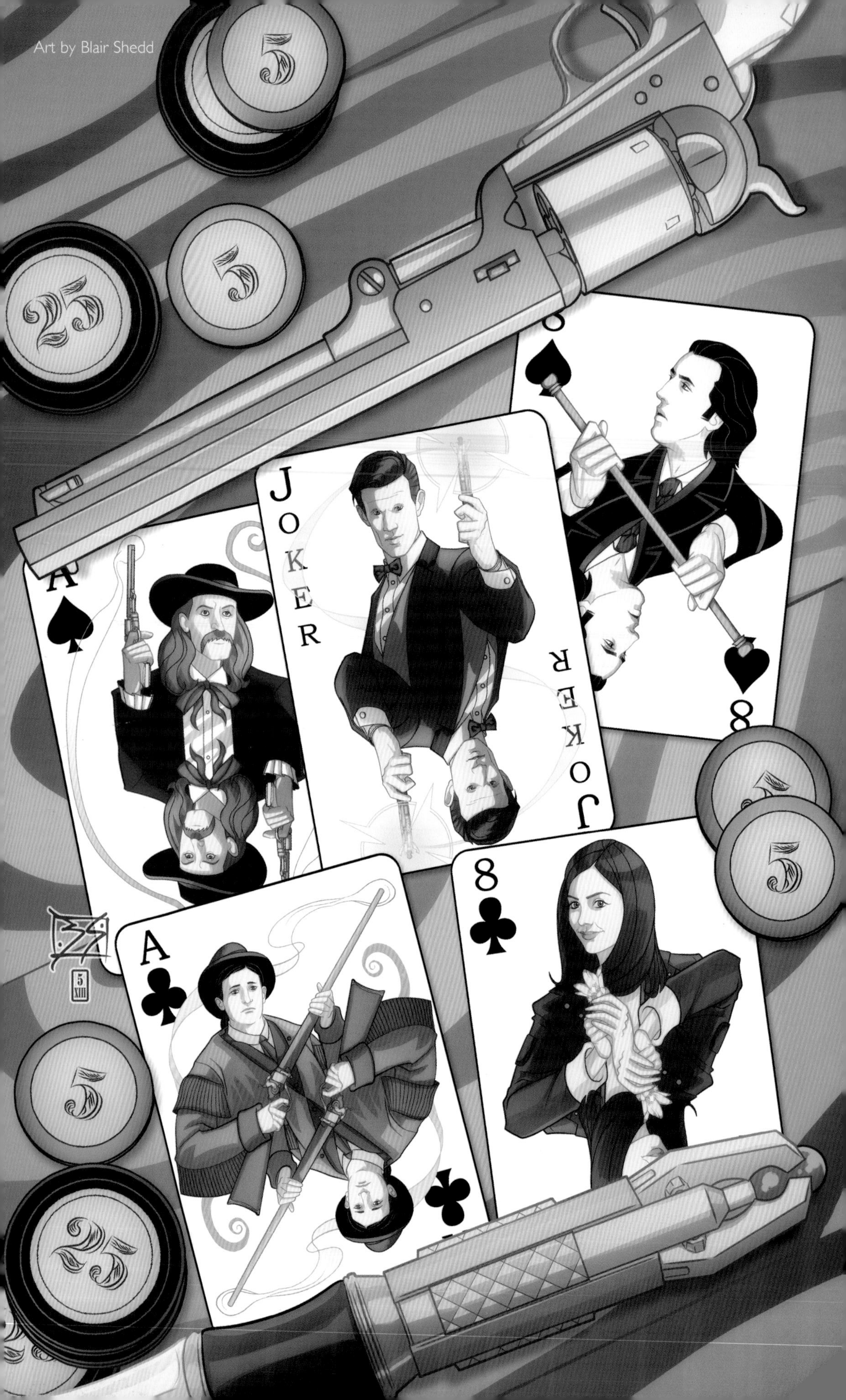
JOKER
Art by Blair Shedd

Art by Blair Shedd

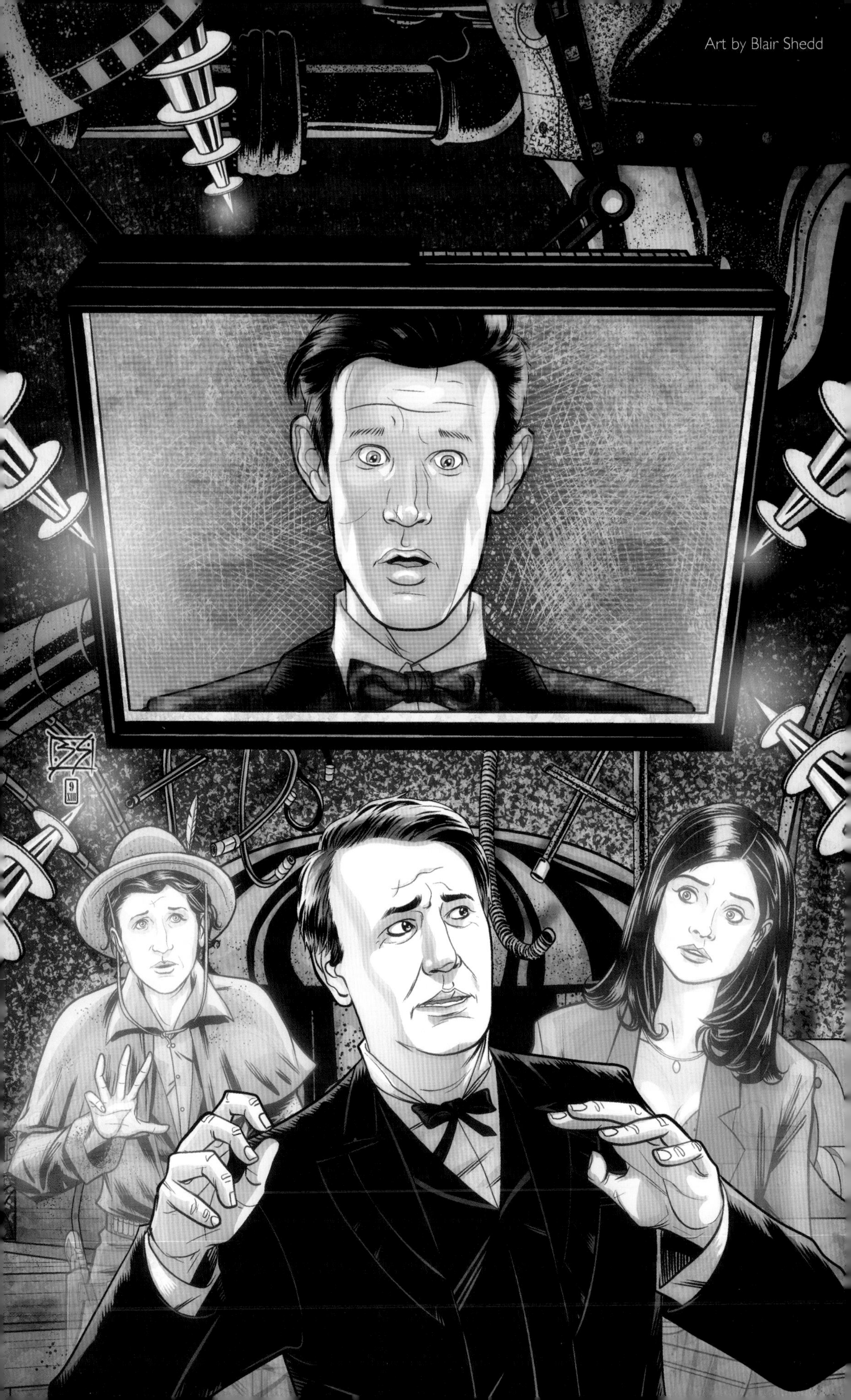

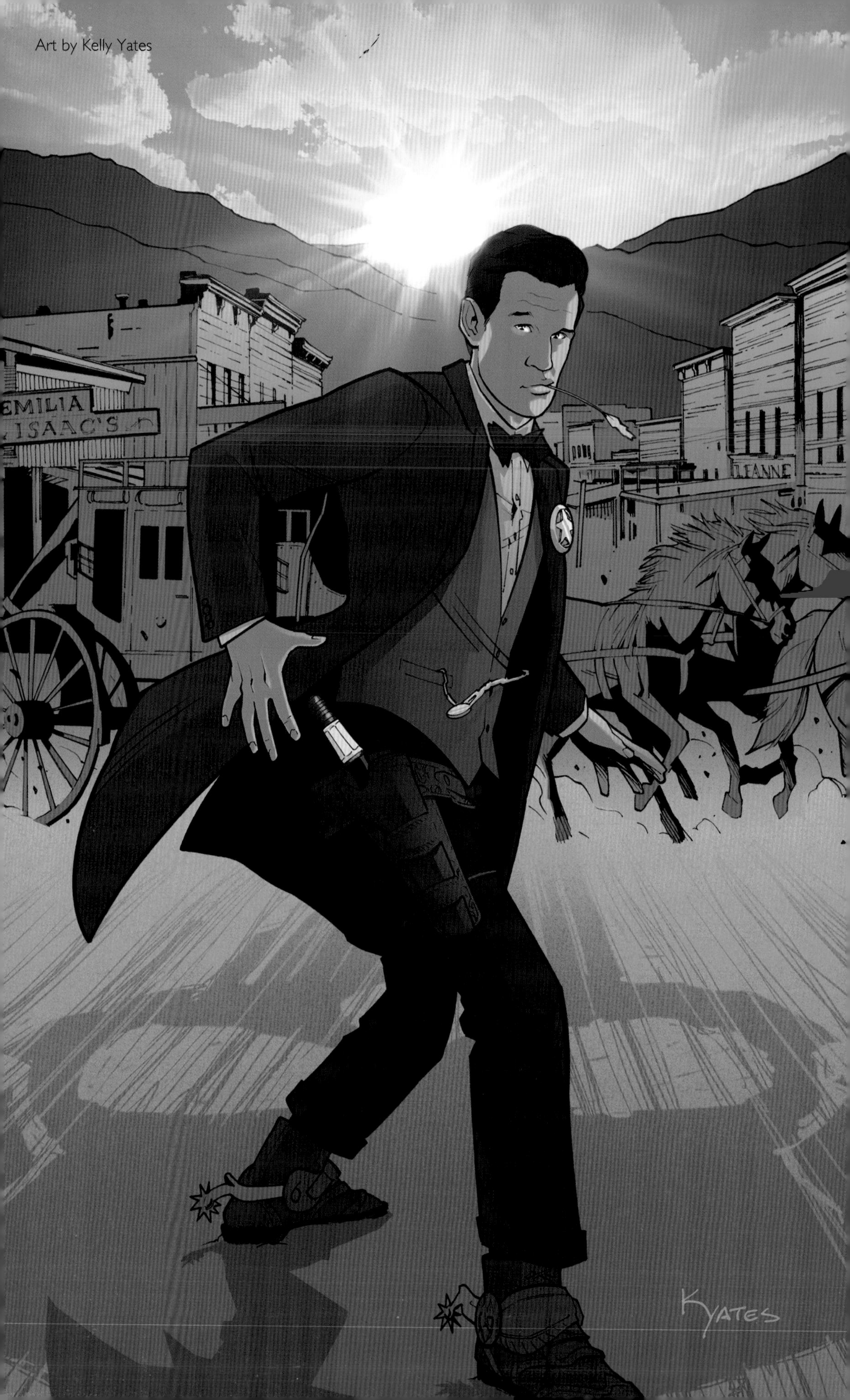
EMILIA
ISAAC'S
KYATES
Art by Kelly Yates

Art by Mike Collins

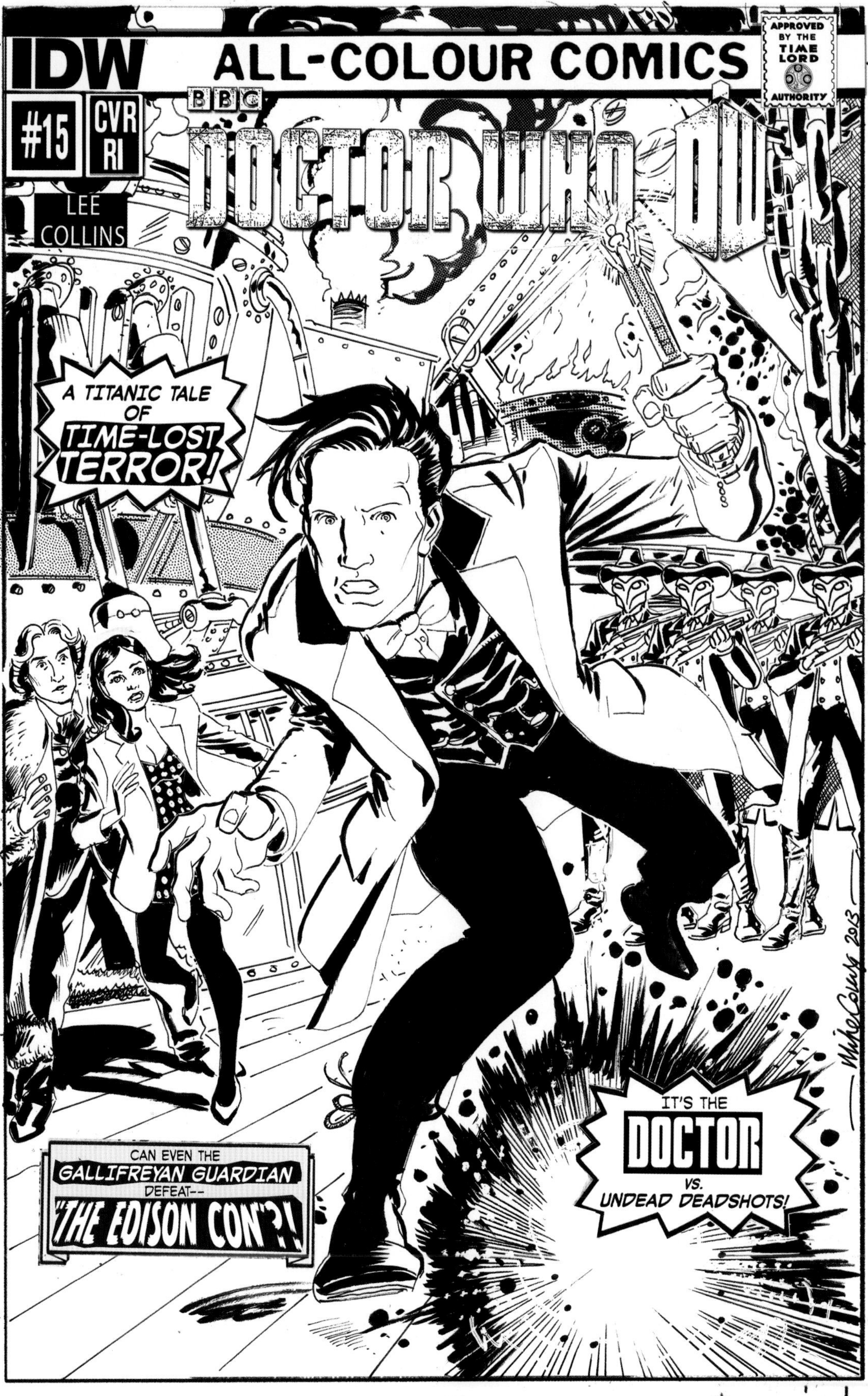
IDW
ALL-COLOUR COMICS
APPROVED BY THE TIME LORD AUTHORITY
#15
CVR RI
BBC
DOCTOR WHO
LEE COLLINS
A TITANIC TALE OF TIME-LOST TERROR!
CAN EVEN THE GALLIFREYAN GUARDIAN DEFEAT--
"THE EDISON CON"?!
IT'S THE DOCTOR VS. UNDEAD DEADSHOTS!

Art by Robert Hack

BBC

DOCTOR WHO

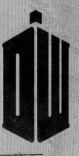

Vol. III No 16 March, 1882 Price, T ents

VARIANT EDITION CVR RI

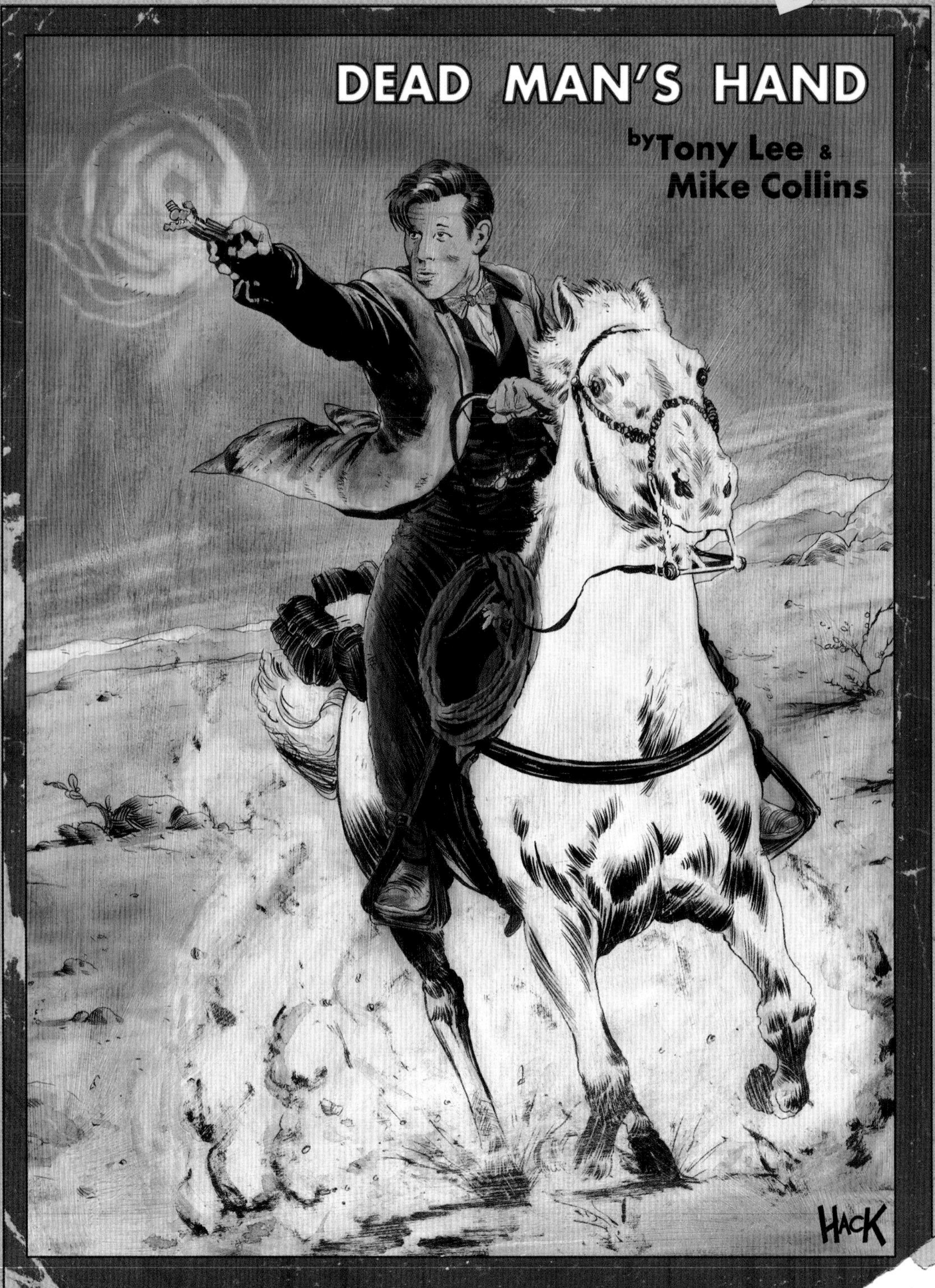
DEAD MAN'S HAND
by Tony Lee & Mike Collins
HACK

"Hooves spit dirt into the Dakota sky as the last Time Lord galloped toward th